THE OFFICERS

Other National Historical Society Publications:

THE IMAGE OF WAR: 1861-1865

TOUCHED BY FIRE: A PHOTOGRAPHIC PORTRAIT OF THE CIVIL WAR

WAR OF THE REBELLION: OFFICIAL RECORDS
OF THE UNION AND CONFEDERATE ARMIES

OFFICIAL RECORDS OF THE UNION AND CONFEDERATE NAVIES
IN THE WAR OF THE REBELLION

HISTORICAL TIMES ILLUSTRATED ENCYCLOPEDIA OF THE CIVIL WAR

CONFEDERATE VETERAN

THE WEST POINT MILITARY HISTORY SERIES

IMPACT: THE ARMY AIR FORCES' CONFIDENTIAL HISTORY
OF WORLD WAR II

HISTORY OF UNITED STATES NAVAL OPERATIONS IN WORLD WAR II
by Samuel Eliot Morison

HISTORY OF THE ARMED FORCES IN WORLD WAR II
by Janusz Piekalkiewicz

A TRAVELLER'S GUIDE TO GREAT BRITAIN SERIES

MAKING OF BRITAIN SERIES

THE ARCHITECTURAL TREASURES OF EARLY AMERICA

For information about National Historical Society Publications, write:

The National Historical Society, 2245 Kohn Road, Box 8200,
Harrisburg, Pa 17105

THE ELITE
The World's Crack Fighting Men

THE OFFICERS

Ashley Brown, Editor

Jonathan Reed, Editor

Lisa Mullins, Managing Editor, NHS edition

A Publication of
THE NATIONAL HISTORICAL SOCIETY

Published in Great Britain in 1986 by Orbis Publishing

Library of Congress Cataloging-in-Publication Data
The Officers / Ashley Brown, editor, Jonathan Reed, editor.—NHS ed.
    p.   cm.—(The Elite ; the world's crack fighting men)
  ISBN 0-918678-54-4
  1. Military biography. 2. Armed Forces—Officers—Biography.
3. Generals—Biography. 4. Military history, Modern—20th century.
I. Brown, Ashley. II. Reed, Jonathan. III. National Historical
Society. IV. Series: Elite (Harrisburg, Pa.)
U51.O33   1990
355'.0092'2—dc20
[B]   90-5613
                                                              CIP

CONTENTS

INTRODUCTION

Guderian . . . Kesselring . . . MacArthur . . . Montgomery . . . Nimitz . . . Patton . . . Rommel . . . Tedder . . . Yamamoto . . . Zhukov . . . Bradley. The names of the ELITE leaders are legion, and legendary. Some of them commanded only small units, even loosely organized partisans, such as Fidel Castro. Some led substantial commands, such as Wolfram von Richthofen and his VIII Fliegerkorps. And then there were the very few, men like Eisenhower, who led virtual continents in waging war, with all of the ELITE commands and commanders at his beck.

Whoever they were, and whatever their level of command, these were the men that their nations looked to for the ultimate in leadership—the men who faced the toughest decisions, challenged the hardest foes, overcame the most desperate odds, and prevailed. Here in this volume of THE ELITE can be met a host of such leaders, the men who, like their commands, went "against all odds."

Meet Air Marshall Arthur William Tedder, who rose from obscurity to be Deputy Supreme Commander of the AEF on World War II. Not popular with Churchill at first, Tedder won the confidence of everyone around him by his herculean efforts and achievements in the Mediterranean, and later by his bombing campaign that paved the way for the successful invasion of France. Meet General Vo Nguyen Giap, primarily responsible for the strategies that stymied two great powers—France and the United States—in Vietnam. Meet General Courtney Hodges, the quiet, unassuming, and unfailingly able First Army commander who took the bridge at Remagen and was among the first to cross the Rhine.

They came from every nation—America, Britain, France, Germany, South Africa, Southeast Asia. Bravery and inspiration know no geographical bounds. What did bind all these leaders together was what they shared with some of those select men they commanded. They were a part of the real "few," a part of THE ELITE.

WHO ARE THE ELITE?

EVERY MILITARY, naval and air force unit is different, reflecting its role, recruitment, training and record of service and, with very few exceptions, all regard themselves quite legitimately as something special, carrying out tasks that only they can do, in ways which no-one else can match. It is therefore difficult to define an 'elite' unit without causing offense – someone, somewhere will always ask why his unit has not been singled out or why a rival has received attention – but it is possible to provide a basic working definition. For the purposes of this publication, the idea of an elite has been taken to mean those military, naval or air force units which stand apart, by virtue of either their outstanding fighting record or their specialist skills.

This concept is nothing new. Armed forces throughout history have had their elites, from the Roman Army's Praetorian Guard to Frederick the Great's Prussian Grenadiers, and all have shown by their physical attributes or their prowess in battle that they are worthy of special attention. But it is in the present century that elite units have proliferated, occupying centre-stage in a wide variety of conflicts and a plethora of armed forces. The reasons for this are many and varied. One of the most obvious is that armed forces have become more widespread, reflecting the massive increase in the number of independent states in the modern world. In 1900, for example, the major armed powers could be counted virtually on the fingers of one hand and, although each contained elite units, the fact that they represented the cream of only a limited number of armed forces inevitably restricted their growth. By 1945, there were still only 53 independent countries in existence (not all of which maintained large or effective armed forces), but 40 years later this number had rocketed to 167, chiefly as a result of the Western European powers shedding their colonies. Again, not all produced large armed forces, but the fact that so many countries existed necessarily increased the numbers of military, naval and air force units from which elites could (and often did) emerge.

Combatant nations were forced to devote large amounts of men and material to the conduct of war

There is more to it than that, however, for the desire to create so many armed forces merely reflected the tensions of the modern world, made more acute as additional states competed for territory, resources, power and influence. On its own, such rivalry did not guarantee the emergence of elites, but the changes in the nature and impact of war in the 20th century have increased the need for more specialised units. As early as World War I (1914-18), it was obvious that new methods of warfare were beginning to emerge, and although it is perhaps premature to describe that conflict as a 'total war', it had many of the attributes associated with that concept. For the first time, combatant nations were forced to devote large amounts of men and materiel to the conduct of war, mobilising vast portions of their populations and economies in order to survive. This, in turn, made the industrial and population centres of a state into worthwhile targets and, as new technology emerged, the expanding nature of the war opened the way for specialised units, capable of using new weapons or of fighting in unfamiliar combat conditions. Among the elites that emerged to cope with such new demands were the Zeppelin formations which bombed England between 1915 and 1918, as

The 20th century has seen a vast escalation in the scale of armed conflict worldwide. Millions of men have answered the call to arms, and many have died serving their nation. With so much at stake, the tactics and technology of warfare have undergone a rapid evolution, giving birth to a new breed of fighting man. We conclude our series with a survey of the modern battlefield, attempting to define the qualities that set the elite apart from the traditional soldier

The modern elite force is required to play a global role and must have the capability of rapid deployment to potential trouble spots anywhere in the world. Background: Men of CENTCOM, the American Rapid Deployment Force, burst into action from a Lockheed C-130.

The elite troops of today are often helicoptered in to the point of action. Background: American forces rappel from a Sikorsky UH-60 Blackhawk.

well as the Royal Flying Corps (RFC) fighter units that opposed them. Comprising men and machines that operated at the frontier of developing technology, these were pioneering elites, requiring a mixture of specialised skills and personal bravery to be effective. Similar attributes were demanded of the airmen responsible for more tactical roles, gaining or maintaining air supremacy over the battlefield itself, and their actions in units such as No.56 Squadron, RFC, or Baron Manfred von Richthofen's Jagdstaffel 11, laid down traditions that were to be refined and developed over the ensuing years.

The process reached a horrific climax with the dropping of atomic bombs on Hiroshima and Nagasaki

Many of these traditions were reinforced during World War II (1939-45), a conflict that may, with some justification, be termed a 'total war'. The unrestricted use of weapons and new technology spawned a number of air force elites, as squadrons contributed to both strategic and tactical attacks. In terms of bombing, the process reached a horrific climax with the dropping of atomic bombs on Hiroshima and Nagasaki in August 1945, but before then units such as No.617 Squadron, RAF (the 'Dambusters') and the 379th Bombardment Group, Eighth US Army Air Force (USAAF) had devised new techniques of bombing that earned them the title of elite. At the same time, fighter squadrons belonging to all the combatant powers contributed to the concept of air supremacy, either by defending airspace against the bombers – something that No.92 (East India) Squadron, RAF, achieved during the Battle of Britain in 1940 but which the Luftwaffe's Jagdverband 44, equipped with Messerschmitt Me 262 jet fighters,

Far right: The nose-gunner of a B-17. Elite armour has included the German PzKpw III (right above) and the Israeli Centurion of the Six-Day War (right below).

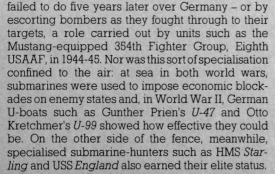

failed to do five years later over Germany – or by escorting bombers as they fought through to their targets, a role carried out by units such as the Mustang-equipped 354th Fighter Group, Eighth USAAF, in 1944-45. Nor was this sort of specialisation confined to the air: at sea in both world wars, submarines were used to impose economic blockades on enemy states and, in World War II, German U-boats such as Gunther Prien's *U-47* and Otto Kretchmer's *U-99* showed how effective they could be. On the other side of the fence, meanwhile, specialised submarine-hunters such as HMS *Starling* and USS *England* also earned their elite status.

But it was on land that the majority of elite units emerged, often in response to the demands of total war fought in a wide variety of combat conditions. During World War I, for example, tanks were developed specifically to cope with the realities of trench deadlock on the Western Front, and the units that carried out the daunting task of supporting infantry across the fireswept nightmare of No-Man's Land were so obviously different, particularly in terms of technology, that they soon emerged as elites. Their role became even more unique when it was realised that they could do far more than merely support infantry, for once they assumed responsibility for Blitzkrieg ('lightning war'), using their firepower, mobility and flexibility to exploit lines of least resistance in enemy defences, demoralising defenders by appearing far to their rear, the tank units, particularly of the German Army, became the arbiters of battle – an undeniably elite characteristic. The success of General Erwin Rommel's 7th Panzer Division in France in 1940, the impact of Waffen-SS armoured units on the Eastern Front in 1941-42 and even the near success of Kampfgruppe Peiper in the Ardennes in 1944, all highlight the strategic potential of armour in the history of modern war. Allied tank units could never match this record (although formations such as the British 7th Armoured Division achieved enough to earn the title elite), and it was left to the Israelis in the post-1945 period to achieve comparable success. The fact that Israeli armour has won victory after victory, helping to ensure the survival of the state against Arab attack, shows that the potential of this particular elite has not diminished.

World War II witnessed the development of similar elites in other spheres of conflict. The use of airborne troops was pioneered by the Germans when gliders deposited infantry and engineers on the roof of the Belgian fortress at Eben Emael in May 1940, and thereafter most combatant nations developed the concept of 'vertical envelopment'. Success was not always guaranteed, as the British discovered at Arnhem in September 1944, but the

elite nature of such units, based upon their special-ised training, dramatic new role and hard fighting skills, could never be denied. Once again, the fact that airborne units have continued to exist in many armed forces highlights their military value; even if the number of combat jumps that have taken place since 1945 is small, the value of highly trained fighting units, invariably composed of volunteers who have been through a rigorous selection process, is indisputable. When, in addition, the concept has been taken one stage further, into the realms of heliborne 'airmobility', practised effectively by the US 1st Cavalry Division (Airmobile) in Vietnam, it is

obvious that a lasting elite has emerged.

Other units from World War II did not survive that conflict, or were forced to change their roles to fit the demands of 'peacetime fighting', but this does not alter their elite status. In North Africa, for example, units such as the Long Range Desert Group and Popski's Private Army emerged in response to a desperate need for long-range reconnaissance, and although they continued to carry out that role else-where in the Mediterranean theatre, they were disbanded in 1945. In the jungles of Burma, units such as the Chindits or the US Merrill's Marauders fol-

Background: An American soldier deploys the awesome firepower of the McDonnell Douglas Dragon anti-tank weapon while the Royal Marines (right) pack the smaller-scale but equally deadly 5.56mm L85 Enfield Individual Weapon.

lowed a similar pattern, disappearing into history as their specialist roles diminished. Only in selected cases – most notably those of the Special Air Service (SAS) and Special Boat Squadron (SBS) – were new roles found that guaranteed survival, although it is interesting to note that the SAS suffered disbandment in 1945 before being revived as a specialist long-range penetration unit in Malaya seven years later. Finally, some units saw their specialist roles reinforced by the experience of World War II, emerging from that conflict with skills which could not be allowed to lapse. In Britain, the Royal Marines perpetuated the skills of commando raiding and amphibious assault, using them in places as far apart as Suez (1956), Brunei (1962) and the Falklands (1982), while their counterparts in the US Marine Corps not only fulfilled a similar role from Korea (1950-53) to Grenada (1983), but also spawned a number of more specialised elites, most notably in Vietnam (1965-73).

An important aspect of the role of modern elites is involvement in counter-terrorist activities, where speed of assault is vital. Above: A helicopter carries members of the French RAID anti-terrorist force to their objective while another member is rapidly lowered down the facade of the target building (right).

Political subversion as well as the military actions of the enemy had to be defeated

Conventional warfare, from the full-scale experience of the two world wars to the more limited engagements of the modern era, has therefore helped to establish the role of elite units, but this is only part of the picture. Since 1945, a more invidious form of warfare has emerged, based not on the size of rival armed forces meeting on the field of battle but upon the politically inspired actions of small groups of guerrillas, intent on the subversion of existing governments and the imposition of political change. Pioneered by Mao Tse-tung in China in the 1930s and 1940s, this concept of insurgency proved well suited to the host of national liberation groups that fought for an end to colonialism, posing problems to the Western European imperial powers as they strove to maintain their global possessions or, at least, ensure a transfer of power to governments friendly to the West. The new techniques of counter-insurgency (COIN) evolved slowly, requiring military units able to adapt to the realities of low-level, unconventional campaigning, in which the political subversion as well as the military actions of the enemy had to be defeated. Some existing units proved well suited – the record of the 1st Battalion, The Suffolk Regiment, in Malaya in the early 1950s is particularly impressive – while others found the transition difficult. In both Indochina (1946-54) and Algeria (1954-62), for example, French regular units – particularly the paras – had some difficulty in adapting to low levels of combat, while in Vietnam many US main-force units concentrated on the conventional war against the North Vietnamese and neglected the need for COIN techniques such as 'hearts and minds', persuading the ordinary people to support the government in preference to the insurgents.

What was needed in most cases were units specifically trained for COIN, earning their status as elites by virtue of their expertise in particularly difficult methods of warfare. In Britain, the SAS rapidly became the COIN experts, and their record of service in a host of campaigns – from Malaya (1952-58) and Borneo (1963-66) to Dhofar (1970-75) and Northern Ireland (post-1969) – is second to none. Other countries produced similar units – the American Green Beret/Special Forces in Vietnam, the Selous Scouts in Rhodesia, 32 Battalion, South Africa Defence Force, in Namibia – and although their

success rate has not always been as high as that of the SAS, the need for specialised elite units of this type has been widely recognised.

The threat of terrorism has considerably reinforced this need, for although the basic principles of counter-terrorism are not significantly different to those of COIN, many states have come to value the existence of hard-hitting elites, specially trained in the delicate art of breaking sieges or rescuing the victims of hijacks. In Britain the role is, once again, an SAS preserve, and the dramatic rescue mission at the Iranian embassy in London (May 1980) remains a classic example of success. Elsewhere, other elites

have enjoyed equal effect – France's GIGN at Djibouti (February 1976), Israel's paras at Entebbe (July 1976) and West Germany's GSG9 at Mogadishu (October 1977) all spring to mind – but other, similar units do exist, acting as quick-response forces in case of trouble. Some, like the US Delta Force, with its unfortunate failure to rescue American hostages in Tehran (April 1980) behind it, have yet to enjoy the success they deserve; while others, such as Spain's GEO, have only participated in domestic rather than international incidents. The fact that they exist at all should act as a useful terrorist deterrent.

The threat of international terrorism is unlikely to diminish in the forseeable future, requiring the retention and further refinement of elite counter-terrorism units. But the process has to be carried out with care, for if such units either fail in their role or appear too violent for the political sensibilities of their democratic sponsors, they could find the tide of public acceptance turning against them. Delta Force, for example, desperately needs a dramatic success like Entebbe or Mogadishu to quieten Congressional pressure for more restricted funding, while the record of Egypt's Sa'Aqa commandos, who not only failed to rescue hostages from a hijacked DC-8 at Larnaca in Cyprus (March 1978) but also inflicted what many regarded to have been unacceptable casualties among the passengers of a Boeing 737, stormed at Luqa in Malta (December 1985), is a salutary lesson in the need for careful planning and flawless execution. Up to now, with the exception of Delta Force's mission to Tehran in 1980 (which failed as much through inadequate equipment as careless preparation), the West has not suffered the consequences of failure in counter-terrorism operations, and although this is, to a large extent, a tribute to the selection, training and skill of the elite units involved, it is also down to luck. If a failure should occur and hostages should be killed in large numbers, domestic and international condemnation would be overwhelming, leading to a loss of confidence in the idea of counter-terrorist elites. They must maintain a fine balance between effectiveness and over-zealous or poorly prepared operations, something that can come only through detailed training.

But this is only one aspect of the elites of the future, for they are now so well established as integral parts of modern warfare at every level that they can be neither organised nor retained for a single counter-terrorist role. In a world made smaller by the impact of international travel, and more interdependent by the exploitation of key resources, many states now take a much more global view of potential threats to their security, concentrating significant parts of their defence assets on the maintenance of resource areas or 'choke points' on the routes of world trade. If these areas should be threatened, the states involved must be able to react quickly and with effective force: for this reason, elites such as airborne and amphibious forces have been refined into quick-reaction formations, capable of deployment to almost any trouble-spot at very short notice. The American Rapid Deployment Joint Task Force/ CENTCOM, stationed at Fort Bragg but capable of rapid movement worldwide, is a case in point, combining ground, air and naval forces in a highly efficient framework. The same is true of Britain's 5 Airborne Brigade, created in the aftermath of the Falklands campaign. In both cases, a tradition of intervention, laid down by men such as Belgium's paracommandos at Stanleyville (1964) and France's Foreign Legion paras at Kolwezi (1978) is being perpetuated.

No amount of specialisation will compensate for the traditional virtues of regular fighting units

Finally, with the likelihood of a major nuclear arms deal between the superpowers, the possibility of large-scale conventional operations in Europe between the forces of NATO and the Warsaw Pact cannot be ignored. If this should ever happen, specialised units on both sides would have important roles to fulfil – for the Pact, Soviet Spetsnaz troops would mount rear-area disruption attacks while ground, air and naval elites would spearhead the main assault; for NATO, similar units would carry out surveillance as well as hit-and-run attacks and main-force actions – but once again, care must be taken. No amount of specialisation will compensate for the traditional virtues of regular fighting units, especially in terms of close co-operation between the various elements of a state's armed forces. Elites clearly have integral parts to play at all levels of combat and, in most cases, they can be depended upon to carry out their duties efficiently and well, but without the other fighting units, whose traditions or records of service preclude them from our definition of 'elite', the war will not be won. No-one can ignore elites, but at the same time no-one can afford to devote a disproportionate amount of money or manpower to their retention. Balance is the key, as indeed it has always been throughout the history of war.

THE AUTHOR John Pimlott is Senior Lecturer in War Studies at the Royal Military Academy, Sandhurst. He has written *Strategy and Tactics of War* and edited *Vietnam: the History and the Tactics*.

The face of things to come. Left: The elite soldier of the future may find himself equipped with a head-up display visor unit allowing off-line sighting of his weaponry, and chameleon camouflage which can be adjusted to suit his surroundings. Below: Two RAF pilots in NBC kit.

Originally a regiment of painters and sculptors, the Artists Rifles provided a backbone of high-calibre officers on the Western Front in World War I

'BY DAY AND BY NIGHT, almost under the enemy's guns, and very often under close rifle fire in the trenches they commenced, they carried on, and they developed their work to the very highest standard of efficiency... they showed us what men of energy and skill could do when they knew how.'

These were the words used by Field Marshal Sir John French, the commander of the British Expeditionary Force, to express his gratitude for one regiment's unique contribution to the Allied effort during World War I. Speaking at a reunion dinner after the Armistice, French was referring to the 28th County of London Regiment (Artists Rifles), a territorial unit that had proved itself both as an exceptional ground-

Below: A file of soldiers moves across the devastated landscape near Passchendaele. The 1st Battalion, Artists Rifles, saw action for the first time as a unit during the protracted Passchendaele offensive of 1917. In November 1914 the battalion provided 50 officers for the badly depleted officer ranks of the 7th Division. The men selected were all privates and NCOs and became known as the 'First Fifty'. In an unprecedented move, they received their officers' stars before joining their new units.

ing for young officers, and as a well-disciplined fighting force on the battlefield.

At the outbreak of war, the 1st Battalion, Artists Rifles, was commanded by Lieutenant-Colonel H.A.R. May, and had already established a reputation as one of the finest volunteer units in the country. The Artists' prowess in military competitions of all kinds was well known, and May was understandably disheartened when his battalion was slated for 'London duties'. Fate intervened, however, and by 26 October 1914 he and his men were embarked on SS *Australind*, bound for France.

Soon after the battalion arrived in France, Lieutenant-Colonel May received orders to proceed immediately to the Ypres salient and take up position in the front line as part of the 7th Division. However, Sir John French, having been informed of the Artists Rifles' exemplary standards of soldiering, intercepted the battalion and informed May that, due to the horrendous casualty figures, the division was in urgent need of junior officers. French tentatively

ARTISTS RIFLES

suggested using the Artists as a training corps through which officers would pass before being sent out to the regular regiments in the line. May fully appreciated that sending his battalion into the line would be a tragic waste of first-class material – one crack unit added to the firing line would have no dramatic effect, whereas 1000 highly trained officers distributed throughout the British Army would be of incalculable value.

May selected 52 privates and NCOs from the ranks of his battalion for instant promotion to officer status, and, together with Regimental Sergeant-Major Peter Emslie, he set about the task of preparing them for their new-found responsibility. On 12 November, an officer's star was affixed to each man's khaki uniform, and three days later the men joined their new regiments and set off from Bailleul for the front line. Shortly afterwards, May received a letter from Sir Thomas Capper, the divisional commander: 'The young men you have sent have done splendidly...they are keen fighters...their men almost

worship them.' It was French's response, however, that led to the 1st Battalion being accorded the honour of providing a school of instruction at the front for officers. His question was simple: 'Have you any more like them?'

At GHQ Cadet School in Blendecques, four miles behind the front lines, the Artists began training candidates for direct commissions. Thousands of potential recruits had been clamouring at the doors of the newly-formed 2nd and 3rd Battalions' headquarters in London, hoping to gain acceptance into the regiment. May was therefore confident that the Artists could supply a steady stream of high-calibre officers for the duration of the war. Indeed, with the help of the home battalions, the Artists Rifles eventually supplied a total of 10,256 officers, gazetted to virtually every regiment in the British Army. All this was accomplished by a unit that had a strength of only 621 men when it first arrived in France.

The Regimental Roll of Honour reflects the leadership qualities of the Artists' officers – eight Victoria

Background: The 1st Battalion, Artists Rifles, form up as guard of honour for George V's visit to the British GHQ at Montreuil in 1917. Above left: Lieutenant D.J. Dean, awarded the VC in 1918. Above centre: Lieutenant-Colonel H.A.R. May, who commanded the Artists until late 1915. Above right: Regimental Sergeant-Major Peter Emslie, wearing a goatskin jacket issued to combat the severe cold of the winter of 1914-15.

Crosses and 891 Military Crosses provide strong testimony to the valour of these gallant men under fire. For example, Lieutenant Donald John Dean, gazetted in October 1916 to the 8th Battalion, Royal West Kent Regiment, was awarded the Victoria Cross for conspicuous bravery northwest of Lens, between 24 and 26 September 1918. Having led his platoon forward to establish an advanced post in a captured German trench, Dean worked without rest to secure the left flank against enemy attacks. Contemptuous of the heavy shell and trench-mortar fire, Dean urged his men to stand their ground, and together they succeeded in repulsing a violent onslaught by extremely determined German troops. Consolidation continued in the face of enemy fire, and each attack during the next 24 hours was thwarted by Dean's masterly leadership.

Each man worked tirelessly to absorb what was necessary to operate the Maxim and Vickers guns

The moulding of young men into highly trained officers for the British Army was by no means the sole task of the Artists Rifles. By late 1914, for example, it had become abundantly clear that machine guns would play a crucial role in a struggle dominated by the concept of trench warfare. Although the facility for training infantry NCOs existed, the task of instructing 2000 machine-gunners a month in the arts of maintaining and firing these relatively new weapons was beyond the capabilities of the existing authorities. When May heard of this predicament he lost no time in offering a small cadre of Artists to form the nucleus of a machine-gun school.

News of the 1st Battalion's sterling performance in the role of officer training had spread like wildfire, and 16 men were duly selected for machine-gun training from the reservoir of talent that May had under his command. On arrival at the Machine Gun Corps' headquarters at St Omer, each man worked tirelessly to absorb what was necessary to operate the Maxim and Vickers guns. Within a matter of weeks, the Artists were able to pass on their new skills to others, and the number of instructors grew steadily. Soon, 800 pupils were passing through the school each fortnight.

Following the example set by the Artists, more schools sprang up, and by 1918 the Machine Gun Corps had built up a formidable reputation on the Western Front. Instilled with the vigour of their instructors, and justly proud of their regiment, 18 members of the Artists Rifles who served in the Machine Gun Corps were awarded the Military Cross. One of the recipients of this coveted decoration was Second-Lieutenant Gerald Harman Ball. In command of a machine-gun post near Arleux in February 1918, Ball was able to hold off a fierce attack until his gun was put out of action by enemy shelling. German infantry poured into the trench, but Ball was undaunted and endeavoured to stand his ground. The sound of metal on metal rang through the air as

THE ARTISTS RIFLES

The Artists Rifles (badge shown above) were formed in 1860 as part of a volunteer movement encouraged by the British Government in the aftermath of the Crimean War. The original idea of the regiment occurred to Edward Sterling, a young art student. After mooting the concept of a special corps of 'artists' to a small group of friends, Sterling decided to go ahead with the project. The founding members hoped that the regiment would attract painters, sculptors, engravers, musicians, architects and actors to its ranks. The new corps was officially formed as the 38th Middlesex (Artists) Rifle Volunteers. By 1880, the regiment could claim that each of its eight companies had an artistic specialisation. By this time, the unit had been redesignated the 20th Middlesex (Artists) Rifle Volunteers.

Many members of the regiment went to South Africa to fight in the Boer War (1899-1902) as part of the City Imperial Volunteers, but it was not until 1914 that the renamed 28th County of London Regiment (Artists Rifles) went abroad as a formation. In 1921, when the spirit of the volunteer movement re-emerged and the Territorial Army was slowly re-forming, one of the first battalions to contain enough men to hold a parade was the Artists Rifles. The regiment continued in its role as an officer-producing unit until the end of World War II. It was re-formed in 1947 as 21 SAS (Artists), TA, and a group from that regiment formed the nucleus of 22 SAS in Malaya in 1952.

bayonets clashed in a brutal life-or-death struggle at close quarters. Rallying his men, Ball succeeded in driving the enemy out of the trenches.

When a manpower shortage threatened to hamper commission training, the new commander of the regiment, Colonel Chatfield Clarke, was able to bring the 1st Battalion back up to an establishment strength of 1200 with the help of a large draft from the holding battalion in England. Training and headquarters duties therefore continued right up until 14 June 1917, when the 1st Battalion was informed that it would be joining the 190th Brigade, 63rd (Royal Naval) Division. After overhauling kit and equipment, and drawing gas helmets under the supervision of Quartermaster Freddy Light, the battalion awaited its 'move orders'; these arrived 10 days later. This development had been eagerly awaited by the Artists; although proud of its role as an officer training corps, the battalion was spoiling for an opportunity to forge a reputation as a fighting unit.

In October, the 63rd Division was ordered to the Ypres salient, and the Artists began planning and training for the forthcoming attack on Passchendaele Ridge. B Company was commanded by Captain Bare, A Company by Captain Mieville, C Company by Captain Chetwood, and D Company by Captain Royds. Supported by an artillery bombardment, the attack began on 28 October, with A, B and C

Right: A sketch map of the Passchendaele front drawn by an Artist during the offensive of 30 October 1917.

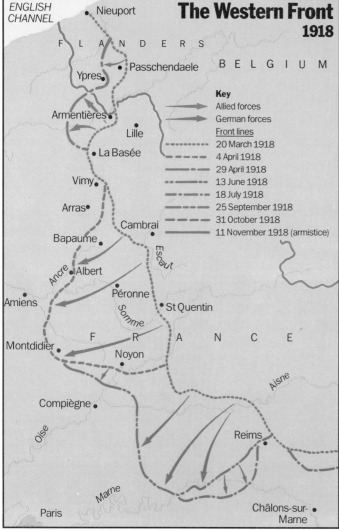

The Western Front 1918

ENGLISH CHANNEL

Key
Allied forces
German forces
Front lines
······· 20 March 1918
– – – 4 April 1918
——— 29 April 1918
– · – · 13 June 1918
– – – 18 July 1918
– · · – 25 September 1918
——— 31 October 1918
——— 11 November 1918 (armistice)

On 21 March 1918 the last great German offensive of World War I was launched. The Allies were overwhelmed at the start and began a hasty retreat which continued in the central Somme area until 4 April. The Germans followed up their advantage to the south and north and it was not until mid-July that the Allies were able to bring the Germans to a complete standstill.

The final Allied offensives that ended the war opened on 18 July. By September the Allies had regained the lost ground, and the war was all but over.

Companies moving up into the front line and D Company staying back in support. The objective lay on the far side of a marshy area known as the 'Paddebeeke', but the Artists encountered heavy machine-gun fire from a number of enemy pillboxes almost as soon as the attack started. Men stumbled through the quagmire, their rifles and Lewis guns hopelessly clogged with thick mud. Captain Royds later remembered watching the three forward companies going into battle:

'The process of digging in when the right spot was found was a nightmare. Fritz had really got nasty and many of the company got buried in more than once. The minutes dragged on as we crouched in the trenches we had dug under a bright moon and a tearing, bitter wind.

'At last our batteries opened up to the second at zero, but then the trouble began. The Hun knew every inch of the ground and put down a counter-

barrage which he kept up for hours. One can imagine the feelings of a man in a successful attack with hand-to-hand fighting and excitement, but that attack with every sort of shell poured upon the advancing lines was as near to Hell as anyone is likely to get. The few who were not killed at once got as far as human beings could get in the mud.'

Within moments of going over the top, the Artists had suffered terrible casualties. From a force of 500, the battalion was reduced to 250 all ranks. Had it not been for the unceasing efforts of the battalion medical officer, Captain David Matthew, the fatalities would undoubtedly have been much higher. During the 72 hours that the battalion was in the line, Matthew tended to the unit's wounded in an advanced dressing station and exhorted his men to send rescue parties across the shell-pitted ground, searching for soldiers who had become trapped in the deep bog. Matthew had continued his work in full

Below: A machine-gun crew in action in 1917. Inset left to right: Captain Bare, Captain Royds and Captain Chetwood, the commanders of B, C and D Companies.

OFFICER TRAINING

The GHQ Cadet School at Blendecques, in northern France, was the only unit in the British Army accorded the honour of being allowed to train candidates for direct commissions without any further training. The 10-week course was rigorous – it had to be if young men were to be moulded into officers destined for the front line.

On arrival at the school, the candidates were given seven days of physical training and bayonet fighting, followed by 16 days of instruction in the art of trench warfare, protection against gas attack and bombing, and close-order drill.

The candidates were then given a three-week attachment to one of the battalions in the front line. They were sent in groups of 20 to each battalion, and were accompanied by an Artist officer or NCO. Back at Blendecques, the candidates were given a short time to rest and write up their first experience of battle. They were then given 16 days of instruction in map and compass work, open warfare tactics, close- and extended-order drill and musketry. The Artists lost no opportunity to provide the candidates with valuable information, and many of the evenings were spent listening to lectures by distinguished military guests from the two Staff Colleges at Hesdin.

During several days at the No.1 and No.2 Training Camps at Étaples, the potential officers were given the chance to test their powers of command and leadership over large bodies of men.

Finally, each candidate was given a personal interview with the commanding officer of the Cadet School. If this proved successful, commission papers were sent in and the candidate received his posting orders to one of the frontline battalions within seven days. Accorded the rank of second-lieutenant, a fresh batch of Artist officers was ready to leave Blendecques.

view of the enemy, and was later awarded the Military Cross for his devotion to duty.

The Passchendaele front was closed down on 10 November, and the 1st Battalion was withdrawn behind the lines for a period of rest and re-organisation. Lieutenant-Colonel John Harrington took over as commanding officer, and the Artists received substantial reinforcements that included six officers and a draft from the regiment's holding battalion in London. Although officers and men from other regiments also joined the battalion during this period, these men very readily assimilated the Artists' esprit de corps.

In December, as a reaction to a German offensive at Cambrai, the 63rd Division was sent to the Somme district. On the night of 15/16 December the Artists moved into the front line in the Marcoing salient, part of the Hindenburg Line. The unit was still sadly under strength, however, and companies were forced to assume organisations comprising either one or two platoons. At 0600 on 30 December, a relatively quiet morning was shattered by the sound of artillery

shells crashing into the front lines and blasting tons of earth and snow skyward. An eerie silence then descended, only to be broken by the news that a battalion of Jägers, camouflaged in white battledress, had overwhelmed the frontline battalion of the 190th Brigade and penetrated the southern flank. The four Artists companies were given the task of recapturing the line. After drawing extra ammunition and gas masks, they moved up the communications trench as enemy shells burst all around them.

Reinforced by a platoon of the 4th Battalion, King's Shropshire Light Infantry, A Company reached the jumping-off point – a sunken road in front of the German position – without suffering any casualties. Having regrouped, the Artists launched their counter-attack. But it was to no avail; greeted by a storm of machine-gun bullets and enfiladed from both flanks, A and B Companies were forced to retire to the sunken road and begin the gruelling task of consolidating their positions. C Company suffered heavy casualties on the way through the communications trench, and the commanding officer, Captain Lepingwell, was seriously injured. Undeterred, Second-Lieutenant Arthur Holland took over command of the company and led his men to the right of the line, where he orchestrated the consolidation of

the position. Venturing forward several times to retrieve men who had fallen in front of this new line, Holland gave a stirring example to the Artists under his command. He was later awarded the Military Cross.

A further three awards of the Military Cross were made to men of the 1st Battalion on account of their valour during the fighting at Marcoing. Lieutenant Raimond Barnett, the commanding officer of D Company, had led a bombing party into one of the trenches that had been captured by the Jägers, and inflicted heavy casualties on the enemy before forcing them to retire. For invaluable reconnaissance work when his position was subjected to a devastating rain of bullets, Captain Walter Mieville was also awarded the Military Cross. The third award was made to Lieutenant Edward Margetson, who had spared no effort to maintain the battalion's lines of communication at a time when enemy attacks were at their peak. Often, when the telephone lines he had laid were severed by shell and mortar fire, Margetson personally carried messages up to his fellow Artists in the front line.

The 1st Battalion was relieved as a frontline unit on the night of 31 December, proud that their stoic defence of the line had prevented the Germans from exploiting their initial success – an event that would have compromised the whole of the Cambrai salient. Depleted by the fighting at Marcoing, the Artists

ere now formed into a composite battalion with the mnants of a battalion of Fusiliers from the 190th igade. The battalion received further drafts from her regiments but, on joining the unit, each man placed his unit badge and shoulder plates with ose of the Artists Rifles.

Following a period of training at Beaulencourt, the t Battalion went back into the front line, again in the builet Wood sector of Marcoing. By the beginning March, intelligence indicated that the Germans ere massing for a huge offensive. Together with the st of the 63rd Division, the Artists waited for the rricane to arrive. It came, on 21 March 1918, in the rm of a massive bombardment by 6000 German ins. The battalion moved forward into its battle osition through a dense cloud of mustard gas and noke. To the south, the British Fifth Army had lost e-third of its strength and was unable to hold on.

The Artists set about clearing the southern section of the Hindenburg Line yard by yard

began the 'Great Retreat' that lasted from March to y 1918. Communications between brigade and visional headquarters were down, and the Artists ere forced to retire to the west, to a line of trenches st of Ypres. The relentless German advance rolled , however, and the battalion conducted a fighting

withdrawal through Gouzeaucourt, Flers and Pozières. By Easter, the Artists had lost 17 officers and 300 other ranks during the retreat.

By the middle of July, with German lines of communication and supply severely over-stretched, the British and French armies launched their counter-attacks. The Artists Rifles now embarked on a series of night marches northwards and, by 31 August, the 63rd Division was only three miles west of Hindencourt; the scene was set for the capture of the Hindenburg Line. Commanded by Lieutenant-Colonel Goldthorp, seconded from the Duke of Wellington's (West Riding) Regiment, the battalion was to lead the assault as part of the 190th Brigade. At 0430 on 27 September, the Artists advanced in drill-perfect order, following on the heels of the frontline troops before swinging south with the artillery. The Germans, expecting an attack from the west, were caught unawares. Supported by two of the 190th's other battalions, tanks and artillery, the Artists set about clearing the southern section of the Hindenburg Line yard by yard.

The attack was a great success, and by the beginning of October the Allies had smashed gaps right through the Hindenburg Line. By 1 October, the Artists had reached the outskirts of Cambrai; the 63rd Division had conducted a fighting advance over

Above: British 60-pounders open up on the German lines during the Passchendaele offensive in which almost a quarter of a million British soldiers died. Heavy rain turned the battlefield into a quagmire and many of the wounded drowned in liquid mud. Left: *Over the Top* by John Nash depicts the Artists going into action at Marcoing. The picture now hangs in the officers' mess of 21 SAS (Artists).

seven miles within the space of four days. Six weeks later, with the Armistice signed, the Artists took part in the First Army's official entry into Mons.

The 1st Battalion, 28th County of London Regiment (Artists Rifles), had been instrumental in providing the British Army with a reservoir of first-class officers in its hour of need, and the battalion's performance in battle had proved equally impressive. In addition to the eight Victoria Crosses and the total of 891 Military Crosses awarded to Artists who had passed through the 1st Battalion's training school, a further 56 ex-Artists won the Distinguished Service Order. Some of these men had been decorated even before they were commissioned. Training and fighting under the watchful eyes of Mars and Minerva – the God of War and the Goddess of Wisdom – the Artists Rifles had proved themselves one of the finest British units serving on the Western Front.

THE AUTHOR David Williams and the publishers would like to thank Gordon Baker, Honorary General Secretary, Artists Rifle Club, Bisley Camp, Surrey, and the Artists Rifles Regimental Museum for their invaluable assistance with this article.

2nd Lieutenant, Artists Rifles 1915

This officer is wearing standard 1915 field service uniform with 1908 pattern webbing, from which hangs his entrenching-tool handle and bayonet. He holds the Field Service Pocket Book that was issued to all newly commissioned officers destined for the front line.

The men of 148 Commando Forward Observation Battery must combine para and commando skills with a wealth of technical expertise

148 COMMANDO Forward Observation Battery, Royal Artillery, is not an easy unit to join. Initially, the selection process is conducted along physical lines, testing the determination, fitness and stamina of each volunteer. Since 148 Battery is the only British unit whose members must be both paratroopers and commandos, each recruit must pass both The Parachute Regiment's Parachute Selection Company ('P' Company) and the Royal Marines' Commando Course. Only then are they allowed to start their specialised training.

Once the volunteer has earned his green beret and parachute wings he is transferred to the 148 Battery headquarters at Poole in Dorset. There he learns the skills of the Naval Gunfire Assistant (NGA), and during the next gruelling six months he becomes familiar with the complete range of army radio equipment and learns, eventually, to receive morse messages at over 18 words a minute (morse is easy to send but very hard to receive). He is taught specialised naval gunfire and artillery adjustment techniques and has to be able to cope with a wide variety of sophisticated code systems.

Apart from mastering the purely technical aspects of his intended role, he learns to perfect the art of camouflage, constructing observation hides out of chicken wire, camouflage netting and vegetation from which to observe without risk of being seen. He practises both abseiling from helicopters, including the 200ft abseil used to breach a jungle canopy and insert a team into tropical rain forest, and a specialised form of parachuting. This latter entails jumping from the tailgate of a Hercules with a 22ft steerable parachute, rather than the more conventional style of using the side doors and wearing a non-steerable chute. Using this technique allows a five-man Forward Observation (FO) team to steer close to each other in the air and land together rather than in a long line. They are thus able to jump into small clearings in woods and a variety of drop zones which would not otherwise be usable by paratroops.

On one dark and moonless night, Sergeant Benfield found himself on his own after a particularly hard landing. The DZ was deserted, and yet he had jumped with five others. There was no-one at the rendezvous (RV), so he packed his chute and equipment and walked to the main road to thumb a lift. A Land Rover came roaring towards him and stopped. Why had he not been at the RV with the rest of his stick? Sergeant Benfield wanted to know why the rest of his stick – and indeed the rest of the battery – were not at the RV! And then he noticed the time. It was two and a half hours after he had jumped and the rest of the battery had been combing the darkness looking for him. He had come down into an unfilled slit trench and the hard landing had knocked him unconscious for over two hours.

The whole selection process for 148 Battery

Kitted out in white camouflage to ensure maximum concealment on snow-covered ground, a 148 Battery forward observation team awaits a parachute drop well within the Arctic Circle. Far right: Stamina and resilience are developed on long marches, an aspect of 148 Battery training that is drawn from the Commando Course and P Company.

TRAIN HARD FIGHT EASY

Below: Observers of 148 Battery can call up heavy barrages from such Royal Navy vessels as this Type 21 class frigate, HMS *Amazon*: its Mark 8 gun can unleash 1760lb of shells a minute.
Right: The A-10 Thunderbolt II blasts anti-tank rounds from its massive seven-barrelled nose cannon.

recruits takes one year, provided the volunteer does not sustain any injuries, and it is a hard grind. The reward is to become the junior member of an FO team, when at last he can begin to learn the actual job that he has already expended so much sweat to gain.

Two of the 148 Battery FO teams are dedicated to amphibious operations. They train as divers and small-boat coxswains and are used either on their own or with the SBS (Special Boat Squadron, Royal Marines). Amphibious operations are the most tricky of all because there are always two hostile elements, the enemy and the sea, and a great deal of experience is needed to cope with dramatic changes in weather and sea conditions. The most experienced 148 Battery men are selected for these teams and have to undergo yet more training.

Apart from teaching repairs and maintenance, boat training aims to develop seamanship and navigational skills, and long transits are practised in the open sea, allowing for tides and winds to make accurate landfalls. It can be very cold, wet and at times tedious. Exercises take place regularly and can develop into real disaster situations.

On a recent NATO exercise in the Baltic, an FO team and I parachuted into a choppy sea five miles from the coast of Denmark, together with a Gemini inflatable assault boat, on a very dark night. We followed the boat's green 'cylume' light down and into the water, realising as we struggled out of our parachute harnesses that the swell (three or four feet high) would not allow us to locate each other – or the boat. After 20 anxious minutes all five were safely aboard, but one of the inflated sections had a leak and the Gemini was full of water.

The engine had to be eased out of its zip-up waterproof bag without dropping it into either the sea or the water at the bottom of the boat. When clamped in place, it refused to start. Lance Bombardier 'Herman' Muncer located the tool kit and removed the spark plugs to dry them off. The swell was quite sharp and he lost his balance, vanishing over the side into the darkness – with the spark plugs. Several harrowing minutes later he reappeared amid the waves with the plugs clasped over his head, like the Lady of the Lake with the sword Excalibur. Bombardier Nick Allin and Lance Bombardier Paddy Ferguson grabbed the plugs and left Muncer in the water until they were replaced. The engine started and we set off towards the distant shore, aligning ourselves by using a compass bearing onto a large red light on top of a coastal tower.

The boat was so full of water that in spite of furious bailing the Baltic Sea flowed over the bow and out of the stern, just below the engine's exhaust. Paddy Ferguson, the coxswain, was being sick over the stern, having his work cut out keeping on the right course as well as avoiding being ill onto the engine. We were all very cold, shivering uncontrollably. The closer we got to the shore, the worse the weather became and for the final few hundred yards, through a forest of long fishermen's poles protruding out of the water, we got out of the boat and swam alongside wearing our fins.

He organises a timed schedule of artillery fire, combining smoke, air-burst, illuminating and high-explosive ammunition

It took an hour to drag everything up the steep beach and into a small wood. The trees were so thick that it was possible to hide the boat completely without having to dig a pit, for which we were thankful as we were exhausted.

This particular exercise lasted for another 10 days, by which time we were more than ready for the 'run ashore' in Copenhagen. Sadly, while we had been struggling at sea in the Gemini, the main landing force was enjoying a 'cultural weekend' in the Danish capital. All we got was the slow trip on HMS *Fearless* after the exercise, back down the English Channel, round through the Straits of Dover and home to Plymouth.

Practice Camps, where artillery training is carried out with live firing, are the most important technical part of the year's training. Along with the observation parties (OPs) of the commando artillery batteries, the FO teams undergo rigorous testing of their artillery control skills under the eagle eye of the Commanding Officer (CO) of 29 Commando Regiment, Royal Artillery. Practice Camp finishes with a CO's test exercise. This involves the observation parties marching long distances at night, digging in before first light and firing the guns, moving often and becoming more and more tired as the days go by.

The co-ordination of artillery is the most important skill to be practised; this reaches its most sophisticated level during a Fire Plan when all the gun batteries within range are used in support of an attack. The commander of the attacking unit or formation takes the advice of the senior gunner, who may hold only the rank of captain or sometimes a bombardier (Royal Artillery corporal). The gunner organises a timed schedule of artillery fire, combining different sorts of ammunition (smoke, air-burst, illuminating rounds or high explosive). Jet fighter-bombers may also be involved.

During the rigorous two or three weeks of Practice Camp, long marches carrying heavy equipment, and the inevitable poor weather and lack of sleep, combined with the complex technical skills and speed of thought required for fire planning, all make heavy demands on every participant. The gun crews spend the time racing with their artillery from one position to the next, fighting off attacks from 'enemy' infantry and coping with calls for immediate and accurate fire from the OPs. The pace is furious – far faster than in war. 'Train hard and fight easy' is the principle – and it works.

148 Battery has two jobs in war: to gather intelligence and to attack enemy positions with naval gunfire, artillery and aircraft. Before an FO team is sent out to locate enemy positions, in order later to bring down fire upon them, it is often provided with good, hard information on the area. For example, during the Falklands War of 1982, I was given town plans of Stanley, detailed photos of all the buildings, and the co-ordinates of a number of the suspected and confirmed Argentinian positions before my FO team was inserted to the north of the town in the last two weeks of the campaign. At other times the team

Left and below: Guided by data supplied by a 148 Battery Forward Air Controller (FAC), a Jaguar sweeps in to deliver an awesome payload of cluster bombs on a dummy tank force.

EARLY SELECTION

Prospective members of 148 Battery are required to undertake the qualification courses of both the Royal Marines and The Parachute Regiment for, although they may seem similar to the outsider, they are designed to test quite different capabilities.

The aim of the commando course is to produce a man who regards being cold, wet and tired as normal and therefore irrelevant. He is also taught specific commando skills, to help him get from the sea to the shore, to work completely by night if required, and to carry on functioning for just that little while longer.

The tests range from the '30-miler' on Dartmoor, the assault course and Tarzan ropes course, the 12 miles of water-filled tunnels, the nine-mile speed march and the load carry. All the tests are preceded by long, uncomfortable and gruelling exercises.

The paratrooper has to be able to turn in his maximum effort for the length of time it takes for his forward parachute drop zone to be re-supplied and his unit relieved. The para tests are therefore designed to produce individual maximum effort and are very severe. The stretcher race, assault course, milling, battle marches, speed marches and load carries cannot be compared with the commando tests because they generally take place straight from camp without the gruelling exercises that precede the commando tests. There are no strict minimum times either; the instructors set more stock by observing the reactions of individuals and ensuring that everyone pushes himself to his own personal limit. For that reason there is much less extra aggravation from the instructors as the paras go through their paces.

Every year, 3 Commando Brigade winters in Norway. The training there is progressive, teaching recruits new to the Arctic the basic rules of survival in a frozen environment and how to ski. Twelve-mile ski races are held carrying heavy bergens and rifles, with a shooting test halfway through. Another, less vital, test is the 'Nigs Race', in which the Arctic novices race in thick snow wearing nothing but boots, gloves and furry hats. Artillery practice is held at Hjerkinn ranges, 3000ft above sea level and well inland where the weather is bitterly cold. 148 Battery also spends a week parachuting into remote fjords and onto small clearings in wooded hillsides. Heavy bergens are parachuted down with snowshoes strapped to the outsides, while skis and heavy equipment are carried on sledges known as polks. During a jump involving polks, the first two men jump, then the polk is despatched, followed very closely by the last three men. They all steer in towards the polk and land as close to it as possible. If the snow is deep it is surprisingly difficult to don snowshoes and get to the sledge. Once the team has joined up, they put on skis and haul the polk away, with two on the front and one at the back as brakeman.

The final exercise for 3 Commando Brigade always takes place well inside the Arctic Circle and involves an amphibious assault, parachute insertions of some Forward Observation teams, and a week or more of hard living and fast movement in the mountains.

may have no prior information at all.

If the Forward Observation teams are sent in before the main body of troops, and 148 teams would need to be inserted early, it would then be essential that they should not be discovered if the future landing were not to be compromised. With such a need for absolute secrecy, intelligence gathering has to be very cautious indeed. During the day after their insertion the team stays in a hide, observing the surrounding countryside and the ground it intends to cross that night. When the men reach the observation position, often after some lengthy and very careful movement, they vanish and will only break radio silence, or emerge at night to reconnoitre, for something really important. They are now ready to control the fire on targets ahead.

Naval guns, artillery and ground-attack aircraft are at their most effective when the fire is closely controlled by an observer on the ground. The identification of targets and their exact locations (as well as the evaluation of their relative importance) can be done only by men who have been in the area for some time. The application of firepower – in which enemy locations are attacked by gunnery or aircraft – has only a limited effect if there is no-one on the ground to adjust the fire, evaluate the damage and bring down more fire if necessary.

Techniques of controlling artillery and naval gunfire are broadly similar. A map grid location and a bearing from the observer to the target is given and the gun is fired. The observer adjusts the shell by giving corrections by radio until it lands in line with the target. Actually to hit the target, he must bracket – that is, observe one shell land behind and one in front of the target, then halve the corrections until he hits. This normally takes up to 10 minutes. When an observer has been in a position for an hour or so he should be able to hit targets with his first shell.

Once hit, targets are recorded on the gun position computer with a target number, so that they can be fired upon again accurately and quickly without the need for any adjustment. The maximum damage is done to enemy positions during the first few seconds of a bombardment. However, the deliberate process of adjustment warns an experienced enemy of the imminent danger, so that by the time the 'fire for effect' of all the guns together comes down he is safe in his trench.

Taking advantage of the speed and accuracy of gunnery, the observer is able to carry out 'aerial ambushes' of enemy positions, in which he suddenly hits them in a few seconds with the power of all the guns he has at his disposal. This tactic is particularly useful against enemy convoys moving down roads and against enemy artillery. After one such ambush, enemy gunners become most reluctant to leave their trenches and move back to their guns, and the enemy battery is obliged to move to a new location

Below: 148 Battery personnel at a camouflaged field headquarters of the Dutch Marines in Norway. Top right: Gunner 'Tich' Barfoot and Bombardier 'Thommo' Thomas on patrol with a Dutch Marine. Centre right: A team prepares to move out of their camp, which comprises a Canadian four-man tent and a Swedish Bv202 over-snow vehicle. Bottom right: Directed by 148 Battery observers, a NATO gun crew lets fly.

before it can fire again.

Attacks on enemy positions are generally preceded by a co-ordinated programme of gunfire. The forward positions are neutralised by steady shellfire so that weapons cannot be brought to bear on our troops. Fire is shifted onto different targets and, once the attackers are amongst the enemy trenches, the gunfire will be falling very close. Artillery observers are an integral part of the attack, often out in front, identifying new targets and bringing down fire upon them.

Naval gunfire training has two aspects – helping the Royal Navy to train the crews of the gunships, and training the FO teams themselves. There are naval gunfire ranges all over the world and FO teams regularly fire on them. The wildest is undoubtedly Seven Hills in Belize, which is surrounded by swampy jungle and infested with scorpions. In the UK, most of the firing takes place around the buoys in the sea off St Alban's Head, an area in which yachts insist on racing during the summer. The work entails long days spent peering through binoculars, usually at sea mist, helping the Navy to get their procedures right. Cape Wrath in Scotland is more interesting. There, the FO teams practise all their insertion skills, from boating and swimming to parachuting onto the sands at low tide. They fire the ships' guns onto the range, moving through the rugged hills or peering from dugouts on the other side of the sea loch.

Below left: 148 Battery volunteers during a jungle navigation exercise in Belize in Central America. Jungle navigation is a hard-won skill: maps are inaccurate, patrols may travel only one kilometre a day, and in limestone country streams may suddenly disappear underground, leaving the patrol without water. Far left: A patrol crosses a swollen river, their waterproofed bergens lashed together into a platform for their weapons. Left: The author, Major Hugh McManners, brews up outside his basha. Around his neck are morphine syrettes and a watch.

The techniques of naval gunfire control are basically the same as those of artillery – except when things go inexplicably wrong. The ship has many more problems than an artillery battery; it is at sea, steaming up and down to avoid enemy aircraft and submarines, and its computer is compensating for the pitch, yaw and changing position of the gun platform as well as working out the firing co-ordinates. The first shell of the day is called the 'Navigator's Round' because until it has landed the exact position of the ship and the accuracy of the firing cannot be determined. Thereafter, the fire is extremely accurate, especially so from a single gun, as opposed to an artillery battery deployed over several hundred yards of ground.

When a naval gun system goes wrong it takes the experience of an FO team to analyse the problem and get the system working properly again. The observer on the shore must be able to work through the difficulty, allowing for the error and continuing his task, because the gunfire is always needed.

Controlling ground attack by aircraft is very different from controlling gunfire. The pilot of a jet fighter-bomber, screaming along at 500 knots, 50ft above the ground, sees a green blur and very little else. The Forward Air Controller (FAC) has to navigate the pilot from a known point to the target, talk him onto the precise location to enable him to deliver the weapon load accurately, and then direct him out of the area on a safe route away from enemy anti-aircraft defences. The weapon loads vary from rockets and cluster bombs to cannon fire and 1000lb iron bombs.

The FAC has to be able to talk fast without gabbling, as the attacks take only a few seconds once the aircraft is visible over the horizon. He has also to be able to vary his performance to suit all sorts of aircraft, from the super-fast Jaguar to the super-slow A-10 with its tight turns and baffling aerobatic attack configurations. Both the FO team leader (the captain) and his second in command (the bombardier) are trained as FACs.

The Falklands War, the most recent all-out combat in which the British Army has been engaged, amply demonstrated the enormous tactical value of 148 Commando Forward Observation Battery. Inserting themselves unseen into the midst of the Argentinian positions, the unit's highly trained observers supplied a stream of accurate information to the land, sea and air strike elements of the Task Force, bringing down appropriate fire on a wide range of targets. By optimising the effectiveness of all three armed services' firepower, 148 Commando proved just how indispensable it was to the British fighting machine.

THE AUTHOR Major Hugh McManners, as a captain, was one of the Naval Gunfire Forward Observers of 148 Commando Forward Observation Battery in the 1982 Falklands campaign, where he received a Mention in Despatches. He has subsequently written a book entitled *Falklands Commando*.

ABRAMS
Resourceful US Chief-of-Staff

After the Battle of the Bulge in December 1944, General George S. Patton, Jr, said of then Lieutenant-Colonel Creighton W. Abrams, Jr: 'I'm supposed to be the best tank commander in the Army, but I have a peer – 'Abe' Abrams.' Coming from Patton, a man not known for his modesty, this was the ultimate compliment.

The compliment was well deserved. In the days before Patton's remark, Abrams led his 37th Tank Battalion in the vanguard of Patton's forces to cut off the southern flank of the German Ardennes offensive. His battalion, and the infantry that followed, were the elements that turned northwards, and raced to link up with the 101st Airborne in Bastogne in a three day dash over icy roads, overcoming German resistance, and never slowing down. Abrams was then just past his 30th birthday.

Creighton Abrams graduated from West Point in 1936. There, his classmates called him 'Number One.' This was not because of his class standing – he stood 184th of 276 – but because he came first alphabetically, standing at the head of the line for countless formations.

He was born on 16 September 1914 of a long line of Massachusetts Methodists. Although relatively young as battalion commanders go, he was already

THE ELITE
COMMANDERS

Left: General Creighton Abrams and below, the M1 Abrams which was named after him. Hundreds of M1 Abrams tanks now serve in Europe, where their namesake distinguished himself more than four decades earlier.

Left: Binh Dinh, Vietnam. Members of the 1st Cavalry Division await orders. A point man goes ahead to peruse the area before the troops move onward. Below: Abrams shortly after his graduation from West Point in 1936, where his classmates recognised his intiative, saying in the class yearbook: 'Wherever you find Abe, you'll find action. The two are inseparable.'

own within the US Army as an audacious leader. ve months before, his 37th Tank Battalion in their [?] Shermans had led the 4th Armored Division eak-out from the Normandy beachhead, using lence and speed to telling effect in the ensuing mpaign across France and Belgium. Abrams al- ys led his tank companies himself, his body rising m the turret of his command tank, and a big cigar ually jutted from his mouth. He wore out six Sher- ns during the war, nicknaming each of them underbolt'. He was one of the few leaders whose llantry in action earned two Distinguished Service osses and two Silver Stars in less than ten months of mbat. By 1945 he was a colonel, and only nine ars out of West Point.

n the years after World War II, Abrams continued rapid rise that saw his career culminate at the top, the Army's Chief-of-Staff in 1972. Along the way, e' Abrams blended gallantry and the experience armoured combat with an appreciation of the itical nuances of using armed forces.

Near the end of the Korean War, he was Chief-of- ff of three different Army corps, and sharpened political skills in his dealings with President ngman Rhee and a number of other Korean and US iticians.

By July 1962 he had been a general officer for six years. That summer, he was the chief-of-staff for the Federal troops sent to the University of Mississippi in case civil rights rioting there got beyond the control of state authorities and Federal marshals. He showed sensitivity and aplomb in dealing with an explosive situation. That was particularly true in coping with the many calls and demands from Washington. President John F. Kennedy and his brother Robert, the Attorney General, wanted the situation control- led peacefully. Abrams' calmness contributed greatly to that end.

Sensitive and demanding assignments continued to be given to Abrams, including command of the Army's V Corps in Germany. He won promotion to four-star general and was appointed Vice Chief-of- Staff, in which post he served between 1964 and 1967, during the administration of President Lyndon B. Johnson.

INTO VIETNAM

In 1967 Creighton Abrams was sent to Vietnam as deputy commander of US forces under General William C. Westmoreland, a West Point classmate. His leadership and tenacity were key elements in carrying the fight to the enemy in 1967 – the 'Year of the Big Battles'. His presence at a unit was always welcomed by officers and men alike. He dealt with all of them with dignity, respect, and understanding. This was especially true of units that had fought hard battles and taken serious casualties. Abrams' calm presence, with the cigar and his unexpected bright smiles, inspired the troops to continue the fight. When senior officers did not match up to his expecta- tions, he could erupt like a slumbering volcano to exert his moral force and temper to exhort them to do better. They did so or left.

When Westmoreland was promoted to Chief-of- Staff of the Army in 1968, Abrams took over the top command in Vietnam. There, over the next four years, he met the most difficult challenges of his career: shifting the emphasis of the fighting to the South Vietnamese as the American units began the phased withdrawal ordained by Washington. Again, his ability to deal with politicians and soldiers alike produced results that met the needs of the day. His leadership and programmes are credited with the South Vietnamese forces' ability to meet and hold the North Vietnamese Army Easter offensive of 1972.

He was the obvious choice for promotion to Chief- of-Staff of the Army when Westmoreland retired in mid-1972. In the Army's top job, Abrams inherited a force that was severely demoralised by the Vietnam experience, slated to become an all-volunteer force as conscription came to an end, and subject to the negative influences of drugs and public disdain. General Abrams devoted his energies to turn the Army around.

The frankness and candour with which he met these challenges was appreciated by both the Army and the US Congress. He concentrated on people, and expected the rest of the Army leadership to do likewise. His actions and programmes began to take hold, preserving the Army at a critical time.

However, General Abrams was not to see his measures come to fruition. On 4 September 1974, 12 days short of his 60th birthday, an Army General Order announced his death at 0035 hours that morn- ing. With his passing the Army lost a distinguished and dedicated leader, and the US nation a faithful servant.

THE ELITE COMMANDERS

Left: Avraham, 'Bren', Adan, one of the key commanders of the Yom Kippur War of 1973 and a great leader of armoured troops. Starting out as a company commander in the Jewish forces of the 1940s, Adan was appointed to some of the key positions in the Israeli Defence Forces (IDF) during the 1960s and 1970s. Below: A Centurion of the IDF surges forward in Sinai. Adan's greatest test was when his tanks proved vulnerable to new weapons and tactics in the 1973 War – but he showed himself able to rise to the challenge.

ADAN

Turning defeat into victory in the Sinai desert

Major-General Avraham ('Bren') Adan (born 1927) had a distinguished career in the Israeli Defence Forces (IDF), and was one of the leaders of the forces in the Sinai during the 1973 War (the Yom Kippur War).

Adan's first important command was in the 1956 War, when, as a lieutenant-colonel, he led a battle-group consisting of a battalion of Sherman tanks and mechanised infantry. His force isolated the strong Egyptian positions at Abu Aweigila, captured the El Ruafa Dam and resisted fierce counter-attacks.

In 1968, Adan was appointed to propose a set of defences along the Suez Canal during the 'War of Attrition' with Egypt, and his scheme was used as the basis for the 'Bar-Lev' Line which formed a central part of Israeli defensive planning.

In 1969, Adan was appointed commander of armoured forces within the Israeli Army, an influential position that had formerly been held by Israel Tal. Tal had moulded the Israeli tank units into aggressive, autonomous units, that had used their firepower and armour to dominate the battlefield.

When the Egyptians launched their surprise attack of October 1973, to try to recover Israeli-occupied Sinai, Adan was in command of one of the two reserve armoured divisions directed to reinforce the hard-pressed forces of Israeli Southern Command. He took his forces into the desert, and launched a counter-attack on 8 October, only to meet with a serious check. The Egyptians were using a heavy screen of anti-tank missiles and guns and were not attempting to leave their defensive positions, while the Israeli Air Force, heavily committed in the battle for the Golan Heights in the north of Israel, was in any case finding the Egyptian anti-aircraft screen difficult to penetrate.

These problems caused serious rifts within the Israeli command in Sinai, The GOC Southern Command, Schmuel Gonen, had less seniority than his two reserve divisional commanders, Adan and Ariel Sharon, and Sharon and Adan themselves were mutually antipathetic. Sharon wanted to keep on the offensive regardless of initial losses, while Adan realised that different tactics had to be worked out to deal with the new Egyptian approach.

The solution that Adan came up with was for the tanks to operate far more closely with mechanised infantry, in their 'Zeldas' (the Israeli name for the American M113 armoured personnel carrier). A mix of arms was to take on the Egyptians.

On 14 October, the Egyptians decided on an offensive, and were decisively defeated in a series of engagements in which superior Israeli tank gunnery played a major part. Now the Israelis themselves held the initiative and on 16 October the first Israeli forces crossed to the west bank of the Suez Canal. Adan's division was the one chosen to exploit this initial bridgehead, and his men began to move into position for a crossing, shattering an attempted Egyptian flank attack as they took up their positions: Adan's units destroyed 86 of a force of 96 Egyptian T62 tanks.

Once over the Canal, Adan's forces swept south to the Gulf of Suez, and although the final action, an attempt to take the town of Suez itself, was a failure, victory lay with the Israelis. Adan had demonstrated great fortitude when his armoured forces were under pressure, and had refused to panic.

THE ELITE COMMANDERS
ALEXANDER

Theatre Commander and Strategist

The British commander who was to become Field Marshal Lord Alexander of Tunis was born in 1891 and educated at Harrow and Sandhurst before being commissioned into the Irish Guards. He served in France during World War I, commanding his battalion at the age of 25, and held a variety of commands in the period between the wars.

With the outbreak of war in 1939 Major-General the Honourable Harold Alexander became commander of I Division of the British Expeditionary Force (BEF) under Lord Gort. When the BEF was obliged to evacuate and Gort was ordered back to Britain, Alexander was appointed as his successor and supervised the final evacuation at Dunkirk. When this was safely concluded he was given charge of the Southern Command, tasked with preparing for the expected German invasion. When it became clear that that invasion had been indefinitely postponed, Alexander was sent to Burma, but once again, Alexander found himself in charge of the withdrawal of British forces.

In August 1942 Churchill decided to dismiss General Sir Claude Auchinleck as Commander-in-Chief, Middle East. Alexander was appointed his successor and thus became the titular superior to Montgomery, who, as commander of the British Eighth Army, was now preparing to deliver a crushing blow to Field Marshal Rommel's German and Italian forces. Alexander handled his subordinate with the charm and tact for which he was noted throughout his career, seeing it as his main role to ensure that Montgomery was given the men and supplies that he needed.

Montgomery's victory at El Alamein in November 1942 is no longer seen by historians as quite the unqualified triumph of arms that it was hailed as at the time. With huge Anglo-American forces landing behind his back, Rommel would have been obliged to retreat eventually; he was outnumbered in men and tanks by more than two to one, the Allies had near-total supremacy in the air, and he was desperately short of fuel. Nonetheless, the end had come for the Axis powers in North Africa. In May 1943 it fell to General Alexander to cable to Churchill as follows: 'Sir: it is my duty to report that the Tunisian campaign is over. All enemy resistance has ceased. We are master of the North African shores.'

In July 1943, Sicily became the stepping-stone for the conquest of mainland Europe. Under the overall command of Eisenhower as Commander-in-Chief, Mediterranean, Alexander took command of the 15th Army Group, comprising the British Eighth Army under Montgomery and the American Seventh Army under General George S. Patton. Once again the Germans put up fierce resistance, and by the time the Allies entered Messina on 17 August, they had managed to evacuate more than 100,000 troops and 10,000 vehicles to the mainland.

Under Alexander's command, British and Canadian troops of the Eighth Army now crossed the Straits of Messina to make the first landing on the European mainland since 1940. On 9 September American and British troops of the US Fifth Army under General Mark Clark landed at Salerno. Meanwhile, the Italians had signed an armistice, Mussolini had been dismissed, and the Allies found themselves facing hardened German veterans in their struggle to conquer Italy.

With the Eighth Army on the Adriatic coast and the Fifth Army on the west coast, the Allies began an

Page 33: Lord Alexander in his capacity as Allied Supreme Commander in the Mediterranean. Right: At a conference in Italy, Churchill and Alexander discuss the battle situation. Below right: Staging through Tunis, victorious Allied troops are greeted by the local population.

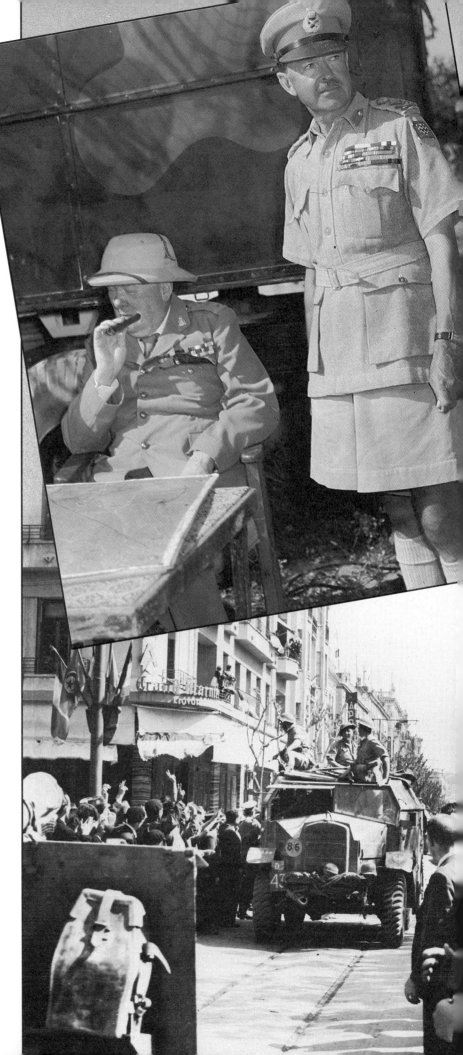

arduous and costly struggle north towards Rome. Their German opponents fought a brilliant defensive action, falling back in carefully planned retreats from one defensive line to the next. Unable to outflank them, the Allies finally ground to a halt at the Gustav line, the key point of which was the town of Cassino, dominated by the ancient monastery on the mountain-top above. For almost five months, the Fifth Army battered at the German defences. In an attempt to break the stalemate Allied troops landed behind the Geman lines at Anzio, but once again the landing was not followed up, the Germans rushed in troops to stop the gap, and the Allied troops were virtually besieged on their beachhead for four months. It was during one of his many assaults on Cassino that Alexander authorised the air-strike on the monastery, in the belief that it was being used by German artillery observers.

At last, in May 1944, Alexander brought troops over from the Eighth Army in preparation for a massive assault. Simultaneously he reinforced the positions at Anzio in readiness for a break-out to the north, with the intention of pinning the Germans between the two Allied forces and eliminating them.

GERMANS CRACK

Under the force of this two-fold assault the Germans finally cracked and withdrew northwards, but Alexander's overall plan was frustrated when General Clark ordered General Lucian Truscott to change the direction of his advance from Anzio and head straight for Rome. American troops entered Rome on 4 June 1944, but the Allies had failed in their more important aim of destroying the German army in Italy. Having fought their way into Europe through Italy, albeit at immense cost, both Churchill and Alexander now proposed to forego the landings in southern France that had been planned earlier as a follow-up to the invasion of Normandy. Instead, in their view, the Allies should press on up through Italy and then either into France or into Eastern Europe. In a decision that was to alter the face of Europe, they were overruled by Roosevelt, who now insisted that it was time to honour their commitments to Stalin, who had no particular wish to have strong Allied forces in Eastern Europe. The landings in southern France went ahead, Italy became a secondary theatre, Allied resources were withdrawn, and the Germans were able to hold the Gothic line in the north virtually until the end of the war. Nevertheless, Alexander had the honour of being the first Allied commander to receive the surrender of a German army group in April 1945.

After the war Alexander became Governor-General of Canada, and between 1952 and 1954 he served as British Minster of Defence. He died in 1969.

ARRIAGA

|THE ELITE| COMMANDERS|

Defender of the Colonies

Kaulza Oliveira de Arriaga was born at Oporto on 18 January 1915 and, after education at the University of Oporto, was commissioned into the Portuguese engineers. Thereafter, his military career, until he took command of Portuguese ground forces in Mozambique in May 1969, was in a succession of administrative or educational appointments. The nature of many of these appointments, however, indicates the manner in which many Portuguese officers were able to combine purely military offices with quasi-civilian posts under the Salazarist regime that dominated Portugal from 1933 until its overthrow by the Armed Forces Movement (MFA) in April 1974. Of that Salazarist system, Arriaga was a dedicated and lasting supporter – as Colonel in 1961 he had actually been instrumental in foiling one plot against Salazar.

His first significant appointment was as an instructor at the Field School for Military Engineering from 1939 to 1945, Portugal being a neutral power during World War II. Arriaga then served at Military Headquarters in Lisbon and on the Army General Staff. From 1950 to 1954 he served in various posts in the Ministry of Defence and from 1955 to 1962 he was under secretary, then secretary of state for aeronautics. He became professor of strategy and tactics at the Institute for Higher Military Studies in 1964, with the rank of Brigadier; director of the Centre for Staff Studies in 1966; and chairman of the Atomic Energy Board in 1967. He was promoted General in 1968.

THE PORTUGUESE ANSWER

Arriaga was posted to Mozambique in 1969, when the colony was under threat from nationalist guerrillas of the Frente de Libertaçâo de Mocambique (FRELIMO). Initially, he commanded only ground forces, but by 1970 he was Commander-in-Chief of all Portuguese forces in Mozambique. Arriaga was the only Portuguese commander to seek to develop a personality cult and to introduce political instruction for his own troops. Arriaga also introduced an extensive campaign to win the 'hearts and minds' of the local population and expanded black units such as the elite *Grupos Especiales*.

The opening of a new FRELIMO front in the Tete region of Mozambique in 1968, had increasingly presented major problems for the Portuguese. Much effort was put into defending the prestigious Cabora Bassa dam project, but at the expense of FRELIMO infiltration from their strongholds in the north into central and even southern Mozambique. Thus, in the summer of 1970, Arriaga launched Operation Gordian Knot, with 10,000 troops to clear the northern provinces of Niassa and Cabo Delgado. Although seriously damaging FRELIMO infrastructure, Gordian Knot did not stop the guerrillas' ability to infiltrate from their sanctuaries over the border in Tanzania. Coupled with the repercussions of allegations of Portuguese massacres of Africans at Wiriyamu, which surfaced in July 1973, the situation led to Arriaga's recall to Portugal in August 1973.

Above: General Kaulza Oliveira de Arriaga, who was in charge of Portuguese forces in Mozambique from 1969 to 1973. In 1970, Arriaga launched Operation Gordian Knot which, although dealing a massive blow to the FRELIMO nationalist guerrilla organisation, failed to affect the movement at its source – in its bases across the border of Tanzania – and Mozambique was given independence in June 1975.

Arriaga, who became President of the Council for Nuclear Energy, flirted with the MFA until it became apparent that it was not a conservative movement. As an ultra right winger, Arriaga was outraged by the condemnation of Portugal's colonial role by the former Portuguese commander in Guinea, Antonio de Spinola, in February 1974. Arriaga had, in fact, published his own views on the need to continue the wars in the colonies in *The Portuguese Answer,* a book privately printed for him in England in 1973. It was not, therefore, surprising that he was retired by the new Spinola regime after the MFA coup. When more radical elements forced Spinola's resignation as president in September 1974, Arriaga was arrested and remained in detention until June 1976. In the following year he founded a right wing party but his influence has remained slight.

THE ELITE COMMANDERS

The Indian Army officer who stopped Rommel in the Desert

Field Marshal Sir Claude John Eyre Auchinleck (1884-1981) was born in India, the son of a colonel serving there. Educated at Wellington College, the young Auchinleck then went on to the Royal Military Academy Sandhurst and was commissioned into the Indian Army in 1903.

After service in World War I in Aden, Egypt and Mesopotamia, and then a period of action in Kurdistan in 1919, Auchinleck had collected a mention in dispatches, a DSO and an OBE. He was noted as the outstanding Indian Army officer of his generation, and, having attended the Imperial Staff College in Britain in 1927, returned to India to assume command of the 1st Battalion, 1st Punjabi Regiment. In 1930 he was appointed instructor at the Staff College at Quetta and in 1933 was given command of the Peshawar Brigade—a much-coveted post. By 1936 he was a major-general and in 1937 was appointed Deputy Chief of Staff.

In 1940, as the Indian Army's most renowned general officer, Auchinleck was recalled to England (by now a most unfamiliar country) and immediately found himself launched into action. First of all he

AUCHINLECK

Page 36, inset: Field
Marshal Sir Claude John
Eyre Auchinleck, soon after
the end of World War II.
Page 36, main picture:
South African troops in the
desert in a Stuart light tank.
Above: Auchinleck during
the period of desperate
fighting that saw the defeat
of Rommel at the Alamein
position in summer 1942.
Above Right:
Commonwealth troops
under Auchinleck's
command move cautiously
forward in North Africa.

served in Norway, where troops under his command retook Narvik before being shipped home to meet the threat of German invasion of Britain itself. Auchinleck took up command of V Corps on the south coast, and then took over all of Southern Command – a key post. His efficient, business-like manner did not endear him to all his contemporaries, but there was general respect for his obvious ability – except in the case of one of his subordinates, Bernard Law Montgomery.

In November 1940, Auchinleck was promoted full general and recalled to India, as Commander-in-Chief of the army there – the summit of the career of an Indian Army officer in normal times. His reputation was high, and when British Prime Minister Winston Churchill decided to relieve Sir Archibald Wavell as GOC Middle East Command in June 1941, Auchinleck was chosen for this critical post.

Like Wavell before him, Auchinleck realised that the British forces in Egypt were hardly ready to drive the Axis out of North Africa and he resisted Churchill's requests for an offensive until November 1941, when he ordered the newly created Eighth Army, under Lieutenant General Sir Alan Cunningham (brother of the Admiral and victor over Italian forces in the Sudan earlier in 1941), to move forward to relieve the besieged port of Tobruk.

The resulting battle was a confused affair, and a typical thrust deep into British lines by Rommel's armour placed the Allied forces in some danger. Auchinleck was forced to replace Cunningham, who wanted to call off the operation, and replaced him with Lieutenant-General Neil Ritchie; Rommel was eventually made to pull back. The Axis forces retreated around the 'bulge' of Cyrenaica, but made a surprise attack in their turn in January 1941, pushing the Eighth Army back to positions at Gazala. Late in May Rommel struck again, winning perhaps the greatest of his desert victories, sending the Eighth Army reeling back into Egypt and taking Tobruk.

Now Auchinleck took up direct command of the Eighth Army from Ritchie. He extricated X Corps from a difficult position near Mersa Matruh, and stopped the Axis drive in its tracks at the El Alamein position, where he established a defensive line making use of the fact that an area of soft sand to the south hindered the movement of armoured vehicles.

Auchinleck's conduct of the defence of the Alamein position – making constant attacks on the weaker Italian forces and maintaining the morale of an army that had just suffered a heavy defeat and been forced into precipitate retreat – marked him out as a commander of high calibre when it came to leading an army in the field. The initial success of Rommel's offensive had, however, lost Auchinleck credibility with Churchill, and early in August 1942 the British Prime Minister flew to Egypt and relieved Auchinleck of his command. Middle East Command was split in two parts, and Auchinleck was offered command of Iraq and Persia; but he refused this post and returned to India.

In June 1943, Auchinleck was given his second great command: he was again appointed Commander-in-Chief of the Indian Army, with responsibility for the training and organisation of the British, Empire and Commonwealth forces in the Far East. He conducted this enormous administrative task with great skill. Auchinleck was created Field Marshal in 1946, and he still had one further crucial role to perform. An Indian Army officer all his life, he was charged with dividing the Indian Army between the newly emergent states of India and Pakistan – a painful, difficult job that he discharged very well.

Following the partition of India, Auchinleck withdrew from public life. He refused a peerage and lived in North Africa until his death and refused to indulge in the public debate about the conduct of operations in the Western Desert. Despite criticism, most pertinently, perhaps, of his choice of subordinates, there can be no doubt that Auchinleck was an excellent commander.

THE ELITE COMMANDERS

The GIs' General

'Bradley has many of the attributes which are considered desirable in a general. He wears glasses, has a strong jaw, talks profoundly and says little, and is a shooting companion of the Chief of Staff.' So wrote Lieutenant-General George Patton when he learnt that he was to serve under Bradley in northwest Europe in 1944 – a reversal of the command chain that had existed in Sicily a year before – and, like all ironic statements, it contains a grain of truth. Omar Nelson Bradley (1893-1981) was a quiet, almost unassuming man, who did not look like a fighting general, and there is no doubt that he owed his promotion, at least in part, to friends in high places. But Patton was a biased witness. In reality, Bradley was a very able commander, leading his army group from the shores of Normandy to the heart of Germany in 1944-45 and going on to hold the highest military offices in the United States.

Bradley began his career at West Point as a member of the 'Class of 1915', sharing the experience with, among others, Dwight D. Eisenhower. Like Eisenhower, he failed to see action in World War I, but this did little to hold him back. By 1929 he was an instructor at the Fort Benning Infantry School, where he attracted the attention of another useful mentor, George C. Marshall, the future Chief of Staff. In 1940, under Marshall's guidance, Bradley moved to Washington as Assistant Secretary of the General

BRADLEY

Left: Lieutenant-General Bradley's troops scour the streets of Messina, looking for snipers after capturing the town in July 1943. Right: Omar Nelson Bradley, who commanded over a million and a quarter men, the largest number of troops ever commanded by an American field commander.

Staff before transferring back to Fort Benning, this time as Commandant. By then, he was clearly marked for higher command.

As soon as the United States entered World War II in December 1941, Bradley was given command of the reactivated 82nd Infantry Division (soon to be trained for the airborne role), and this was followed by a stint as commander of the 28th Infantry Division, raised from the Pennsylvania National Guard. In both cases, his command skill, tact and efficiency were noted so that when, in early 1943, Marshall felt that Eisenhower, commanding US forces in North Africa, needed a 'trouble-shooter', Bradley seemed the obvious choice. His task was not easy – when he arrived in Tunisia the US II Corps had just been mauled at Kasserine Pass – and it took a mixture of ruthlessness and diplomacy to restore morale. One of Bradley's decisions was to sack the existing corps commander and replace him with Patton. The latter, wary of having Eisenhower's representative peering over his shoulder, insisted that Bradley should be his second-in-command; it turned out to be a good command team. Patton, intent on glory, was occasionally reckless and constantly disdainful of such mundane matters as logistics; Bradley was more practical and acted as a useful moderating influence. When Patton took over the US Seventh Army for the planned invasion of Sicily, Bradley assumed command of II Corps, gathering around himself a staff of particularly able men.

OPERATION OVERLORD

During the Sicily invasion, II Corps constituted the field formation of the Seventh Army and Bradley was beginning to experience problems controlling the zeal of Patton, particularly during the 'race to Messina' in August 1943. The result was a reversal of fortunes for the two men, especially after Patton had been discredited by the notorious 'soldier-slapping' incidents, and when Eisenhower began to put together his command team for Operation Overlord (the invasion of Europe), he looked with favour on his old classmate, by now highly experienced and renowned for calmness under pressure. As Patton kicked his heels and remained firmly at the level of army command, Bradley was transferred to Britain to

Top: A US machine gunner strategically positioned with his 0.30in Browning in the hedgerow country of France. On 25 July 1944, Bradley launched Operation Cobra (the Allied Normandy breakout), which he later described as 'the most decisive battle of our war in Western Europe'. Below: M4 Sherman tanks prepare to come ashore in support of Allied troops in 1944.

prepare the US First Army for the invasion, on the clear understanding that, once the forces were ashore, he would take over full command of an army group.

First Army units, under Bradley's leadership, stormed ashore on Utah and Omaha Beaches on 6 June 1944, experiencing some problems for which Bradley has been held to blame. His lack of confidence in the British-designed amphibious tanks, for example, was probably misplaced – they would have been particularly useful on Omaha as the American troops clung precariously to the beachhead – but, once the initial crisis was over, Bradley carried out his task of building up forces on the Allied right without delay. Under the overall command of General Sir Bernard Montgomery, the Americans captured Cherbourg, cleared the Cotentin peninsula and, in late July, began the process of break-out, attacking south from St Lô. By then, Patton had reappeared, this time as commander of the US Third Army which, together with the First, formed 12th Army Group, under Bradley. By 1 September, with Eisenhower assuming supreme command of all Allied forces, Bradley found himself on a par with Montgomery, with Patton under his charge. It was a volatile mixture of personalities.

The fact that Bradley was able to command effectively in these circumstances says much for his skill. He was one of the few American commanders who could co-operate with Montgomery, for although the latter viewed Bradley as inexperienced, he grew to respect his quiet efficiency and command ability. Their relationship even weathered the storm of December 1944, when Bradley's army group, caught by the surprise German offensive in the Ardennes, had to be split, with the US First and Ninth Armies shifting temporarily to Montgomery's command. The relationship with Patton was less smooth, but by then Bradley was used to the recklessness of his subordinate and fully aware of his brilliance if allowed a certain degree of tactical freedom. As Allied forces crossed the Rhine – with Bradley's men leading the way through Remagen in early March 1945 – the precarious balance of command personalities was being maintained by Eisenhower, ably supported by Bradley.

Once the war was over, Bradley acted as Administrator of Veterans' Affairs before being appointed Army Chief of Staff in 1948. A year later, he became Chairman of the Joint Chiefs of Staff and, as such, presided over US efforts in Korea. He retired, as a five-star General, in 1953.

THE ELITE COMMANDERS

Brilliant strategic planner

Alan Francis Brooke was born at Bagnères-de-Bigorre in the French Pyrenees on 23 July 1883. His parents, both from old Ulster families (his father was third Baronet of Colebrooke) had taken to spending the winters in the south of France, and it was there that Alan Brooke was brought up and educated, speaking French before he spoke English. Though his blood was Anglo-Irish, like that of so many distinguished British soldiers, his biographer General Sir David Fraser believes that it was possible to detect the influence of this French upbringing and early environment in the quickness and clarity of his mind.

Coming as he did from a family with a long military tradition, it was determined when he was in his teens that he should have an army career. He entered the Royal Military Academy at Woolwich, which trained cadets for the Royal Artillery and Royal Engineers. In December 1902 he was commissioned into the Royal Regiment of Artillery, serving initially in Ireland and India, and learning his trade in France and Flanders in World War I.

Between the wars Brooke distinguished himself as a brilliant instructor at the Staff College and the Imperial Defence College and developed an interest in technical innovations, especially the use of armour, which made him one of the more far-sighted young officers of that period. On the outbreak of World War II he went to France as a lieutenant-

ALAN BROOKE

general in command of II Corps, British Expeditionary Force, playing a major part in the evacuation at Dunkirk. Recognised already as a brilliant planner, he then became Commander-in-Chief, Home Forces, organising Britain's defences against the expected German invasion.

On Christmas Day, 1941, Brooke became Chief of the Imperial General Staff (CIGS). There was already strong regret that a man who had shown himself to be an excellent field commander should be removed from active service to a desk in Whitehall.

The judgement of General MacArthur that 'Alanbrooke [he became Viscount Alanbrooke in 1946] is undoubtedly the greatest soldier that England has produced since Wellington' may come as something of a surprise. As CIGS, Brooke was denied the public glamour that fell on Montgomery and the other fighting generals. The battles he fought, as Chairman of the Committee of the British Chiefs of Staff, were Whitehall battles, battles with Churchill, with his fellow planners, with the politicians and the senior commanders. Yet Brooke was responsible, with Churchill, and later with the American Chiefs of Staff, for the conduct of the war at the highest level and for its ultimate successful conclusion.

AT THE WAR OFFICE

On a typical day, on almost every day from December 1941 until the end of the war, Brooke would arrive at the War Office at 0900 hours. On his desk he would find overnight situation reports from all theatres, land, sea and air. All of these he would absorb at astonishing speed before his briefing team arrived at 1000, bringing him briefing folders for the 1030 meeting of the Chiefs of Staff. This would take place at Great George Street, in the warren of subterranean rooms where the War Cabinet also met. With him would be the First Sea Lord, the Chief of Air Staff and, for a time, Lord Mountbatten as Chief of Combined Operations. On the agenda would be a host of items that might relate to any of an almost infinite number of different aspects of the war.

After a brief interval for lunch, Brooke would return to the War Office for an afternoon of interviews with visiting commanders, then there would be more briefings before the meeting of the War Cabinet at 1830. After dinner he would return to Great George Street for the 2230 meeting of the Defence Committee of the Cabinet, with Winston Churchill in the chair and the other Chiefs of Staff also present. When that meeting was at last over, Churchill would detain Brooke for further discussions that frequently went on into the small hours.

Without Brooke the tide might never have turned and there might never have been a triumph in the West. The clarity and discipline of his mind, his grasp of the total picture of the war at any given time, and his brilliance as a planner enabled him to turn the

Committee of the Chiefs of Staff into the most efficient war machine that Britain, and perhaps the world, had ever seen. Though it was naturally not infallible, the plans that flowed from it, to be broken down stage by stage into orders that would eventually reach the smallest units in the field, ensured that Britain's always limted resources would be deployed to maximum effect. But it was Brooke's relationship with Winston Churchill that was the most crucial, and ultimately the most valuable. The two were complementary and, though they quarrelled frequently, they knew it. Once Churchill told General Ismay, a valued friend to both, that Brooke hated him and would have to go. Brooke, when told this, said 'I don't hate him, I love him, but when the day comes that I tell him he is right when I believe him to be wrong, it will be time for him to get rid of me.'

WORKING WITH CHURCHILL

Brooke rightly saw it as his job to turn Churchill's vision of ultimate victory into practicable policies – to talk him out of the madder schemes, to restrain him when the time was not ripe and the resources not ready, to take the responsibility of turning a perception of the ultimate course of the war into plans that could be put into effect, while Churchill's mind leapt forward to its next intuition. All this, calmly and imperturbably, Brooke did, day after day. Churchill frequently argued with him and with the other Chiefs of Staff, but on essentials he scarcely ever overruled them. When Brooke was convinced that his professional judgement of a situation was correct, and Churchill's wrong, he simply refused to budge.

Brooke is said to have been disappointed that he was not appointed Supreme Allied Commander for the invasion of Europe. That may be so, but in other respects he showed himself remarkably free from personal ambition. Though he worked himself to a point beyond exhaustion, his overriding desire was to do what he could to end the war as speedily, and with as few casualties, as possible. He retired as CIGS in 1946, in which year he also became Viscount Alanbrooke. Field Marshal Sir Alan Brooke died in 1963.

Page 40, left: Soldiers of the Royal Ulster Rifles, on a makeshift pier at Bray Dunes, about five miles from Dunkirk, await evacuation from the French coast in 1940. Then a lieutenant-general, Alan Brooke played a major part in co-ordinating the withdrawal. Bottom right: Viscount Alanbrooke's cool brilliance was an invaluable foil to Winston Churchill's impulsive genius. Many of Churchill's schemes would never have been realised without his assistance. This page, above: Alanbrooke (wearing spectacles) confers with his service chiefs and their US opposite numbers at Casablanca in January 1943. Below: Long lines of British troops queue to be evacuated from Dunkirk. Codenamed Operation Dynamo, the evacuation lasted from 26 May to 4 June 1940.

THE ELITE COMMANDERS

Father of modern Cuba

At the beginning of December 1956 a tall bearded lawyer called Fidel Castro was hiding in a sugar plantation from the forces of the Cuban dictator Fulgencio Batista. Three days before he had arrived from Mexico in the yacht *Granma* with his revolutionary army of just 81 men to launch the struggle for Cuban liberation. Running into an ambush his army had been thoroughly defeated and dispersed. Now reduced to three or four companions, practically devoid of weapons and supplies, he might easily have concluded that his revolution was over before it had begun. Just over two years later, on 8 January 1959, Castro marched into Havana and took over the government that he has held ever since.

Fidel Castro was born on 13 August 1927 and given an orthodox Catholic education by his middle-class parents. He graduated in law from the University of Havana in 1950 and had become active in politics from his student days. Political feelings intensified and moved further to the left after Fulgencio Batista, a former army sergeant, overthrew the government prior to democratic elections in 1952 and established the corrupt and repressive dictatorship that gave Cuba its political flavour in the early 1950s, virtually sharing power with gangsters, suppressing all dissent and trade union activity, but supported by the United States.

On 26 July 1953 Castro led a group of 111 men in a dawn attack on the Moncada barracks housing 1000 government troops, killing 19 of them. The revolutionaries were eventually forced to retreat and Castro was sentenced to 15 years in prison but he had established himself as a leading figure in the struggle against Batista. Released in an amnesty in 1955 he went to Mexico, met Che Guevara, who was to become his lieutenant, and started forming and training what he called, in honour of the Moncada venture, the 26 July Movement.

At that time, and subsequently, Castro maintained contacts with other revolutionary groups, then almost entirely urban, and his arrival in Cuba was intended to be co-ordinated with activity in Santiago de Cuba in Oriente province at the eastern end of the island. But the landing took place some distance away near the port of Niquero and Castro's small force was entirely unassisted when it ran into a unit of Batista's army. There were few casualties—four dead and one wounded – but inexperience led to panic and dispersal.

In mid-January Castro and about 20 followers regrouped in the Sierra Maestra, the mountainous region of Oriente province at the opposite end of the island from Havana and one of the poorest parts of the country. Castro's link with the urban guerrilla groups was known as *el llano* and there is no doubt at all that without it Castro would not have survived, let alone succeeded, for the evidence is that at that time in the Sierra Maestra his local support was practically nil. Castro did not win the support of either the urban proletariat or of the peasantry until his revolution was well on the way to success. When Castro felt strong enough to attack the El Uvero barracks on 28 May 1957 his force numbered 80 guerrillas, of whom 50 had probably been sent to him from Havana in

CASTRO

February of that year. For most of his two-year war he concentrated on small-scale lightning attacks on police and army barracks, combined with sabotage and bombing attacks organised by his revolutionary contacts in the cities.

It was during 1957 that stories about Fidel Castro began to appear in the American newspapers, where he was portrayed as a romantic Robin Hood-style figure. On the whole he fought a 'clean' war, treating his prisoners mercifully, caring for his followers and behaving with courtesy towards the local people. Although it became clear later that even at this stage he was planning a Marxist revolution after his victory, he was politically shrewd enough to keep that to himself, recognizing that until he had established his revolution he would need a wide range of political support, including that of liberals and the Church. Cuba was later to take massive financial aid from the Soviet Union, although at that time he was fighting his war with no help whatsoever from outside the country, frequently using weapons captured from Batista's American-equipped army.

By the end of 1957, though still numbering perhaps only 200 guerrillas, Castro's 26 July Movement was

THE ELITE COMMANDERS

Page 42. Top: Fidel Castro, the man who led the revolutionary army in Cuba to victory. The war resulted in Castro leading the first communist state in the region. Below: Members of Castro's army take a break, rifles at the ready.
This page. Top: Seated left to right; Brezhnev, Castro and Khrushchev. In the aftermath of revolution, Castro turned to the Soviet bloc for aid. Below: The Bay of Pigs, 17 April 1961, brought humiliation for the US and further prestige for Castro.

well established in the Sierra Maestra. In February 1958 the rebels in the Sierra declared 'total war against tyranny'. Events began to move rapidly. Recognising that the foundations of the Batista regime were beginning to crumble, the US government withdrew military supplies in March 1958. At the same time, detached columns from Castro's forces were beginning to operate on the north coast (under Fidel's brother, Raúl) and in the Escambray mountains in the centre. Deciding that he could no longer slight this challenge to his power, Batista ordered an all-out offensive, involving perhaps as many as 11,000 government troops against perhaps 300 of Castro's. But Batista's forces were already demoralised, ill-led and deeply riddled with corruption. Within two months the Batista forces were in retreat.

THE REGIME CRUMBLES

By the summer of 1958 Castro virtually controlled the eastern part of the country, drawing his supplies from local agriculture and business and running his own newspaper and radio station. The whole country was beginning to turn to his cause. In August he went on the offensive in the centre of Cuba, by now commanding an army of perhaps 1500 men, but with the moral and material support of a major part of the population of Cuba. On 28 December, Che Guevara took the western provincial capital of Santa Clara. Batista fled into exile on 1 January 1959 and Che's men moved into Havana on the night following that day. Fidel Castro made his triumphal entry seven days later.

In the honeymoon period following his seizure of power, Castro indicated a liberal-democratic programme, including free elections. There is now very little doubt that during that period he was running a parallel government, working behind the facade of liberal government while he established the structures of a radical regime on his own very personal neo-marxist lines. In 1961 he humiliated the US by repulsing the CIA-sponsored Bay of Pigs invasion. In the following year he probably suffered less of a defeat than the Russians when President Kennedy forced a climb-down in the Cuban missile crisis. Subsequently Cuba has stepped outside of the Caribbean to play an important part on the world stage in Africa and elsewhere. Economically it depends heavily on aid from the Soviets. It has removed the corruption and brutality of the Batista regime and given its people decent standards at least at the basic levels of health and elementary education. Castro, fighting against all odds, defeated Batista's army both strategically and psychologically.

THE ELITE COMMANDERS

CHALLE

The counter-insurgency expert whose own rebellion failed

Maurice Challe (1905-1979) has the distinction of having led one of the most enterprising and important counter-insurgency campaigns of modern times. He also has the rather less fortunate claim to fame of having led an unsuccessful revolt against the government he was committed to obey.

Challe went to the officer school at Sancerre, and after joining the French Air Force rose rapidly in rank. After the defeat in 1940 he was prominent in the Resistance, and led the famous Free French 'Marauder' squadron in the final year of the war. During the turbulent years of the Fourth Republic, he was associated with the policies of the socialist Guy Mollet, and was frequently entrusted with delicate diplomatic missions. In 1956, however, he came under a cloud when he made serious criticisms of the organisation of French forces during the Suez crisis.

The overthrow of the Fourth Republic and the return to power of Charles de Gaulle in 1958 marked a change in Challe's fortunes, for de Gaulle put him in charge in Algeria, where the French Army was engaged in a bitter struggle against the nationalist guerrillas of the FLN (Front de Libération National).

Challe decided to utilise the fact that very effective frontier defences (*barrages*) had cut the rate of infiltration into Algeria from Tunisia and Morocco. He formed a strong reserve of elite units, such as the Foreign Legion and parachute regiments, to act as a striking force, while the mass of conscripts held a pattern of more static posts across the country. He wanted to attack the FLN in its traditional strongholds in the mountains. 'Neither the mountains nor

Above left: Maurice Challe, the air force general who proved that he could master the intricacies of counter-insurgency. Above: Challe with his fellow conspirators in April 1961. From left are generals André Zeller, Edmond Jouhaud, Raoul Salan and Challe himself. All these senior military men felt intense disquiet about the policy being pursued by the government of Charles de Gaulle. They believed passionately that France should not give in to the FLN, and were especially concerned that the pro-French Moslems (*harkis*) who had fought for the French forces should not be abandoned to the mercies of the nationalists. In the event, the French forces in Algeria decided to stay loyal to the French government, and the 'coup of the generals' collapsed after four days.

the night must be left to the FLN' was his slogan.

In the area chosen for attack, small groups of fast pursuit troops (*commandos de chasse*), guided by special tracker units composed of Moslems loyal to the French (*harkis*), would follow and engage FLN bands. Then, large units of the mobile reserve would be swiftly brought in, often by air. Concentrated air strikes would add to the problems of the guerrillas, and the French would remain in an area for long enough to clear it completely, secure in the knowledge that the enemy was cut off from reinforcement. During 1959, French forces moved steadily across the hinterland of Algeria, in what became known as the 'Challe Offensive'. From April to July, Operation Courroie destroyed the FLN in the eastern Ouarensis; then, in July, a move into the Hodna devastated the FLN there, while in Operation Jumelles (completed by October) the Kabylia was cleared.

By January 1960, the imperturbable, pipe-smoking Challe was preparing for his final large-scale move, against the guerrilla concentrations in the Aurès. But now, however, de Gaulle was rethinking his whole policy toward Algeria. In May, Challe was removed from command, and the final offensive never took place as events began to swing inexorably towards independence for Algeria. In common with many other senior officers, Challe was disenchanted with the new policy. He resigned from the armed forces, and, in April 1961, joined three other generals in Algiers trying to rally the army to overthrow de Gaulle's regime. Support was not forthcoming, however, and Challe surrendered to the authorities. He was tried and sentenced to a long period of imprisonment, but was pardoned after only five years. It was a sad end to a brilliant career.

THE ELITE COMMANDERS

Shrewd and innovative Soviet Army commander

Vasili Ivanovich Chuikov was born near Moscow in 1900. Joining the Red Army in 1918, he rose to command a regiment during the Civil War (1919-21) and was quickly earmarked for a long-term military career. Between 1925 and 1927 he attended the Frunze military academy, and by 1938 he was commanding a rifle corps. After service in the Russo-Finnish 'Winter War' of 1939-40, he was promoted to lieutenant-general and given command of the Fourth Army in western Russia. Fortunately for his future, he was sent to China in early 1941 to act as head of the Soviet military mission to Chiang Kai-shek's Nationalist forces, missing the disasters which followed the German invasion of Russia in June.

Returning home in March 1942, Chuikov was appointed to command the Sixty-Fourth Army, in the process of being formed in the Don sector. It proved to be an important task, for as the German offensive towards the Caucasus developed, Chuikov's men found themselves in the forefront of battle. On 25/26 July 1942, German forces attacked towards the Don river, forcing Chuikov to commit all his reserves and, when they failed to stem the tide, to pull back to positions astride the Volga to the south of Stalingrad. As his first taste of action in the new war, this was hardly a success, but Chuikov's combination of calmness and resolution soon brought him to the attention of Stalin. On 10 September, as the German advance on Stalingrad gathered momentum, Chuikov was

Above: Vasili Chuikov displays his military regalia. Below: A line of Russian rocket launchers opens up on German positions as the prelude to a Soviet night attack.

transferred to command the Sixty-Second Army, desperately clinging to positions in the western suburbs of the city with his back to the Volga.

Chuikov assumed his new command just in time to witness a ferocious German assault, clearly designed to seize the west bank of the river. Under a murderous hail of shellfire and dive-bomber attack, his already depleted units held on in small pockets of resistance, forcing the enemy to fight for every house and street corner. At one point, German assault squads penetrated to within 800yds of Chuikov's command bunker, but he kept his nerve. The timely arrival of the 13th Guards Division, fed across the Volga in penny-packets late on 14 September, prevented a Soviet collapse, but the situation was desperate.

CHUIKOV

The battle for the west bank, centred on fortified positions around the railway station and the factories of Krasnya Oktyabr, Barrikady and the Tractor Plant, continued at a ferocious pace throughout the autumn months. The Sixty-Second Army, reinforced piecemeal, refused to crack, gradually drawing the German Sixth Army into the jaws of a trap. Although the tenacity of individual Soviet soldiers, living amid the rubble of their ruined city, was a key to eventual victory, the command skills of Chuikov were impressive. Moving his command post as far forward as possible, his constant presence acted as a boost to morale and enabled him to 'see' the battle with remarkable clarity, moulding his forces to fit the tactical needs of the conflict. By mid-October, he had abandoned traditional unit formations and introduced the concept of small 'assault teams', ideally suited to urban combat. Armed with light weapons and commanded by junior officers or NCOs, these teams were able to infiltrate German positions and engage in attritional battles which prevented enemy concentrations of force and broke the back of his attack formations. By mid-November, German attention (and reserves) had been drawn into the centre of Stalingrad, enabling Soviet armies to mount counter-attacks to the north and south, encircling the city.

ELITE SPEARHEAD

Chuikov's men – soon to be renamed Eighth Guards Army in recognition of their bravery – continued to fight in Stalingrad until the German surrender in late January 1943, but thereafter they rapidly assumed

Below left: Chuikov (left of picture) in Stalingrad, the scene of one of the Red Army's, and Chuikov's, great achievements. Below right: Polish troops enter Berlin in 1945.

the role of an elite spearhead of Soviet assaults. By October 1943, Chuikov was leading his units in a fight to establish bridgeheads across the Dniepr river at Zaporozhi; eight months later he and his men had been shifted further north to join Rokossovsky's 1st Belorussian Front, poised for an advance into eastern Poland. After a period of intensive training to familiarise them with the marshes of Belorussia, Eighth Guards Army took up positions to lead the breakthrough on the left flank of the forthcoming Operation Bagration, scheduled for 18 July 1944. Chuikov was still introducing new tactical ideas. Recognising a German pattern of pulling back to prepared positions as soon as artillery strikes heralded a Soviet attack, he limited his preliminary barrage to 30 minutes, then committed 'reconnaissance forces' to move deep into the enemy rear, preventing pre-emptive withdrawals. It worked well, enabling Eighth Guards Army to achieve an immediate and decisive breakthrough. By 26 July, Chuikov had reached the Vistula river, close to Warsaw, and pushed forces across to the west bank.

Unfortunately, the Soviet advance then stalled, chiefly because of a shortage of supplies, and Chuikov did not break out from the bridgehead until January 1945, having done nothing to prevent the German suppression of the Warsaw Uprising the previous August. By the new year, German defences were crumbling fast and Chuikov's men forged ahead, taking Lodz and Poznan before pausing on the banks of the Oder, close to Berlin. Their final campaign began on 16 April, aiming to take the enemy capital, but the fighting was hard. The move into Berlin was opposed every step of the way and all the experience of street-fighting, gained in Stalingrad and reinforced more recently in Poznan, had to be brought to bear. Once again, Chuikov introduced the 'assault team' concept and, as other Soviet armies closed in from north and south, his men inched forward towards the Reichstag. The Red Banner was raised over the ruins late on 30 April and, two days later, Chuikov had the satisfaction of negotiating the final surrender of a beaten enemy. It was a fitting end to his fighting career.

Chuikov went on to hold a variety of higher command posts in the postwar period, culminating in his appointment as Commander-in-Chief, Soviet Land Forces in 1960. He retired in 1972 and died ten years later.

THE ELITE COMMANDERS

US Commander in Italy

General Mark Wayne Clark, who was to command American forces in Italy in World War II, was born in 1896 and graduated from West Point in 1917. Tall, lean, with considerable personal charm, he was known to his friends as 'Wayne'. Winston Churchill nicknamed him 'The American Eagle'. Eisenhower described him as the 'best organizer, planner and trainer of troops that I have met'.

Between the wars Clark became a staff officer and with American entry into World War II he was promoted rapidly, becoming the commander of US ground forces in Europe as second-in-command to Eisenhower in July 1942. In October of that year he made a secret journey to North Africa in the British submarine HMS *Seraph* for a meeting with French officers in preparation for Operation Torch. After the successful Allied landings in North Africa (8 November 1942) and the subsequent advance into Tunisia, he negotiated with the Vichy commander, Admiral Darlan, whom eventually Eisenhower and Clark accepted as 'Head of State' in North Africa.

Clark became a lieutenant-general in November 1942 and in January 1943 was given command of the US Fifth Army which, from July of that year, began preparations for the invasion of mainland Italy. At the Casablanca Conference of 14-23 January 1943 and the Washington Conference of 12-25 May 1943, the Americans, while still pressing for a cross-Channel invasion of German-occupied Europe, had somewhat reluctantly accepted Italy as an interim objective that would at least compel the Germans to divert forces from the Eastern Front and thus ease the pressure on the Russians. This lack of commitment, which meant that the Allies were never to devote adequate resources or to provide thorough follow-up planning, was to combine with the terrible terrain through which it was fought, to make the Italian campaign one of the most bitter and costly of the war. Although the Allies had cleared Sicily and reached the Straits of Messina by August 1943, the Germans were surprised at the ease with which they were able to extricate virtually their entire force of 40,000 men plus 62,000 Italian troops.

INTO ITALY

On 3 September 1943, Montgomery's Eighth Army landed (Operation Baytown) near Reggio in the toe of Italy. Six days later, following the Italian surrender, Clark's Anglo-American forces landed at Salerno, meeting surprisingly fierce resistance from the hardened German troops who had been rushed in to meet them. The Allies only just managed to establish and maintain their beachhead, and by the time the Germans withdrew on 20 September they had succeeded in their objective of once again enabling the German forces in the southern tip of the country to withdraw to safety. Clark's Fifth Army finally entered Naples on 1 October.

The Germans now withdrew to the formidable defensive positions known as the Bernhard and Gustav Lines, which combined massive natural obstacles with superbly designed man-made defences. By January 1944 Clark's forces had managed to batter their way through the Bernhard Line to the Rapido river, the crossing of which would have enabled the Fifth Army to break through the Gustav Line and into the Liri valley. The attempt to cross the Rapido with the 36th Division, 'The Texan', against equal or superior German forces in strong defensive positions, was a disastrous and costly failure for which Clark, with some justice, was strongly criticised after the war. On 22 January 1944, Allied forces made a relatively easy landing at Anzio, some 75 miles

CLARK

behind the Gustav Line, but Hitler rushed forces from as far away as France and Yugoslavia to counter-attack, and once again only a desperate defence and heavy reinforcement enabled the Allies to hold on to the position.

General Harold Alexander, the Supreme Allied Commander in Italy, now brought a British and a New Zealand division over from the Eighth Army to reinforce Clark's forces, and Clark ordered an assault on the strong-point of Monte Cassino in the Gustav Line. General Bernard Freyberg, tasked with the attack, asked for a massive bombardment of the famous monastery on top of the mountain. Clark at first refused, for both tactical and religious reasons, but was overruled by Alexander. The controversial destruction of the monastery if anything probably helped the Germans rather than hindered them, and it was not until most of the Eighth Army was combined with the fifth for a massive assault in May 1944 that the Allies, led by General Alphonse Juin's heroic French Corps, finally broke through the Gustav Line.

Alexander now ordered Clark to drive eastwards from Anzio to block the German retreat. The Allies had another chance to trap the Axis forces in Italy and annihilate them, but Clark, eager for the symbolic prize of Rome and distrustful of British intentions, disobeyed the order and despatched the major part of his forces towards the Italian capital. Once again the Germans were able to withdraw with their command structure intact, leaving Rome to be occupied by Clark's Americans on 5 June.

Clark's entry into the first of the Axis capitals to fall to the Allies was a hollow victory, and the triumph was brief. The following day the invasion of Normandy took place, and the Italian campaign became a secondary consideration. In January 1944 Clark had been given command of the planned invasion of Southern France, Operation Anvil, but had been relieved a month later at his own request. Now the requirements of Anvil meant that his forces in Italy were further weakened as they pursued the Germans northwards. As the winter of 1944 fell and the enemy dug into their strong position in the Gothic Line, just south of Bologna, Clark found himself in command of units from more nationalities than at any time in modern history, including Brazilians, Italians, French, New Zealanders, Poles, Jews from Palestine and Indians. In November he took over from Alexander to head the entire 15th Army Group, comprising both the Fifth and the Eighth Armies.

Fighting in northern Italy in the winter of 1944-45 was out of the question due to the unusually severe weather, but in the spring of 1945 the Fifth and Eighth Armies finally broke through the Gothic Line, increasingly supported now by Italian partisans. On 2 May the German forces in Italy surrendered.

After the end of the war, General Mark Clark commanded the US occupation forces in Austria before returning to command the Sixth Army. He was the commander of the United Nations forces in Korea from May 1952 until the armistice was signed in July 1953. He retired from Army service in October 1953.

The Italian campaign had achieved the limited objective of obliging Germany to divert large forces from the Eastern Front and, after June 1944, from France. It had failed in its greater aim of annihilating Axis forces in Italy entirely, but for that the ultimate blame must lie with the higher political powers, which yielded to pressure from Stalin to open a second front in France and not to make a major thrust up through Italy and into Central Europe. The shape of the map of Europe today is the result of those decisions.

This page. Above: Troops of the US Fifth Army, commanded by Clark, take Rome on 5 June 1944. Below: Shermans of the 46th Royal Tank Regiment at Anzio during the Italian campaign.

Page 47: General Mark W. Clark aboard a PT boat carrying him to the beachhead, near Anzio, a small port on the west coast of Italy. This amphibious landing was code-named, 'Operation Triangle'.

Canada's inimitable commander

Henry Duncan Crerar, one of the most distinguished officers ever to serve in the Canadian forces, was not always intent on a military career. Born in Hamilton, Ontario on 28 April 1888, he attended the Royal Military College, Kingston, but on graduating in 1910 he chose to become a civil engineer, continuing part-time soldiering as an artillery lieutenant in the Canadian militia. On the outbreak of war in 1914, however, Crerar was one of the first contingent of the Canadian Expeditionary Force to arrive in France. He proved an outstanding officer and by 1918 was a lieutenant-colonel on the staff of the Canadian Corps artillery. When the war ended, he stayed in the army, belatedly completing his training at Camberley Staff College.

From the start of World War II, Crerar dedicated himself to the creation of a Canadian Army equipped and trained to carry out major offensive operations against the enemy, part or all of which he might himself lead into battle. He first went to London to set up the Canadian Headquarters there and then, in 1940, was recalled to Canada to take up the post of Chief of General Staff. His administrative ability and depth of experience were fully demonstrated in the taxing task of expanding and reorganising the Canadian forces, but Ottawa was too far from the front line for Crerar's taste. In late 1941 he accepted demotion from lieutenant-general to major-general so that he could be posted back to Britain as acting commander of the Canadian 2nd Division Overseas.

In April 1942, Crerar took command of I Canadian Corps, a post he was to hold for the next two years. At this stage of the war the Canadian troops were rendered inactive by their government's decision that they should play no part in the Mediterranean theatre, the only scene of land fighting against the Axis (outside the Soviet Union). Both Crerar and the overall Canadian commander, Lieutenant-General A.G.L. Macnaughton, were therefore delighted by the leading role allotted to their troops in the projected raid on Dieppe, although neither had played any part in planning the operation. Executed on 19 August 1942, the raid was a disaster – over half the Canadians involved were either killed or taken prisoner. Crerar always defended the Dieppe raid against its critics, however, claiming that it constituted 'A Canadian contribution of the greatest significance to final victory'.

THE ELITE COMMANDERS

Below left: Canadian troops on a tank landing craft peer anxiously over the raised ramp, shortly before landing at Dieppe. Below right: Henry Duncan Graham Crerar, the first Canadian general to command Canadian troops in the field.

In 1943 I Canadian Corps was at last transferred to the Mediterranean, joining the Allied forces in Italy. While Crerar was playing his part in the slow slog up towards Rome, Macnaughton remained in Britain with the First Canadian Army. Relations between Macnaughton and the British High Command were stormy, however, and in March 1944 he was recalled to Canada. Crerar was designated to take his place and, leaving his corps in Italy, he returned to Britain to prepare his new command for the invasion of Normandy. Even-tempered and always ready to see the other man's point of view, Crerar established good relations with his fellow commanders – even the notoriously difficult Montgomery, who described him, significantly, as a 'loyal subordinate'.

CRERAR

Crerar was not involved in the Normandy landings. It was not until 23 July that he established his army headquarters on the left flank of the British Second Army, taking under command not only the Canadian II Corps but also I British Corps and other Allied formations. On 7 August First Canadian Army launched a successful offensive from the Caen sector towards Falaise, and it then forced its way rapidly along the coast as far as Antwerp – having the satisfaction of taking Dieppe en route on 1 September. In control of the Antwerp sector, Crerar faced the task of clearing the banks of the Scheldt, held in strength by the Germans who were thereby able to deny the Allies use of Antwerp as a port. By 23 September, Crerar had completed his plans for the Scheldt operation, but due to illness he was not able to oversee their execution.

Arriving back at his headquarters on 9 November, Crerar could begin preparations for his greatest battle: a thrust from the Nijmegen salient into Germany, through the Reichswald and the northern end of the Siegfried Line to the Hochwald and on to the Rhine. The logistical build-up for this massive offensive was impeccably organised, showing Crerar's exceptional flair for this vital aspect of warfare. On 8 February, XXX British Corps led the way into the Reichswald. Despite the support of outstandingly well-organised artillery fire and powerful air attacks, the fighting was hard and grim. Weather conditions were appalling and enemy resistance was fierce. On 3 March, however, First Canadian Army made contact with Ninth US Army, and the two advanced on a combined front to the Rhine, which they reached seven days later. General Dwight D. Eisenhower wrote to Crerar shortly afterwards: 'Probably no assault in the war has been conducted under more appalling conditions of terrain than was this one. It speaks volumes for your skill and determination and the valour of your soldiers that you

carried it through to a successful conclusion.' At the height of the battle for the Reichswald, Crerar had 13 divisions under his command, nine of them British, a total force of over 500,000 men.

On 1 April, First Canadian Army resumed its advance, pushing north into the Netherlands, where Crerar encircled German forces with a bold pincer movement. At this late stage, I Canadian Corps arrived from Italy to join their compatriots, so Crerar was able to end the war with all Canadian land forces united under his command. He retired the following year, having proved himself to possess in the highest degree the qualities he himself required of an officer: 'vision, courage, purpose and tenacity'.

THE ELITE COMMANDERS

Below left, from left to right: General Crerar, Lieutenant-General Dempsey and General Montgomery at the Second Army headquarters in 1944. Below right: Crerar and Wyman.

THE ELITE
COMMANDERS
CUNNINGHAM

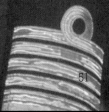

Master of the Mediterranean

Andrew Browne Cunningham (1883-1963) was the outstanding British naval commander of World War II, whose consummate ability made an abiding impression on all who sailed with him. Educated at Edinburgh Academy, he was commissioned into the Royal Navy in 1898. His first command was torpedo boat *No. 14* in the Home Fleet, but he left this vessel in 1910 to take over the destroyer HMS *Vulture*.

When World War I broke out, Cunningham was commanding HMS *Scorpion* in the Mediterranean. Together with HMS *Wolverine, Scorpion* opened Britain's account against the Turkish Navy by sinking a Turkish minelayer in the Gulf of Smyrna in October 1914. *Scorpion* went on to play an important part in the Dardanelles campaign. By the end of the war, Cunningham was a commander, and received promotion to captain during destroyer operations in the Baltic in the aftermath of the war. After serving in the Naval Inter-Allied Commission of Control, he returned to destroyer service in 1922, leading the First Flotilla Home Fleet

By 1934, Cunningham had worked his way up to vice-admiral. Chances of further elevation seemed remote, but two strokes of luck launched him onto a wider stage. First, Vice-Admiral Sir Geoffrey Blake was taken ill and Cunningham was chosen to replace him as acting second-in-command of the Mediterranean Fleet. Then, in November 1938, Cunningham was appointed deputy chief of naval staff at the Admiralty, under Sir Roger Backhouse.

Early in 1939, Backhouse was also struck down with illness, and Cunningham had to assume much of the responsibilities of his chief. Backhouse's eventual replacement was Sir Dudley Pound, and Cunningham was given Pound's former post as comman-

THE ELITE COMMANDERS

Above: Sir Andrew Browne Cunningham, great fighting admiral and superb strategist. Page 51, top: Battleships of Cunningham's Mediterranean Fleet (followed by a cruiser) in line ahead on their way to bombard Axis positions in North Africa. Page 51, left below: Next to a Vickers anti-aircraft mounting, an observer anxiously scours the sky for German aircraft. Back cover, right below: Cunningham in his uniform as Admiral of the Fleet.

der of the British Mediterranean Fleet.

In 1939 the Mediterranean seemed an easy posting: between them, the French and British fleets enjoyed an easy superiority over any possible enemy. The events of the summer of 1940, however, changed all that. The defeat of France and the entry of Italy into the war left the British Mediterranean Fleet perilously exposed and outnumbered, and the main fleet base at Malta was within easy range of Italian aircraft.

Cunningham was nothing if not a vigorous commander, however. In the best traditions of the Royal Navy he took the fight to the enemy, using the torpedo bombers of his fleet to cripple three Italian battleships at Taranto in November 1940, and then, in March 1941, risking a potentially hazardous night action to sink three cruisers and two destroyers at the Battle of Cape Matapan.

Cunningham saw his task in very clear-cut terms. He was to assert superiority over the enemy fleet, and to prevent supplies reaching the Axis forces in North Africa. The possession of Malta, lying across the direct route from Italy to Libya, was the key to the latter operation, and much of Cunningham's attention was devoted to keeping the island supplied. The convoys that regularly battled their way to Valetta suffered heavy losses, but the Allies held Malta.

In spring 1941, German armies invaded the Balkans, and a British Expeditionary Force sent to help the Greeks was compelled to pull back to the island of Crete. Eventually, the Germans landed airborne forces on the island, and this too had to be evacuated. In spite of the dangers from German air power, Cunningham did not hesitate to undertake the operation, 'It takes the Navy three years to build a ship. It would take 300 years to rebuild a tradition,' was his comment. Two destroyers and an AA cruiser were lost during the operation.

Throughout the rest of 1941, Cunningham had to cope with the increasing German build-up in the Mediterranean, including the deployment of U-boats, and he also had to arrange for the resupply of the port of Tobruk, which held out against Axis forces until relieved late in the year. Early 1942 saw Cunningham continue to juggle the conflicting priorities of his command, this time in the face of a sustained air offensive against Malta and Rommel's spring offensive in the Western Desert.

DIRECTING THE ALLIANCE

In May 1942, Cunningham went to Washington to become a British representative on the Joint Chiefs of Staff, a critical post in the new alliance. He returned to more active service soon after, however, as commander of the naval forces involved in Operation Torch, the Allied landings in French North Africa. This was the prelude to the final defeat of the Axis in North Africa and the triumph of Allied naval power in the Mediterranean; indeed, in September 1943 Cunningham had the satisfaction of receiving the formal surrender of the Italian fleet on board HMS *Warspite*, his original flagship in the Mediterranean Fleet.

Following this success, Cunningham reached the highest command in the Royal Navy when he was appointed First Sea Lord in October 1943. He spent the rest of the war in overall charge of all British naval operations, overseeing the victory in the Battle of the Atlantic and the preparations for D-day.

Cunningham retired in 1946. Given the changes in technology that have revolutionised naval warfare since 1945, he may well be seen as the last of Britain's great fighting admirals.

THE ELITE COMMANDERS

DAYAN

Dynamic leader of the Israeli Defence Forces

The modern state of Israel has had to struggle to survive. Created in May 1948 in the aftermath of a bitter guerrilla war, it has faced constant pressure from more populous Arab neighbours, fighting six major conflicts and defending its existence through a combination of luck, political judgement and remarkable military skill. Moshe Dayan (1915-1981) became synonymous with this struggle, helping to create and protect the state and displaying a rare mixture of military innovation, political acumen and boundless energy.

Dayan was born on 4 May 1915 in the kibbutz of Daganiah, to the south of the Sea of Galilee, and grew up imbued with the Zionist dream of a Jewish homeland in the then-Turkish province of Palestine. As early as 1929 – by which time the British had replaced the Turks – he had joined the Haganah, an unofficial Jewish defence organisation, and by 1936, when an Arab Revolt threatened Jewish settlements, he was already a platoon commander. He first saw

Above: Moshe Dayan sporting the famous black eyepatch that he wore after losing his left eye during the campaign in Syria in 1941, when he was fighting for the British against Vichy-French forces. Dayan was always an exponent of officers in the field leading from the front. It was a doctrine that proved one of the mainstays of Israeli success in the wars fought against neighbouring Arab states from 1948 to the present. **Top:** Men of the 89th Commando Battalion celebrate their capture of Lod in July 1948 during the War of Independence. Under Dayan's energetic leadership the unit totally outwitted the Arab defenders.

action as a member of Orde Wingate's 'Special Night Squads', raiding Arab camps, and he supplemented his training by joining the British-sponsored Jewish Settlement Police Force, although this did not prevent his arrest in October 1939 for illegal possession of firearms. Sentenced by the British to 10 years in gaol, he served only 15 months before being released to help fight the Axis forces in World War II. On 8 June 1941, while leading a reconnaissance team across the border into Vichy-French Syria, Dayan was badly wounded, losing his left eye. Thereafter, a black eyepatch was his personal trademark.

Once recovered, Dayan joined the Haganah General Staff as an intelligence officer, in which capacity he served throughout the guerrilla war against the British (1944-48). By May 1948 his skills had been recognised and, as Arab armies invaded the new state, he was given command of a special unit, soon to be known as 89th Commando Battalion. In July he led this unit into battle, capturing the town of Lod in a stunning display of tactical flexibility that contained all the ingredients of future Israeli success. Recognising that Israel could never hope to match the size of the Arab armies, Dayan always advocated a concentration of force and firepower in short, sharp attacks designed to demoralise the enemy by shock action, and stressed the need for officers to lead from the front.

SUCCESS IN THE FIELD

A proven record of success in the field, coupled with his previous staff experience, made Dayan a natural choice for high command in the fledgling Israeli Defence Forces (IDF), and, in December 1953, he was appointed chief of staff. He devoted his time in office to the creation of a formidable fighting force, based upon the swift mobilisation of reservists, shock action and dynamic combat leadership. The IDF that routed a numerically superior Egyptian Army in Sinai in late October 1956, thrusting deep into enemy lines and spreading chaos throughout the command chain, was very much Dayan's creation.

Leaving the army immediately after the 1956 campaign, Dayan moved into the sphere of politics. Elected to the Knesset (Israel's parliament) in

Right: General Moshe Dayan (left) entering the Old City of Jerusalem on 8 June 1967. After a heavy artillery barrage on 6 June, Israeli troops supported by Sherman tanks stormed into the city and, after bitter fighting, broke through St. Stephen's Gate and reached the West Wall (Wailing Wall) of the Temple Mount by 1000 hours on the 7th. The Israelis suffered their heaviest losses of the war on this front: 550 killed and 2500 wounded. Below, inset: A youthful Dayan (left) poses for the camera when he was a member of the Haganah, a Jewish defence force formed in 1920 to resist Arab attacks. By 1947, the movement could call on the services of over 45,000 men in its campaign to create a Jewish homeland. After a skilfully conducted war, the State of Israel came into being on 14 May 1948. Below: Dayan studies the road to Damascus during the Israeli counter-attack against the Syrians in Yom Kippur War in 1973.

November 1959, he was appointed minister of agriculture in David Ben-Gurion's government, holding the post until 1964. A period in the political wilderness ensued, but as the 1967 crisis developed, public disquiet forced Prime Minister Levy Eshkol to recall the 'victor of 1956' to the cabinet, this time as minister of defence. It was a wise move: Dayan enjoyed the full confidence of the IDF and, in a four-day burst of frenetic activity, he recast Israel's war plans for a conflict that now seemed inevitable. The subsequent Six-Day War (5-10 June 1967) was won by the IDF on the basis of Dayan's ideas for a blitzkrieg-style assault using a combination of armour and airpower; tactics to which neither the Egyptians, Jordanians nor Syrians could provide an adequate response.

COMPLETE VICTORY

Seldom in the history of war had so complete a victory been achieved in so short a space of time; it took the Israelis a mere four days to wipe an army of seven divisions from the map. Over 10,000 Egyptian soldiers were killed, 20,000 wounded and 5500 captured; 500 tanks were destroyed and 300 captured intact; 450 artillery pieces of various calibres were taken, along with 10,000 vehicles of every type. In comparison with these losses, the Israelis suffered only 275 killed and an estimated 800 wounded. As they held the battlefield, they were able to repair the great majority of their damaged tanks. This overwhelming triumph fully justified Dayan's hasty reorganisation of Israel's war strategy and vindicated his belief that wars are won by keeping the initiative and never allowing the enemy time to reorganise.

A degree of complacency then set in, however, and although Dayan remained as minister of defence, he was caught by surprise on 6 October 1973 when both Egypt and Syria mounted a co-ordinated attack on Sinai and the Golan Heights. During the Yom Kippur War (6-24 October 1973) Dayan displayed his usual energy, visiting both fronts to ensure

recovery and eventual counter-attack, but his credibility, both in the IDF and among the wider public, had been damaged. As opinion turned against him, he resigned in June 1974 and re-entered the political wilderness.

In 1977 Menachem Begin appointed Dayan foreign minister, in which capacity he helped to negotiate the Camp David agreement with Egypt (September 1978), but his proposals for civilian administration in the 'occupied territories' of Sinai, Golan, the West Bank and the Gaza Strip proved unpopular. He resigned for the last time in late 1979; when he died two years later, on 16 October 1981, he was justly mourned as a founding father of the Israeli state.

THE ELITE COMMANDERS
DE GAULLE

The embodiment of France

Charles de Gaulle (1890-1970) has a military importance on two quite distinct levels. First of all, he was one of those theorists of the 1930s. who advocated the ideas of aggressive armoured warfare, and although he remained a prophet without honour in his own country, he tried to put his ideas into practice during a short period commanding armoured forces during the campaign of 1940. De Gaulle's decision to keep on fighting the Germans from Britain after the Wehrmacht's success in that campaign gave him a much wider importance, however, and had profound consequences for the French Army. Similarly, during the late 1950s, de Gaulle took politico-military decisions that led to fundamental splits within the armed forces.

Until his capture at Verdun in 1916, de Gaulle had served with distinction during World War I, and as a company commander under the then Colonel Henri Petain he had been a model officer. After the collapse of Imperial Germany and his release, de Gaulle volunteered for service under Pilsudski in Poland, where he again saw action as the newly independent nation fought through civil war and Russian invasion.

During the 1930s, de Gaulle began developing theories of warfare that were implicitly critical of the policies of the French government and military establishment. A defensive mentality, born out of the grievous losses of World War I and perhaps symbolised by the construction of the Maginot Line, had taken hold. De Gaulle's book *The Army of the Future,* suggested a different line of thinking. He recommended a small, professional force, using armoured vehicles, as the basis for an offensive strategy that could prevent the deadlock of trench warfare.

In 1939, after war broke out, de Gaulle was given command of the tank units within the French Fifth Army, but was refused permission to amalgamate them into a powerful, unified armoured force until May 1940. And almost as soon as he was able to centralise his tanks, de Gaulle, by now the youngest general in the French Army, found

that the German offensive was sweeping all before it in a style of warfare that he himself had advocated.

During the German offensive, de Gaulle led one of the few effective French counter-attacks, around Laôn, but the strategic victory of the Germans made this isolated effort fruitless. On 6 June, de Gaulle was appointed to the cabinet as Under Secretary of State to the Minister of National Defence, and in this new post, as France's defences were collapsing, de Gaulle argued for the creation of a 'national redoubt' in Brittany, or the continuation of the war from North Africa if France itself fell. But Marshal Petain took over the government for the rump of the nation at Vichy.

THE 'FREE FRENCH'

De Gaulle had flown to London shortly before the armistice, and he denounced its signature as a betrayal. Some French forces rallied to his call, but those in France itself (with little choice) obeyed Petain. The Vichy regime proclaimed de Gaulle a traitor, and his 'Free French' (or 'Fighting French' as they were later renamed), a group of mutineers. Indeed, there were problems of all kinds involved in the establishment of Free France. Petain's cabinet was the constitutionally agreed government of France – and an obedient officer should have obeyed that government's order to lay down his arms. The other European nations conquered by Hitler's Germany – such as Poland, Holland, Belgium and Norway – had all established governments in exile that were clearly recognised as such. De Gaulle was in no such position.

Events of the summer of 1940 made things even more difficult. The Royal Navy fired on French vessels at Mers-el-Kebir, and the British authorities made it clear that they did not know how to deal with de Gaulle, whose high appreciation of his mission and refusal to be treated merely as a grateful refugee seemed out of all proportion to the resources at his disposal. There were also setbacks. Late in 1940, an attempt to take the colony of Dakar, garrisoned by troops loyal to the Vichy government who had refused to come over to the Free French, was a disastrous failure in which Frenchman fought Frenchman.

FRENCH TROOPS LIBERATE PARIS

The successful Allied invasion of French North Africa not only put more men and resources under de Gaulle's control, it also led to the German takeover of Vichy France. Now that France was occupied totally, he was recognised as the major representative of his nation – although the Americans were still unwilling to see him as the head of a provisional government even in the planning for D-Day. French troops took part in the Italian campaign, and in July 1944 landed in southern France as part of Operation Dragoon. On 25 July, French troops liberated their own capital, Paris, and de Gaulle headed a provisional government. The French Army then played a major part in the defeat of Germany.

Disappointed at being excluded from the Yalta and Potsdam conferences in which the shape of the postwar world was decided, de Gaulle had managed, in the face of manifold difficulties and risking a permanent split in the French Armed forces, to maintain national self-respect.

Although he had embodied his country at war de Gaulle, like Churchill, found that this was no insurance against the vagaries of domestic politics. In January 1946 he resigned from the presidency, and re-entered the political wilderness he had left in 1940. But once again, he was recalled to centre-stage – although not until the late 1950s. The governments of the Fourth Republic had been lurching from crisis to crisis, and after military defeat in Indochina, faced another war of national liberation in Algeria. Here, in

Page 56: General Charles de Gaulle returns in triumph to France in June 1944. The long-exiled leader received a tumultuous welcome from his countrymen. Below: De Gaulle, as President of the French National Committee, salutes the Tricolour, during a tour of the 'Fighting French' forces in Italy. 'Je suis la France' de Gaulle had proclaimed and believed that as leader of the Fighting French, he was preserving the honour of France. Above: De Gaulle served as President of France from 1959 until his resignation in 1969. On his death in 1970, his successor, President Pompidou, declared, 'France is a widow.'

an area of North Africa that was not even a colony (it was officially one of the French *departments*, a part of France itself), the Army was determined to hold the line against left-wing nationalism, and it was the Army that, in effect, toppled an enfeebled republic and called on de Gaulle to restore French national honour.

De Gaulle responded by stepping up military action in Algeria, and by establishing a new constitution, including a powerful executive presidency, as an antidote to the previous political fragmentation. He became the first president.

A series of offensives wore down the military strength of the Algerian insurgents; but then, the new president began to change his mind about the Algerian question. He had formulated a new view of France's international position, in which old-style colonialism had no place. And, as in World War II, he set about putting his beliefs into practice. The result, as in 1940, was a trauma for the armed forces. Many of those who plotted against de Gaulle during this period saw themselves as acting as he had in 1940 – trying to withstand a defeatist government – but de Gaulle won through, resisting coup attempts, avoiding assassins and showing himself prepared to deal with the problem of the exiled European settlers. By the mid-1960s, France was out of Algeria, had set its sights on a different future and was undergoing a period of sustained economic growth; de Gaulle had what one can guess was the pleasure of informing British governments that there was no place for them in the European community of which France was a dominant member.

It is possible to argue that de Gaulle was wrong on many of the issues that he faced; but he was always prepared to fight to the end for what he thought was right for France as a nation.

DE LATTRE

Chivalrous warrior

Jean-Marie de Lattre de Tassigny (1889-1952) was a skilled military commander who, while managing to master the complexities and technicalities of modern warfare, also maintained the chivalrous spirit of the warrior fighting on the side of right. De Lattre believed in France, and its destiny as a great nation.

His military career opened in a manner that prefigured much of what was to come – in 1914, as a young cavalry officer, he was badly wounded in a mounted duel with a German Uhlan. In all, he was wounded four times during World War I. After the war he transferred to the infantry and saw active service in Morocco.

During the 1930s, de Lattre held a number of senior staff positions, and following the outbreak of war in 1939, succeeded in obtaining an active command – of the excellent French 14th Division. In May 1940, his men were thrown into the breach created by the German breakthrough in the Ardennes, and were one of the few French formations to achieve any measure of success, halting the southern thrust of Guderian's advance and making a fighting withdrawal when the whole front crumbled. Eventually, de Lattre pulled the 14th back into the zone that became unoccupied 'Vichy' France.

The conclusion of an armistice with Germany led to a fierce split within the French armed forces. Some, led by Charles de Gaulle, preferred to continue the struggle from Britain, but the majority were prepared to obey the new head of state, Marshal Henri Pétain, and submit to the German success. De Lattre, as a loyal officer of the old school, accepted Pétain's leadership, but with some reluctance. He was appointed to a command in Tunisia, which was still under French control, but was swiftly recalled because of his outspoken anti-German attitudes and pro-Allied sympathies.

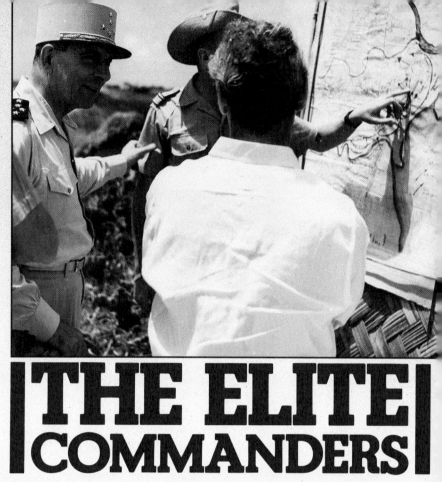

THE ELITE COMMANDERS

Late in 1942, when the Germans took over the previously unoccupied Vichy zone, de Lattre tried to organise some resistance to this move, and was imprisoned. A year later, however, he escaped from Riom prison and made his way to London where he joined de Gaulle. The German occupation of Vichy France had released French officers from any obligation to the Vichy regime, and although the rift within the French armed forces was still felt, it did not seriously affect operations during the rest of the war. De Lattre was appointed commander of the French First Army in North Africa during the autumn of 1943, a formation raised from both Free French and former Vichy units.

De Lattre's men were an important component of the Anvil/Dragoon landings in the south of France in

Above: De Lattre (left) discusses plans for the defence of the Red River Delta with colleagues. Below: A French tank prepares to engage enemy forces at Mao Khe during the second phase of the Viet Minh offensive on the Delta.

August 1944 and his forces liberated Toulon and Marseilles after some hard fighting. By 15 September, de Lattre's formations had raced north up the Rhône valley to link up with, and come under the command of, General Eisenhower, whose armies had landed in Normandy. From then until the end of the year, the French First Army took part in the Allied advance to the German frontier.

In January 1945, the French were a part of the Allied forces that had to hold a German counter-attack on the southern end of the line. Often under great pressure, they resisted well, and distinguished themselves especially during the fighting for the 'Colmar pocket'. Late in the spring of 1945, they launched a surprise attack across the Rhine, and had pushed deep into Germany by VE-day.

After the war, de Lattre was hailed a national hero. He held senior commands, and was appointed to a NATO post when that organisation was set up in 1948. In 1950, however, he was again offered a concrete military challenge – this time in Indochina, where the war between the French and the communist Viet Minh guerrillas was tilting against the French forces. At the time of de Lattre's appointment, the French had just lost control of the northern mountains in Tonkin, and were fighting a losing battle to stem the flow of weapons and supplies coming through to the Viet Minh from across the border with China.

WAR IN THE DELTA

De Lattre arrived in Hanoi in December 1950, and immediately set about restructuring the French forces which, in his opinion, were poorly organised. He recognised that the Viet Minh, under the leadership of Ho Chi Minh and Vo Nguyen Giap, were preparing for an offensive on the Red River Delta, the heart of the northern province of Tonkin. To meet this threat, de Lattre assigned his units to a variety of tasks: some were organised into 'Groupements Mobiles' (mobile strike forces), while others were deployed to garrison a chain of small posts, the so-called 'De Lattre Line', that he set up to defend the Delta. He also created small commando units, with a high component of hill tribesmen, to take the war back to the communist guerrillas in the hills.

During the first half of 1951, the communist forces launched their offensive on the Delta in three phases: the first in January, the second in March, and the third in May-June. The final phase almost caught the French off-guard, but by relying heavily on air support, de Lattre won through and inflicted heavy losses on Giap's troops. Although a military success, the Red River Delta campaign was a personal tragedy for the French commander – his own son died at Ninh Binh in June.

Having defeated a Viet Minh offensive, de Lattre was keen to take the initiative. His method was to send a large force into Viet Minh-held territory on the Black River, at Hoa Binh, and to challenge the communists to an engagement where superior French firepower could win the day. Hoa Binh lay astride what were assumed to be vital communist supply lines, and it was thought that the enemy could

not avoid a battle.

In the event, however, the descent on Hoa Binh in November 1951 was a failure, and the French troops, demoralised and having suffered heavy losses, were pulled out in February 1952.

At this juncture in the war, de Lattre was clearly a very sick man, suffering from the cancer that would kill him later in the year. But, despite his failing health, he was still a commander to be wary of; his adversary, Vo Nguyen Giap, described in 1951 how 'we had thought that in de Lattre de Tassigny we would find a general enslaved by his background and training, incapable of adapting to a form of war not taught in imperialist military academies. But de Lattre is, in fact, a brilliant professional soldier. The death of his son has hardly affected his aggressive spirit. Our forces, which are so superior in guerrilla actions, must not . . . engage in full-scale battles.'

Above: Men of de Lattre's First French Army occupy Collobrières, a French town east of Toulon, during World War II. Below: French artillery in Indochina engages Viet Minh positions in the battle for the Red River Delta.

DIETL

Commander of mountain troops

Eduard Dietl (1890-1944) was a favoured officer in the Wehrmacht of World War II. He had supported Hitler from the 1920s, and although he disagreed with the Führer's instructions of 1941, he never lost favour with the Nazi propaganda machine.

After service with the German Army in World War I, Dietl's right-wing political leanings led him, in 1919, to join one of the Freikorps, or Free Companies, bands of disaffected ex-soldiers. Dietl was, like Hitler, a Bavarian; he joined the fledgling Nazi Party in 1920, gave Hitler military information and took part in the failed putsch of 1923.

This record of sympathy for the Nazis stood Dietl in good stead when Hitler became Chancellor of Germany. By 1939, he was a major-general in command of the 3rd Mountain Division. He led this formation during the attack on Poland, and the following year was given the task of occupying northern Norway.

The Germans encountered a considerable setback when the Royal Navy destroyed the flotilla that had escorted the invaders into Narvik fiord, but Dietl acted energetically to restore his difficult situation, enlisting survivors from the German flotilla and arming them with captured Norwegian equipment. Outnumbered (although reinforced with some paratroops) Dietl was forced out of Narvik by early June. His resistance, however, had not been in vain, for the Allied forces re-embarked soon after.

After his hard-won success at Narvik, Dietl was promoted to lieutenant-general, and his command was expanded to comprise a mountain corps, based in Norway to guard against Allied attacks. Then, in April 1941, Hitler invited Dietl back to Germany to discuss the role his troops would play in the coming invasion of the Soviet Union. The intention was for the mountain troops to take over the Petsamo region, and to cooperate with Finnish forces to cut the railway linking Murmansk with the rest of Russia. The distance that Dietl's men would have to cover to isolate Murmansk seemed small on paper, but the physical conditions and the climate were against any offensive movements; Dietl, therefore, counselled caution, and less ambitious plans.

Although he appeared to accept this advice, Hitler soon changed his mind and Dietl's troops were

Top: Ski troops under Dietl's command on the move in Norway. Mountain troops, many of whom came from Austria, were well equipped to take on the daunting Norwegian terrain, and Dietl, himself a mountaineer, understood how to use them perfectly. Above: Dietl in his command post in Lapland.

condemned to a fruitless advance that got them to within 40km of Murmansk before retreat became a necessity. The war in this sector soon settled down to a stalemate.

In January 1942, Dietl was promoted to colonel-general leading all German forces in Lapland; in this position he became popular not only with his own troops but also with the Finns (Marshal Mannerheim in particular was an admirer) and the population of Lapland. This popularity was made much of by Göbbels and Nazi propagandists, before Dietl was killed in an air crash in summer 1944.

U-boat commander supreme

Karl Dönitz was born on 16 September 1891 in the suburbs of Berlin and went on to become Reichsführer following the suicide of Adolf Hitler. After joining the German Navy he first saw action during World War I aboard the cruiser *Breslau*, which operated in Turkish and Russian waters. After submarine training, he was given command of *U-68*, operating in the Mediterranean. On 4 October 1918, *U-68* was stalking a British convoy when the longitudinal stabilisers failed. Dönitz' U-boat was forced to surface and was captured by the Royal Navy.

Following the end of World War I, Dönitz remained in service and gradually earned a series of promotions. In November 1934, having reached the rank of captain, he was given command of the cruiser *Emden* which deployed into the Indian Ocean until July 1935. At the end of the cruise, Dönitz was posted to command the U-boat section of the navy. Under the 1935 Anglo-German Treaty, Germany was allowed to develop her U-boat strengths to within 45% of British submarine strength.

Dönitz was keen on both technical and tactical innovation and in 1939 he published a work which drew attention to the tactical weakness of U-boats operating singly against convoys; this was Dönitz' first contribution to the development of the 'wolfpack'. The implication of his ideas was that large numbers of cheap craft were more important than small numbers of better-armed craft, and so he concentrated on the production of the simple and reliable Type VII U-boat, which, in its various Marks,

Admiral Karl Dönitz, who turned the German U-boat force into a deadly weapon that almost won the Battle of the Atlantic and could have starved Britain into submission.

DÖNITZ

was to remain the German Navy's mainstay for the duration of the war.

Germany entered the war with 57 U-boats, of which only 39 were seaworthy; Hitler was still not convinced of the importance of submarine warfare. Despite this early lack of strength, Dönitz personally supported his crews to such an extent that their early achievements were spectacular. The successes of the U-boats reached even greater heights after the fall of France, and, in mid-1940, Dönitz moved his headquarters to Lorient on the Atlantic coast. By the end of 1941, his U-boats had sunk over 1000 Allied naval and merchant ships.

The 'happy time'

Dönitz had a very clear and direct idea of the strategy that the U-boat arm should pursue: a steady war of attrition against Britain's sea lanes in the North Atlantic. He realised that all other considerations should be subordinate to this long-term strategic aim. Hitler, however, was always prepared to look for short term advantages that took U-boats away from what Dönitz saw as the crucial theatre: Hitler insisted on the introduction of U-boats into the Mediterranean, for example, and although this had immediate results, the vessels were then trapped.

The most fruitful time for the U-boats came just after the Japanese attack on Pearl Harbor, and the entry of the USA into the war. Operating along the US Atlantic coast, against a US merchant marine that had not yet learnt the value of the convoy system, the U-boats enjoyed what they called a 'happy time', and Dönitz further enhanced the rich pickings by de-

THE ELITE COMMANDERS

Top: A U-boat ploughs through the icy waters of the North Atlantic. Dönitz was particularly insistent upon the application of a coherent strategy in which the North Atlantic theatre should not be subordinated to short-term advantage available elsewhere; but in many cases he was overruled by Hitler. Above: Dönitz greets a U-boat crew just arrived back in France from an Atlantic voyage. He was a commander who believed in keeping in close touch with the men who had to undertake the perilous missions that proved so costly in men and machines.

veloping methods for supplying the U-boats across the Atlantic with 'milk cow' submarines that replenished the attack vessels thousands of miles from their bases.

On 30 January 1943, Dönitz was appointed Commander-in-Chief of the German Navy, in succession to Admiral Raeder. In this position, Dönitz was able to devote naval production to U-boats, and to divert towards the 'wolves of the sea'. By mid-1943, there were 212 operational U-boats and 181 in training.

The spring of 1943, however, also saw the decision in the Battle of the Atlantic. New technology, better escort vessels and, above all, more air support inflicted severe losses on the U-boats, and henceforth they were fighting a losing battle. Dönitz spent the remaining period of the war desperately seeking technical solutions to the problem of Allied superiority: the Type XXI and XXIII submarines were developed, and with the use of hydrogen peroxide as a fuel and the schnorkel as a device enabling the boats to stay submerged indefinitely, something might have been achieved, had not Allied land victory intervened before the new vessels could enter service in appreciable numbers.

In the collapse of Germany, Dönitz emerged as head of civil authority in the north, and was invested with the title of Führer until his arrest on 23 May 1945. He was sentenced to 10 years imprisonment for war crimes at Nuremberg, and was released in 1956.

THE ELITE COMMANDERS

Organiser of victory and commander of 'The Few'

Air Chief-Marshal Sir Hugh Dowding (1882-1970) was the man who directed Fighter Command during the Battle of Britain, and it is possible to argue that without his clear understanding of the nature of that aerial conflict, the 'Few' would have been defeated by the might of the German Luftwaffe. Nevertheless, at the time Dowding received little credit for the decisive victory won by his Spitfire and Hurricane pilots and it is only since 1945 that the crucial role he played has been fully recognised.

Dowding had joined the Royal Flying Corps in World War I, and saw active service in France. From 1930 to 1936 he was Air Council Member for supply and research, then was promoted to Air Officer Commanding-in-Chief Fighter Command. He was involved in the critical decisions that led to the deployment of monoplane fighters, and the armament that they carried (wing-mounted machine guns), and was also instrumental in the establishment of a chain of radar stations along the coastline, a crucial defence in the early years of the war.

When the German breakthrough in Western Europe took place in May 1940, Dowding was, therefore, in the rare position of having built up himself the force which he was to lead in the coming battle. And like certain of the German Panzer commanders (Guderian, for example), Dowding proved as competent in the deployment and direction of his force as he had in taking the technical decisions surrounding its formation.

Dowding had some very difficult choices to make, and there were many critics of him at the time, but in

Below right: Air Marshal Dowding in pensive mood. His unshakable if rather humourless character earned him the nickname 'Stuffy', but he proved rocklike in a time of extreme danger for Britain and may well deserve much of the credit for preventing the Germans from launching Operation Sealion – their master plan for the invasion of Britain in 1940. Friction between his senior Group Commanders, Park and Leigh-Mallory, over the deployment of fighter squadrons placed a great strain on Dowding, and many junior members of the Air Ministry held the view that at 57 he was too old for the job. Below: Squadron scramble for fighter pilots.

retrospect, it is difficult to fault his basic approach. First of all, there was his refusal to send more than a token force to France to aid the defeated French armies that were retreating after the German breakthrough at Sedan. The quixotic Churchill was enthusiastic to shore up a battered ally, but Dowding, realising the consequences of losing valuable machines and even more valuable pilots in what he assessed as a lost cause, took the cruel but necessary line that Spitfires were to be saved for the defence of British interests alone.

After the surrender of France in June, Britain was isolated in Europe. Dowding, closely supported by Air Vice-Marshal Keith Park who commanded No. 11 Fighter Group, stuck to a strategy based upon retaining Fighter Command in being as a force capable of covering attacks on any German invasion fleet. The key to success was not to lie in decisive victory in a few engagements, but in a refusal to allow the Germans to claim mastery of the skies. This view was opposed by some in Fighter Command (notably by Wing-Commander Douglas Bader of 12 Group Wing) and Dowding's reluctance to use large formations ('big wings' as their proponents called them) was seen as a lack of resolution in some quarters.

After the Battle of Britain, in November 1940, Dowding was replaced by Sholto Douglas, a man with far more aggressive ideas on the employment of Fighter Command's squadrons. Dowding retired from active service in 1942; not under any particular cloud, but certainly not with the unswerving confidence of his political masters, and certainly not with the accolades that should have been due to the man who had created and then led the forces that won one of the decisive battles of the 20th Century.

DOWDING

THE ELITE COMMANDERS

EISENHOWER

Supreme Allied Commander

Dwight David Eisenhower (1890-1969) was a soldier in the tradition of those US military men whose wartime successes were the prelude to a political career culminating in the US presidency – a tradition going back to Andrew Jackson, Ulysses Grant and George Washington himself. But unlike Jackson and Grant – the one a ruthless populist politician and the other an implacable general who understood that victory in the American Civil War must be paid for in blood – Eisenhower has usually been portrayed as an emollient, tactful figure whose abilities lay in diplomacy, rather than in the formulation and execution of strategy. The typical photographs of 'Ike' taken during World War II show him wearing the practised, friendly grin that became almost the symbol of the American presence in Europe. But there are other pictures of him taken off guard. In these, the face is harder. The steel beneath the relaxed public image is only too apparent – as are the strains of the command he had to bear.

Eisenhower was born into a poor, religious Texan family. He proved an excellent sportsman at West Point, particularly on the American football field. During World War I, Eisenhower remained in the US, rising to the rank of lieutenant colonel in charge of a tank training establishment. During the 1920s, he was recognised as an extremely able staff officer and came to the attention of Douglas MacArthur, on whose staff he served during the early 1930s. Late in 1941, with American involvement in the war looming, he performed particularly well on manoeuvres as

Left: Dwight Eisenhower
displays his relaxed public
image which masked the
immense pressures of being
supreme commander of the
Allied forces in Europe.
Above: Eisenhower, a
Lieutenant Colonel at the age
of 28, in 1918.

THE ELITE COMMANDERS

Above: Allied Commanders. Seated to the left, Air Vice-Marshall Sir Arthur Tedder with whom Eisenhower had a close relationship. After meeting in North Africa, he later became 'Ike's' deputy for Operation Overlord. Seated centre is Eisenhower, and to the right is General Bernard Montgomery. Eisenhower and he did not always see eye to eye and, consequently, relations between the two men were always strained.

chief of staff to the Third Army, and when war was finally declared, the head of the Army, General Marshall, brought him to Washington to head the Operations Division of the General Staff.

In April 1942, Eisenhower was sent to London to discuss the build-up of US troops in Britain with the British military authorities and political leaders; in June he was appointed to command US troops in Europe, and in August was given command of those Allied forces assigned to the Torch landings in French North Africa. The decision to go for the landings had not been taken until late July and, consequently, there was a great deal to do in a short time; and the planning had to take into account the differences in American and British methods. Eisenhower formed an Allied Force Headquarters that had some novel features – for example, he paired British and US officers in many of the staff jobs, to ensure that both sides of the alliance knew exactly what was going on and how decisions were reached.

In common with many US officers, Eisenhower believed that the Mediterranean theatre was a sideshow – but the landings were very successful. In spite of some initial problems, the Allied forces got ashore and soon asserted control. Eisenhower now had some tricky political decisions to make, connected with the status of the Vichy administrations of Algeria and Morocco, and with the position of the 'Fighting French' under General Charles de Gaulle. He came to an agreement with Admiral Darlan, deputy to Vichy leader Marshal Pétain, who happened to be in Algiers when the invasion took place. This arrangement was criticised in some quarters – but it did solve an immediate problem.

The German decision to hold on in Tunisia posed more problems. Eisenhower was not commanding a well-knit army – US troops lacked combat experience, while the French forces that he controlled did not want to serve under British command. Early in 1943, Eisenhower was made Supreme Allied Commander in North Africa, and the British General Harold Alexander assumed direct control of ground operations. Eisenhower now had huge responsibilities, putting Allied grand strategy into effect in a vast theatre of war. It was during this period that he first worked with Air Vice-Marshal Arthur Tedder, the man responsible for British air operations in North Africa. The two got on extremely well, and Tedder became Eisenhower's deputy when the invasion of Europe was being planned. Eisenhower's relations with other Allied commanders were not so good. In particular, he found Montgomery, commander of the British Eighth Army, a trying subordinate.

After the final victory in North Africa, the British pushed for an invasion of Italy. Once again, the Americans reluctantly agreed to what they saw as a further dispersal of effort – since his posting to the Operations Division of the general staff in 1942, Eisenhower had argued strongly for a concentrated effort against Germany and was against spreading available resources over a variety of theatres. After some discussion, it was decided that Sicily (rather than Sardinia) would be the first objective. Operation Husky, the invasion of Sicily, was the largest amphibious operation of the entire war, and it is greatly to Eisenhower's credit that it worked as well as it did. By August 1943, the island was in Allied hands.

Eisenhower was supreme commander of the Allied forces in Italy during the opening months of the Italian campaign, but in January 1944 he returned to the US, and later that month went to Britain, where he was to take over supreme command of the Allied forces preparing for Operation Overlord – the invasion of Europe.

During the build-up in the lodgement area in Normandy, and the hard fighting against the German forces there, command of Allied forces on the ground was vested in Montgomery. Eisenhower gave his subordinate full support during this period, even though little headway was made for some time. After the breakout, when the Germans were forced back, Eisenhower went over to the European mainland, to take direct control of ground operations from 1 September 1944. This move had been decided on long before, but Montgomery clearly hoped to be left in sole command.

CONTROVERSY AFTER D-DAY

It is the period just after Eisenhower's arrival in France that is the most controversial in his career. Both Montgomery and General Patton, commanding respectively the 21st Army Group and the US Third Army, wanted to be given all available supplies – especially fuel – to enable their forces to pursue the retreating Germans to the utmost, and both were bitter about what they saw as Eisenhower's failure to appreciate their views. Eisenhower decided that Montgomery was to have priority, although not total support, in the allocation of resources – but the result was the defeat and check at Arnhem.

During the rest of the autumn of 1944, Montgomery persisted in his resentment of Eisenhower's decisions. In the fighting of December 1944, when the Germans counter-attacked through the Ardennes, Montgomery was given control of all Allied forces, including US troops, north of the salient that had been created; and although this was only a temporary measure, Montgomery used it to try to bring up the possibility of his taking control of all ground forces again. Eisenhower was forced to threaten to take the matter to the Joint Chiefs of Staff before it was settled.

During 1945, the Allied armies advanced steadily against the battered Wehrmacht, adopting a 'broad front' strategy – Eisenhower's chosen approach – rather than the 'single thrust' that Montgomery and Patton favoured. There were more political disputes to come, however, for Eisenhower did not prevent the Red Army's occupation of Prague and Berlin.

Eisenhower proved himself a master of dealing with a coalition army – not since Marlborough had a military man managed his allies so effectively. In addition, Eisenhower had taken important, large-scale decisions that could have had catastrophic consequences had they been wrong. He had received much criticism, but essentially his contribution to final victory in World War II was very great.

THE ELITE COMMANDERS

Chief of Staff of the IDF

On 2 April 1974, the Agranat Commission, set up to investigate the reasons for Israel's apparent lack of preparedness for the Yom Kippur War of October 1973, presented an interim report. The main findings were blunt: the Commission, it was stated, had 'reached general agreement that the Chief of Staff, David Elazar, bears a personal responsibility for what happened on the eve of the war, both in the matter of evaluating the situation and in the state of preparedness of the Army'. With great reluctance, the Commission recommended that Elazar, together with the Chief of Military Intelligence, Major-General Eliahu Zeira, should be relieved of command without delay. Elazar, protesting his innocence, tendered his resignation as soon as the report was published. It was an untimely end to what had been, until then, a brilliant military career.

David Elazar ('Dado') was born in Yugoslavia in 1928, travelling to Palestine when he was 12 years old. Like so many young men, he was attracted to the Haganah – the unofficial Jewish 'army', dedicated to the creation of a state of Israel in territory administered by the British – and, by 1946, he was an active member of its 'shock' force, the Palmach. During the 'War of Independence' of 1948-49, he commanded a Palmach company in Jerusalem, gaining a reputation for bravery on the night of 18/19 May 1948 when he led his men through the Zion Gate into the Old City, to link up with the embattled Jewish Quarter. Counter-attacks by the Arab Legion soon forced him back, but this incident, together with others of a similar nature in Sinai against the Egyptians later in the year, brought him clearly to the attention of his superiors and ensured him a place as a regular officer in the

Below left: General David Elazar (left), talking to his troops on the Golan Heights at the Syrian border, after Israel had launched an operation against Syria in January 1973. The operation was in retaliation for Syrian attacks on the settlement of Merom Hagolan. Below right: Elazar shortly after his promotion in 1971 to Chief of Staff of the Israeli Defence Forces.

newly formed Israeli Defence Forces (IDF). By 1961, after a period of training and university education, he was Deputy Commander of the Armoured Corps, and three years later he took over as General Officer Commanding Northern Command, with responsibility for defending Galilee against Arab attacks from Lebanon, Jordan and Syria.

He was still in this post when the Six-Day War broke out on 5 June 1967, commanding a total of seven brigades covering the northern borders. As early as the afternoon of 5 June, Elazar ordered his armoured forces to advance into northern Samaria (part of the West Bank) to neutralise Jordanian artillery positions around Jenin, and four days later he organised the successful assault on the Golan Heights, ousting the Syrian defenders from seemingly impregnable positions. His co-ordination of forces and management of two virtually simultaneous campaigns earmarked him for further promotion. In 1969, he was transferred to IDF Headquarters and two years later, backed by the powerful figure of Prime Minister Golda Meir, he was appointed Chief of Staff – the

ELAZAR

highest position of command in the IDF.

Elazar's duties as Chief of Staff included responsibility for evaluating military intelligence of Arab intentions, preparing the IDF for war and advising the Cabinet, through the Minister of Defence – at that time Moshe Dayan – if he felt that Israel was about to be attacked, so that mobilisation of reserve forces could be ordered. According to the Agranat Commission, he failed in these duties in October 1973, showing an unquestioning dependence upon unsubstantiated intelligence reports and allowing Israel to be taken by surprise, with only partially mobilised reserves, when the Egyptians and Syrians crossed the borders. These were grave charges which Elazar hotly contested, arguing that he did not receive a full intelligence picture or adequate backing from Dayan for early mobilisation, but the fact remains that on 6 October Israel's borders in Sinai and on the Golan were poorly defended, the call-up of reservists was chaotic and the IDF was very nearly defeated. As Chief of Staff, Elazar had to bear a large measure of the responsibility for all this, and he should have been aware of the weaknesses.

CRUCIAL TIMING

Nevertheless, as the war developed, Elazar quickly showed his command skill and it is not unreasonable to argue that without his calm response to what was, for the first few days, a desperate situation, Israel would have been hard-pressed to survive intact. As the Arab attacks intensified, it was Elazar who initiated the decision to give priority to the Golan, where a Syrian victory would have threatened Israeli territory very quickly indeed, and his orders for Major General Peled's armoured division to move north onto the Golan instead of south into Sinai on 7 October proved to be of crucial importance. At the same time, Elazar's insistence that Israeli forces stand firm on both fronts, at a time when Dayan was advocating strategic withdrawal, was fully vindicated by subsequent events.

It was in Sinai that Elazar faced his greatest command test, for it needed a man of his skill to impose strategic sense onto a confused and chaotic battle. His initial reaction to the Egyptian crossing of the Suez Canal was to organise a counter-attack, but when this failed on 8 October, amid bitter arguments between the GOC Southern Command, Shmuel Gonen, and his subordinate, Ariel Sharon, Elazar not

only imposed a decision to assume the defensive (at least until the Syrian threat had been countered) but also sent Chaim Bar-Lev to sort out the command problems as his personal representative. A few days later, it was Elazar who vetoed plans for a counter-attack across the Canal until the Egyptians had committed their armour to the east Bank and been defeated. It was a key decision, without which Sharon's crossing at Deversoir and the encirclement of the Egyptian Third Army would have been impossible.

Elazar's resignation was therefore a major loss to the IDF, although in the final analysis he was probably better suited to war than peace, preferring the pressures of combat to the tedium of administration. He did not get a chance to redeem himself: in April 1976 he died of a heart attack, brought on in part by the strains of the Yom Kippur War and its aftermath.

THE ELITE COMMANDERS

Below right: General David Elazar (right) arrives at headquarters on the Golan Heights. Elazar was eager to launch an offensive in the northern sector to crush the Syrian Army before the IDF concentrated its efforts against the Egyptians in Sinai. This plan went ahead despite reservations from Moshe Dayan. Below left and above: Israeli troops in the front line during the fighting on the Golan.

THE ELITE COMMANDERS

A Soldier's General

General Sir George Erskine was born on 23 August 1899, the son of a Major General in the Indian Army, and educated at Charterhouse before entering the Royal Military College at Sandhurst. Commissioned into the Kings Royal Rifle Corps, the young Erskine saw service in the closing year of World War I. He progressed through the usual regimental appointments during the interwar years and began World War II as CSO1 (chief staff officer) of the 1st London Territorial Division. By 1944 he had won the DSO and had reached the rank of Major-General, having successively commanded a battalion of his regiment, 69th Infantry Brigade, and the celebrated 7th

Below left: Major-General Sir George Erskine commanding the famous 7th Armoured Division in the Western Desert during World War II. Erskine went on after the war to become C-in-C East Africa in June 1953. In Africa he faced the challenge of dealing with the Mau Mau insurgency which had erupted in Kenya in 1952. Erskine galvanised the demoralised police and armed forces into action, with raids (below) into the Mount Kenya forests, to hit at Mau Mau strongholds.

Armoured Division in the Western Desert and Normandy. It was in the latter campaign, however, that his career was temporarily stalled when Montgomery controversially removed him from command of the division after it had failed to take Aunay in the attempted breakout from the Normandy beachhead. Nevertheless, he commanded British forces in Hong Kong and served with the army of occupation in Germany before being appointed Director-General of the Territorial Army in 1948.

Erskine then commanded British forces in Egypt and the Mediterranean and was GOC of Eastern Command before being summoned to the post of Commander-in-Chief in East Africa in June 1953. Erskine had experience of pre-war 'Imperial policing' in India and of tackling Egyptian terrorism in the Suez Canal Zone which, coupled with his political experiences in post-war Germany, made him an ideal choice to assume command against the Mau Mau insurgency which had erupted in Kenya in 1952. Based primarily on the Kikuyu tribe, Mau Mau was essentially a tribal nationalist movement with some

ERSKINE

12,000 adherents operating from refuges in the mountain forests of the Aberdares and the area around Mount Kenya.

When Erskine arrived, he found the security forces almost wholly lacking in offensive spirit and he resolved to go over to the offensive against the Mau Mau gangs at the earliest opportunity. Undoubtedly a 'soldier's general', Erskine's strong, bluff character was ideally suited to raising the morale of the security forces. Indeed, he had left his wife in Britain on the grounds that, as his troops – mostly young national servicemen – could not bring their families to Kenya, he would not do so either. His rather old fashioned appearance sometimes gave the impression that he lacked ability but, in reality, he was a shrewd and perceptive soldier.

If Erskine's plain speaking was admired by his

troops, it found less ready acceptance among the community of white settlers, whom he came to dislike and who frequently attempted to interfere in his handling of the emergency. He had sought similar powers over all aspects of counter-insurgency policies to those enjoyed by the British High Commissioner in Malaya, Sir Gerald Templar, but was refused them by the British government. However, he did have complete control over all military forces, and operational control over the police and local forces. Through his friendship with the British prime minister, Winston Churchill, he also carried a letter authorising him to take over the civil administration from the Governor, Sir Evelyn Baring, and to declare martial law, should he deem it necessary.

SCOURGE OF THE MAU MAU

Erskine's aim was to release the army from static policing duties and move it into action against the main Mau Mau gangs in the so-called Prohibited Areas – regions such as the Aberdares where army and police had authority to use weapons freely. He began hitting back at Mau Mau in June and July 1953. In the following year, his large-scale Operation Anvil succeeded in destroying the political infrastructure of the insurgents in Nairobi, five battalions undertaking a massive cordon-and-search operation which detained 16,500 suspects. Thereafter, the army was in a position to launch sweeping operations in the forests to break up the gangs. Such operations were costly in that they drew heavily on the available

THE ELITE COMMANDERS

Below: As C-in-C East Africa, Erskine conducts a tour of inspection of his troops. Erskine set high standards for his men and did not hesitate to press charges against any who broke his rules. His strict attitude to discipline and his outspokenness paid off, however, winning him the respect and loyalty of the men under his command; so much so, that by the end of his tour of duty in East Africa in 1955, he had curbed the strength of the Mau Mau and the insurgency was being brought under control.

manpower resources, but later on Erskine's successor, Sir Gerald Lathbury, was able to introduce smaller units to hunt down the surviving Mau Mau.

But if Erskine appeared to favour the bludgeon to the rapier, he was careful to avoid massive retaliation against the African population at large. Although appalled by the bestial brutality of Mau Mau gangs in their indiscriminate attacks on white and black alike, Erskine had immediately stopped the 'killing competitions' he discovered in some British and native units when he arrived in Kenya. He made it very clear that he expected the highest disciplinary standards, and he pressed charges against those in the white Kenya Police Reserve or the locally raised Kikuyu Guard and Kings African Rifles who fell short of the discipline expected of the army units. Nevertheless, he had an understanding of the value of raising local units such as the Kikuyu Guard, provided that they were properly controlled, and he also pioneered the use of 'counter-gangs' of former guerrillas who were willing to operate against their erstwhile colleagues.

At the end of his tour of duty in May 1955, the back of the Mau Mau insurgency had been shattered. The army was, in fact, withdrawn from operations as early as the end of 1956, although the emergency did not officially end until January 1960. Erskine then returned to Southern Command in Britain and became Lieutenant-Governor and Commander-in-Chief on Jersey on his retirement in 1958 until 1963. He died on 29 August 1965.

69

THE ELITE COMMANDERS

Implacable commander of New Zealanders

Bernard Cyril Freyberg was born in London on 21 March 1889 and was educated at Wellington College, New Zealand. At the time of the outbreak of war in Europe in 1914, Freyberg was in California but returned to England in order to volunteer for active service. He was commissioned into the RNVR as a sub-lieutenant and joined the Hood Battalion. The battalion was first sent to Antwerp, and then on to

Below: A New Zealand anti-tank gun crew in action against German machine-gun positions on Monastery Hill, near Cassino, in February 1944. Freyberg was later to advocate the controversial destruction of the monastery, on 15 February 1944. Below right: Major-General B.C. Freyberg, VC, in August 1940.

FREYBERG

Gallipoli in the Dardanelles. It was during a diversionary action at Bulair that Freyberg won his first commendation in action, a DSO.

In May 1916, Freyberg was gazetted captain with the Queen's Royal West Surrey Regiment, but remained with the Hood Battalion which he now commanded as an acting lieutenant-colonel. Later that year, the Royal Naval Division was returned to France for the Battle of the Somme and it was at Beaumont Hamel that Freyberg won a Victoria Cross. Freyberg had captured his objectives, 500 prisoners and received four wounds in the space of a two-day operation. World War I was to prove a good war for Freyberg's military career and in September 1918 he won a bar to his DSO. In the final days of the war he won a second bar. He was also credited with six mentions in despatches and a Croix de Guerre.

Freyberg remained in the army following the cessation of hostilities and even found time to make several cross-channel swim attempts, at one point getting to within 500yds of Dover before the tide

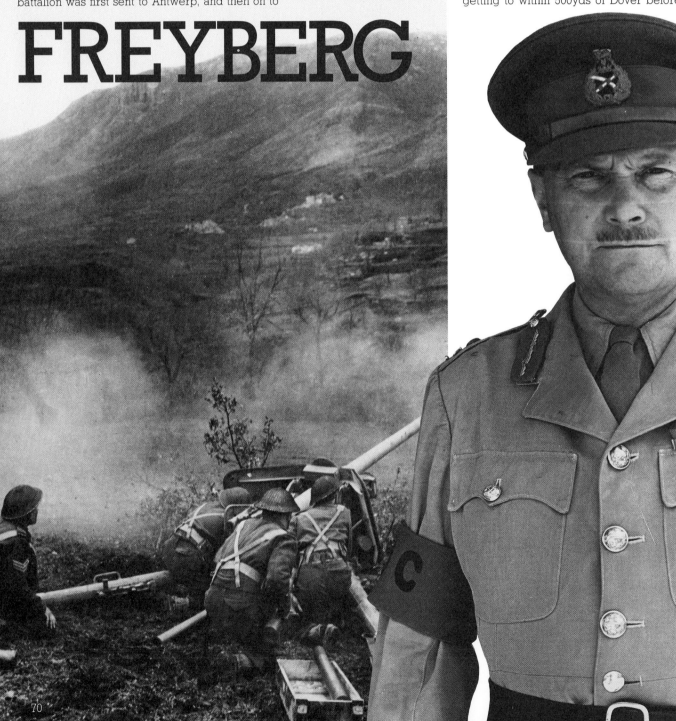

turned and prevented him from completing the swim.

In 1927, he was promoted to major and on his promotion to lieutenant-colonel (in 1929) he took command of the 1st Battalion, the Manchester Regiment. In 1931, Freyberg was appointed Assistant Quarter Master General, HQ Southern Command and in 1933 was made General Staff Officer, 1st Grade, at the War Office. Freyberg was promoted to major-general in 1934, and this posting took him to India as a District Commander; but illness forced him to leave the Army in 1937.

This was not the end of an illustrious career, however, for when World War II broke out in 1939, Freyberg had recovered sufficiently to be recalled and was appointed General Officer Commanding, Salisbury Plain Area. In November of the same year he was given command of New Zealand Forces Overseas.

Freyberg returned properly to active service in 1941 when the New Zealand Divison was sent to Greece to resist the German advance on Athens, taking up positions on the Aliakhmon Line. Freyberg's forces conducted a series of spirited defensive actions and only the fall of Yugoslavia and the defeat of the Greek Army forced a withdrawal to Crete, where Freyberg's forces were to provide the island's principal defensive units.

Freyberg was given command of all Allied forces on Crete, and despite the lack of equipment and air support (much of the heavy artillery had been left on the Greek mainland) his troops inflicted severe casualties upon the German XI Air Corps which had launched a massive operation for the invasion of Crete. Inevitably, the Allied forces were withdrawn from Crete, though Freyberg only managed to evacuate about half of the 30,000 troops on the island.

DECISIVE ASSAULTS

The New Zealand Division was then sent to bolster Sir Alan Cunningham's Crusader offensive in the Western Desert. They acquitted themselves well (taking Sidi Rezegh) but Freyberg was unsatisfied with Auchinleck's Desert Command and their attitude toward the New Zealand Division. He insisted that his men be allowed to retrain and reorganise. The request was approved and Freyberg withdrew his men to Syria for six months.

In June 1942, his revitalised troops were recalled to active service after the fall of Tobruk, in an attempt to block Rommel's advance. Their first action was at Mersa Matruh where Freyberg was badly wounded, his division narrowly escaping annihilation. After redeployment into the Alamein position, Freyberg returned to action in time for Montgomery's offensive and it was he who led the decisive assaults that clinched the Battle of Mareth in March 1943.

In November 1943, Freyberg's New Zealanders were transferred to the Italian theatre and, after taking part in the Battle of Sangro, joined the US Fifth Army. Freyberg was charged to assault Cassino upon which a previous American attack had failed. Freyberg's command was a specially formed New Zealand Corps which also included a US combat group, an Indian division and a British division.

The corps did not succeed in taking the main objective due, in part, to the results of the artillery bombardment of the town and monastery which Freyberg himself had advocated as vital to the assault, but which in the event proved of little value. In February and March 1944, Freyberg conducted two assaults against the objective, taking key positions, but the corps was withdrawn before the final successful offensive in May. However, Freyberg's efforts had earned him another bar to his DSO.

Following the conclusion of hostilities, Freyberg's outstanding career and his affiliation to the people and government of New Zealand resulted in his election as Governor-General to the country. This position he held until his return to England in 1952, where he was appointed Deputy Constable and Lieutenant-Governor of Windsor Castle and was later made 1st Baron Freyberg. His other honours included KBE and KCB in 1942 and GCMG in 1946. He was honorary DCL, Oxford, and an honorary LLD, New Zealand. Freyberg died on 4 July 1963.

Freyberg maintained a remarkable physical and mental strength throughout his military career despite being wounded 12 times and engaged in battle against seemingly insurmountable odds on numerous occasions. His bravery won admiration from many quarters – Winston Churchill described him as a 'salamander' – and one of his greatest adversaries, General Rommel, wrote of his division that he would 'have been happier if it had been safely tucked away in our prison camps instead of still facing us' – such was the resilience of this formidable soldier.

Below: After the fall of Tunis, on 7 May 1943, Marshall Giovanni Messe, the Italian Commander-in-Chief in Tunisia, (second from right) surrenders to General Freyberg (foreground), the GOC of the New Zealand troops serving with the Eighth Army. The capture of Tunis was the final triumph of the Allies in North Africa, after almost three years of warfare.

THE ELITE COMMANDERS

Master of guerrilla strategy and an implacable opponent

General Vo Nguyen Giap (1912-   ) is widely acknowledged as one of the world's great military leaders. Although the system of collective leadership adopted by the communists in Vietnam makes it difficult to attribute responsibility for decisions to specific individuals, Giap is credited with the conduct of the long campaigns which defeated two of the world's major military powers – France and the United States.

Giap always projected a genial public image, with an ever-present smile and a relaxed style of speech in the precise, fluent French of a one-time schoolteacher. Yet his conduct of war displayed the ruthlessness and determination of a man whose entire life was dedicated to a single goal – victory in revolutionary war.

Giap's original concepts of military strategy and tactics were learnt from the example and teachings of Mao Tse-tung, the Chinese communist leader. Giap studied Mao's doctrines in south China during the 1930s, where he had fled after a crackdown on communist movements by the French colonial administration in Indochina. He was given responsibility for raising and organising guerrilla groups, and it was under his leadership that small-scale guerrilla

Right: Vietnam's master strategist, General Vo Nguyen Giap, who triumphed first over the French, then over the Americans, and finally over the forces of South Vietnam. Below: North Vietnamese infantry move forward against US-supported South Vietnamese troops during Operation Lam Son 719 in February 1971. Giap's belief in the value of massed infantry assaults against heavily defended enemy positions was often criticised as unnecessarily wasteful of his troops' lives.

GIAP

operations against both the French and the Japanese were initiated in the north of Vietnam during December 1944.

Giap's Viet Minh forces expanded rapidly, partly through American military aid offered as part of the war effort against the Japanese, but also through Giap's exceptional talent for the organisation of regular and irregular forces. After the Japanese surrender in August 1945, the Viet Minh were able to establish their authority through most of northern Vietnam, and Giap became both minister of defence and army commander in the regime established in Hanoi by Ho Chi Minh. He was responsible for the raising of forces, training, indoctrination, discipline, administration and logistics – at which he was to excel. By the time the French reoccupied Hanoi in December 1946, a military structure had been set up which would prove capable of sustaining a prolonged insurgency against the colonial forces.

Giap had a close understanding of Maoist guerrilla doctrines. His strategy was based on the need to move through three stages of warfare – clandestine preparation, open guerrilla warfare, and finally, the transition to conventional forces. Similarly, there were three levels to the guerrilla army – local self-defence militia, regional forces with a somewhat higher level of equipment, and regular forces which were given rigorous training in safe areas until the time came for large-scale operations. At all levels, political motivation and education were regarded as of fundamental importance. Indeed, Giap's whole concept of warfare was dominated by politics; he always conceived the aim of military action in terms of its effect on his enemy's political will to fight.

Giap's conduct of the Indochina War against the French was not flawless. Depending on the absolute security of his base area in the mountainous Viet Bac region, and exploiting a safe supply line from China,

Below: Giap congratulates North Vietnamese soldiers at a ceremony in Hanoi during the Vietnam War. Giap's public appearances always showed the benign, relaxed side of his character, keeping his implacable willpower and determination well hidden.

he directed a highly successful guerrilla campaign in which thousands of small-scale assaults threatened the French throughout the country, tying down the majority of their forces in static defence posts. He was tempted, however, to move into the conventional phase prematurely in early 1951, and lost almost a third of his men in three major engagements in the Red River Delta.

Yet in the aftermath of these defeats, Giap's ability as a leader showed clearly. Realising (and willing to admit) that he had made a mistake, Giap reverted to guerrilla warfare and regained the strategic initiative. When the French moved 12 battalions to garrison an outpost at Dien Bien Phu, he sensed the chance for a decisive victory. In March 1954, a force of 40,000 Viet Minh put Dien Bien Phu under siege, and the defeat of the French garrison two months later effectively ended colonial rule.

The establishment of North Vietnam as an independent communist state could not satisfy Giap and his colleagues, however, who aspired to govern all of Vietnam. From 1959, the North Vietnamese were progressively drawn into support for an insurrection in South Vietnam. Giap masterminded the creation of a superb logistics network from the North to the South, which was to become ever more sophisticated through the following decade. Guerrillas from the South were trained north of the border and returned to the battlefield, but Giap did not commit North Vietnamese Army (NVA) formations to the South in any great numbers until after US combat troops began to arrive in 1964.

The conflict with the Americans in South Vietnam was the most severe test of Giap's abilities. He faced an enemy enjoying total technological superiority, but short on the political willpower required to fight a long and costly campaign. Never losing the strategic initiative, Giap drew the Americans into a war of attrition that he believed they could not sustain.

Once again, the wisdom of some of Giap's decisions has been queried. The Tet offensive of 1968, in which Viet Cong guerrillas and NVA troops seized towns and cities throughout South Vietnam while, simultaneously, a large NVA force besieged US Marines at Khe Sanh, has been described as a costly failure. Certainly, the seizure of the towns did not provoke the expected popular uprising, Khe Sanh was eventually relieved, and losses of both guerrillas and regular troops were extremely heavy. Yet Giap was indisputably correct in his assumption that this offensive would destroy the American will to fight.

From late 1969, Giap devoted most attention and resources to a build-up of NVA forces and equipment, preparing a conventional invasion of the South, which followed at Easter 1972. The Easter invasion was in one sense another costly failure – 130,000 men lost for little territory gained. Giap has been criticised for dispersing his forces in three separate lines of advance, and for underrating the impact of US airpower. Yet once more, this view neglects wider political and strategic considerations. It was vital for the North Vietnamese to hold territory in the South prior to the conclusion of peace negotiations with the Americans (which followed in January 1973), and a toehold in three separate strategic areas.

By 1975, Giap had been forced through illness to hand over command to General Dung, but the final NVA victories in that year were the culmination of his grand strategy. Giap had proved himself a master of revolutionary warfare, not only in the organisation and supply of both regular and irregular forces, but also in the political dimension of military strategy.

THE ELITE COMMANDERS
GORSHKOV

Architect of the Soviet navy

Born in the Ukraine in 1910, Sergei Georgievich Gorshkov entered the Leningrad Naval Academy at the age of 17. He seems to have been an exemplary student and he rose rapidly through the ranks after graduation, but it was probably due as much to Stalin's purges of senior commanders as to professional ability that he became a rear admiral with the Black Sea Fleet at the early age of 31. For reasons that remain unclear, he delayed joining the Communist Party until 1942, but all his pronouncements reveal him as a dedicated communist, with orthodox ideological leanings. He survived Khrushchev's fall from power in 1964 to become a deputy defence minister, a member of the Central Committee, a deputy of the Supreme Soviet and a Hero of the Soviet Union. In October 1967 he became the first Soviet to hold the rank of Admiral of the Fleet. He has rightly been described as the architect of Soviet naval power.

The position that Gorshkov took over in 1956, that of commander-in-chief of the Soviet Navy, appeared to fall far short of its British or American equivalent. Russia, with its limited access to ice-free seas, is not a natural naval power in the way that those countries have been. The Russian Navy had not ventured far from its home ports since the 18th century and it had suffered a disastrous humiliation at the hands of the Japanese at Tsushima in 1905. During World War II Gorshkov himself played a distinguished part in the defence of Odessa, but in that war the Soviet Navy in general had only a minor role, mainly in support of the army.

By the end of the war, Russia's ships and dockyards had been shattered. A major rebuilding programme was started by Stalin, who declared 'every nation that becomes a world power must have a navy', but Stalin's naval strategy was still almost entirely defensive, and somewhat vitiated by the enormous prestige he attached to heavy cruisers. After his accession to power in 1953 Khrushchev maintained the defensive policy, but replaced Stalin's obsession with large surface ships with an obsession of his own: apparently convinced that there was no naval task that could not be performed by submarines, he set out not only to increase their numbers by a huge percentage but also virtually to scrap the entire surface fleet.

When Gorshkov was appointed commander-in-chief he revealed his powers as a naval politician by supporting the submarine-building programme but at the same time quietly side-stepping Khrushchev's policy on surface vessels. As he was to state in *Pravda* in 1962, 'The basis of our Navy are the atomic submarines, equipped with powerful rockets and homing torpedoes with nuclear charges...On a level with submarines are the surface ships, equipped with rockets and the latest technical aids.' He was to be a strong avocate of what he called a 'well-balanced fleet'.

The grand strategic naval policy that Gorshkov inherited and seems to have accepted in the late 1950s was an anti-carrier policy. Since the enemy's main striking power was in the form of carrier-borne aircraft, the Soviet Navy had to counter that threat by arming its submarines and surface ships with missiles: the submarines would shadow the enemy's carriers, the missiles would penetrate the carriers' defensive screen and destroy them. Conversely aircraft carriers were perceived as being so vulnerable in the age of the missile-armed submarine that there was no point in having them. Even if Gorshkov

had wanted a carrier fleet at that time there is very little likelihood that Khrushchev would have let him build one. Instead the Russians began fitting their Kotlin and Krupny class destroyers with missile launchers and pushed ahead with their nuclear submarine programme, especially after US Polaris-armed submarines began to threaten Russia's coastline in the early 1960s.

It was also in the early 1960s that Gorshkov's strategic thinking began to change and develop, perhaps stimulated by the Cuban missile crisis of 1962, when Russia had to back down in the face of America's supremacy in the Western Atlantic, and by the increasing range and defensive ability of Western carrier forces. Gorshkov's re-activation in the mid-1960s of Russia's black-bereted naval infantry, with its capability of long-range amphibious intervention, may have been symptomatic of the new thinking. The Russian Navy as designed by Khrushchev could defend the homeland or launch strategic nuclear weapons in a global war, but it lacked the means to play any part in 'local' wars, as, for example, the US Navy was effectively doing in Vietnam, or to act as an arm of Soviet political strategy on the world stage in peacetime.

CONVINCING NAVAL PRESENCE

Gorshkov had begun to recognise the need, on the one hand, for more flexibility in the structure of his fleets, including possibly a reconsideration of the role of the carrier, and on the other, to have for the first time in his country's history a convincing naval presence in the world's oceans. A step towards the development of Soviet aircraft carriers was taken with the appearance of the helicopter carrier *Moskva* in 1967, soon followed by her sister ship *Leningrad*. The first Kiev class aircraft carrier was laid down in 1971.

However, it was not the size or the composition of the Soviet fleets that began to attract the world's attention in the 1960s so much as their movement out of their home ports to challenge, in Gorshkov's own words, 'capitalist naval supremacy in all the seas and oceans of the world'. In 1964 a squadron from the Russian Black Sea Fleet spent part of the year in the Mediterranean. In 1967 the Soviet Mediterranean squadron became permanent, challenging the US Sixth Fleet, and the first Soviet survey ships appeared in the Indian Ocean. In the same year, Russian-supplied Styx missiles sank the Israeli destroyer *Eilat*, the first time a warship had been sunk by a surface-to-surface missile launched from another vessel. In 1968 a Soviet naval squadron entered the Indian Ocean. In 1970 all the Soviet fleets combined for the first time in Exercise Okean, demonstrating their capacity for a command structure on a massive scale and symbolically telling the West that the Soviet Union was now, in naval terms, a world power. The Soviet Navy under Gorshkov was showing that it had learned about the political power that flows from the ability to show the flag in the oceans of the world.

In the 1980s Soviet naval power is taken for granted. One only has to look back to the situation in the 1950s to see the measure of Gorshkov's achievement. As he himself put it:

'The age-old dreams of our people have become reality. The pennants of the Soviet ships now

Page 74: Two Soviet submarines (top), moored for refuelling. Below: Admiral Sergei Gorshkov in full uniform. This page below: A Midi Mi-8 Soviet helicopter flying over a Soviet torpedo boat.

flutter in the most remote corners of the seas and oceans. Our Navy is a real force and possesses the ability to resolve successfully the tasks of defending the state interests of the Soviet Union and of the whole socialist world.'

Admiral Gorshkov has never commanded his fleet in action, and his triumphs have been over political rather than military opponents, but history will almost certainly recognise that he has been responsible for one of the most massive changes in the world balance of power since World War II. In December 1985 Sergei Gorshkov retired and was replaced as commander-in-chief by Vladimir Chernavin.

GUDERIAN

Architect of the German armoured forces

Heinz Guderian (1888-1954) was an outstanding military commander whose ideas and fighting skills contributed in no small measure to German victories in the early months of World War II. He was a pioneer and practitioner of Blitzkrieg, spearheading the devastating attacks on Poland (1939), France (1940) and western Russia (1941) and, as Inspector of Armoured Forces (1943-44) and Chief of the General Staff (1944-45), he displayed remarkable qualities as a staff officer at the highest levels of command.

A NEW WEAPON OF WAR

Guderian was born in 1888 in East Prussia, and his early education in cadet schools and the War School at Metz prepared him for a military career. He was commissioned into the 10th Hanoverian Jaeger Battalion in 1908 and served throughout World War I, initially as a regimental officer and then on the General Staff. In 1919 he was one of a select band of officers retained in the peacetime Reichswehr, where he soon began to specialise in 'motor transport', a convenient cover for early experiments in tank warfare. Influenced by the writings of the British theorists J.F.C. Fuller and Basil Liddell Hart, Guderian was quick to appreciate the potential of the tank as a fast-moving, hard-hitting instrument of war which, if used to find and exploit weaknesses in an enemy defence, could spread panic in rear areas and achieve strategic victory. By 1931, when he was appointed Chief of Staff to the Inspectorate of Motorised Troops, he was already experimenting with all-arms mobile formations, centered on the tanks

THE ELITE COMMANDERS

Above left: Heinz Guderian, architect of Germany's panzer forces. Below: Guderian leans out of his half-track command vehicle during the invasion of the Soviet Union in 1941. He was an inspiring commander, who believed in leading from the front, and his troops nicknamed him 'Schnell Heinz' because of the pace at which he drove them.

Below and right: Guderian observes the action. Guderian was in the fortunate position of having evolved theories and weaponry that he was able to put to the test on the battlefield, where his ideas were triumphantly vindicated.

but also including motorised infantry and artillery units, and when Hitler gave his support to the concept two years later, Guderian went on to produce the first of the panzer divisions. Backed by the dive-bombers of the nascent Luftwaffe, the basic instrument of Blitzkrieg was available to the Nazis by 1935, thanks largely to Guderian's efforts.

The panzers first saw action during the invasion of Poland in September 1939, and they immediately proved their value. Guderian played a central role in the attack, commanding XIX Corps (comprising one panzer and two motorised infantry divisions) in an advance out of Pomerania towards the Vistula river. XIX Corps cracked apart the thin linear defence of the enemy and swept forward virtually unopposed. Characteristically, Guderian led from the front, mounted on a half-track equipped with radios from which to coordinate his fast-moving units. As other mobile forces converged on Poland from Silesia and the Luftwaffe opened up the lines of advance, the first of the Blitzkrieg victories was complete.

Guderian played an equally important part, still as commander of XIX Corps (by now comprising three panzer divisions), in the invasion of France and the Low Countries eight months later. His task was to break through in the centre, emerging from the 'impassable' Ardennes to cross the Meuse river at Sedan before moving swiftly behind Anglo-French lines to the coast beyond Amiens. The overall plan was audacious and Guderian's part in it was carried out to perfection. As German forces on the right invaded Holland and Belgium, drawing the Allies north, Guderian spearheaded the Ardennes assault: setting out on 10 May 1940, he crossed the Meuse three days later and reached the Atlantic coast on the 21st, leaving an outmanoeuvred and demoralised enemy in his wake. As British units escaped via Dunkirk, the French could do nothing to prevent defeat.

Similar success was achieved in June-July 1941, during Operation Barbarossa, the invasion of the Soviet Union, when Guderian, as commander of 2nd Panzer Group (later 2nd Panzer Army) cooperated with General Hermann Hoth's 3rd Panzer Group in a series of wide sweeping moves designed to encircle vast portions of the Red Army in the area attacked by Field Marshal Fedor von Bock's Army Group Centre. By 29 June the panzers had trapped 300,000 enemy troops east of Minsk and the process was repeated in early July at Smolensk. Hitler then intervened, however, diverting the panzers south to the Ukraine, and the opportunity to take Moscow was lost. As winter weather prevented momentum, Guderian became understandably bitter about the Führer's strategic decision; he was relieved of his command on 26 December.

Confrontation With Hitler

He remained 'inactive' for just over a year, but even Hitler could not ignore his qualities. In March 1943 he appointed Guderian Inspector of Armoured Force, specifically to supervise the development and deployment of the new generation of tanks (the Panthers and Tigers), and in July 1944 he was promoted to Chief of the General Staff. There followed a difficult time, full of confrontations with Hitler over strategic priorities – Guderian always favoured bolstering up the Eastern Front and viewed with growing concern operations such as the Ardennes offensive in the west in December 1944 – and although he achieved a remarkable amount, chiefly by standing up to the Führer, there was a limit to his influence. In March 1945 he was sent on 'sick leave' – a euphemism for retirement – and his military career came to an end. He died in 1954.

Guderian was undeniably one of the most influential theorists and commanders of the 20th Century, and bears comparison with any of the great captains of history.

THE ELITE COMMANDERS

Prophet of Revolt

Ernesto 'Che' Guevara (1928-67) has become a symbol of modern revolution. His face, framed by long dark hair and a thin beard, has stared down from countless posters; his speeches and writings have assured him a place in the history of revolutionary theory; and his death in Bolivia, while still an active fighter, has made him a martyr to the cause of peasant revolt. The French philosopher Jean-Paul Sartre

Below: Portrait of a committed revolutionary. Ernesto 'Che' Guevara trained as a doctor, but shot to prominence as one of Fidel Castro's lieutenants during the successful campaign to overthrow the corrupt regime of Fulgencio Batista, the autocratic ruler of Cuba, in the late 1950s.

GUEVARA

described him as 'the most complete man of his age' and, to many on the political left, that remains his epitaph.

The reality is slightly different. Born in Buenos Aires, Argentina, in 1928, Guevara came from a solidly middle-class background and did not enter the arena of revolution until after he had qualified as a doctor. In February 1954 he travelled to Guatemala where, four months later, he witnessed a CIA-backed coup which overthrew the reformist president, Jacobo Arbenz Guzman. Guevara could do nothing to oppose the coup – indeed, he was forced to seek refuge in the Argentinian embassy in Guatemala City as soon as it occurred – but out of his experience emerged two beliefs that were to be central to his revolutionary thought. On the one hand, he recognized the inevitability of US intervention to prevent left-wing reforms in Latin America; on the other, he advocated arming the 'workers and peasants' to oppose such intervention.

A few months later, Guevara moved to Mexico, where he made contact with a group of Cuban exiles, led by Fidel Castro, who were preparing to return to their homeland to overthrow the government of Fulgencio Batista. Guevara joined them as their doctor, travelling to Cuba aboard the motor-cruiser *Granma* in late November 1956. The aim was to land in the eastern province of Oriente, make contact with members of the 26 July Movement already active on the island and initiate a concerted campaign of political subversion and guerrilla attacks. Unfortunately, things did not go according to plan.

When Castro and his followers landed on 2 December, Batista had already dealt with the threat from the 26 July Movement, leaving the *fidelistas* without support. Moreover, within 72 hours of landing, the latter were caught in an ambush by elements of the Cuban Army and virtually destroyed. Guevara was lucky to survive, having to struggle for days through difficult terrain, before rejoining Castro and a group of no more than a dozen dispirited guerrillas deep in the Sierra Maestra mountains.

The fact that Guevara did survive forced him to become a guerrilla fighter rather than a doctor, and during the ensuing months he began to display remarkable qualities of leadership, not least in terms of determination, inspiration and bravery. By the summer of 1958 he was in command of a column of 200 guerrillas, pushing towards Havana across the centre of the island. Batista was by now in trouble, having alienated vast sectors of the Cuban population through policies of repression, and Guevara was able to exploit the growing weakness of the army to capture town after town without a fight. On 2 January

Page 79: In the war against Batista, Castro's men operated out of the Sierra Maestra highlands. Guevara, seen here operating a radio (below), led the first guerrillas into Havana, the Cuban capital.
Above: After the war, Guevara became involved in schemes to help the country's peasants.

1959 he led his men into Havana, seizing power on Castro's behalf.

He was rewarded with political posts in the new revolutionary government – he served as Minister for Industry and President of the National Bank – but he soon became frustrated. Still a young man, he had a dream of extending the Cuban model of successful revolution to states throughout Latin America, putting forward what was known as the 'foco' principle as the means of doing so. Based upon his experience in Cuba, Guevara believed that the days of protracted revolution, in which vast sectors of the peasant population were laboriously persuaded to support the rebels, were over; instead, dedicated and inspirational guerrilla leaders could be inserted into selected states to act as a focus for discontent, creating rather than exploiting the desire for political change. If this could be done in a number of states simultaneously, US resources would be swamped and a wave of revolution would sweep the continent. It was an ambitious plan.

BETRAYED BY PEASANTS

Guevara disappeared from public view in April 1965, travelling to the Congo (Zaire) and North Vietnam before entering Bolivia in November 1966, disguised as a businessman. He chose Bolivia because of its central position, bordering five other Latin American states, but his campaign was poorly prepared and beset with problems. Moving to a remote farm to the east of the capital, La Paz, he hoped to attract support from the Bolivian Communist Party, but when they refused to accept his leadership, he was left with fewer than 40 armed followers, the majority of whom were Cubans with no particular knowledge of Bolivia. More importantly, the local peasants showed no desire to support the guerrillas, for although the government of President Rene Barrientos was authoritarian and repressive, it had carried out a land reform programme which ensured at least a degree of popularity.

This became apparent to Guevara in March 1967, when he led the majority of his group on a preliminary 'route march' to the north of their base at Nancahuazu. The going was hard, through thick jungle and across wide, raging rivers, many of the guerrillas suffered from disease and Guevara himself began to be affected by chronic asthma. Struggling back to base, moreover, they soon discovered that local peasants had betrayed their presence to the Bolivian Army, elements of which were closing in. Guevara still retained his skill as a guerrilla leader. In April he laid a successful ambush which gave his group a vital breathing space, but the advantage of surprise had been lost.

As the United States poured equipment, helicopters and advisers into Bolivia, the outcome was inevitable. In late August Guevara's 'rearguard' was surrounded and wiped out, and a few weeks later it was the turn of the main group. On 8 October, by which time Guevara was so ill he could hardly move, his small band of less than 20 men was cornered in a wooded ravine close to the Rio Grande river; Guevara was wounded and captured. Early the following morning he was executed on orders from the government and his body displayed before the cameras of the press. The dream was over, only the romantic memory remained.

THE ELITE COMMANDERS

Chief of the German General Staff

Between 1938 and 1942, Franz Halder served Adolf Hitler as chief of the army general staff. Although Halder opposed Hitler's overall strategy and despised National Socialism, this did not prevent him from serving the Führer during three crucial years of the war. After being dismissed by Hitler in 1942, he survived imprisonment following the July Bomb Plot in 1944, and after the war worked closely with the US Army, directing former German officers in compil-

HALDER

Below right: Franz Halder, one of the Wehrmacht's most able and energetic senior staff officers, fell foul of Hitler when he objected to the operational conduct of the war in Russia, and was later dismissed from his position as the chief of the army general staff. Below: German troops during the opening stages of Operation Barbarossa. Initially enthusiastic about this enterprise, Halder soon began to doubt that victory was possible.

ing detailed reports on their military experiences.

Franz Halder was born in Würzburg, Bavaria, on 30 June 1884, into a family with a long tradition of service in the Bavarian Army. In 1902 he entered the army as an officer candidate in the 3rd Bavarian Field Artillery Regiment and became a second-lieutenant in March 1904. Being a very able, intelligent and even academic young officer, he was selected to study at the Bavarian War Academy and was serving on the general staff in 1914. For most of World War I Halder served as a staff officer. After the defeat in 1918, he was considered good enough to serve in the Weimar Republic's Reichsheer. For much of the 1920s he alternated between troop and staff appointments, impressing his superiors with his loyalty, hard work and grasp of detail.

After Hitler came to power in 1933, Halder had an ambivalent attitude towards both the Führer and Nazi policies. He was acquainted with both because of his military service in Bavaria at the time of the Munich Putsch of 1923. Although Halder, as a devout Christian, regarded Hitler as someone who was amoral, he was impressed by his genius and his determination to restore Germany's former glory. After 1934 Halder felt constrained by his personal oath of loyalty to Hitler. Under Hitler, his career

progressed smoothly, with his promotion to major-general and commander of the 7th Division in 1935, and by early 1938 to lieutenant-general and an appointment on the general staff.

DISAGREEMENTS WITH HITLER

By this stage, Halder was deeply concerned that Hitler's aggressive foreign policy would lead Germany into a war that could not be won. He found himself involved in Hitler's purge and reorganisation of the army high command following the removal of Blomberg and Fritsch. Despite Hitler's reservations about Halder – he believed, erroneously, that Halder was a Catholic, and a 'chronic know-it-all' – he appointed him deputy chief of the general staff to Beck. When Beck resigned in the autumn of 1938, at the time of the Munich crisis, Hitler, convinced that Halder was an apolitical professional soldier, appointed him chief of the general staff.

Hitler was wrong in his belief that Halder was apolitical. By 1938 he was prepared to consider joining other military opponents of Hitler in using the army to launch a putsch. But Halder lacked sufficient determination, and gradually his political reservations became subordinated to his professional interest in operational planning. From the summer of 1939, with the preparations for the invasion of Poland, until the crisis outside Moscow in the late autumn of 1941, Hitler relied upon Halder to provide the technical expertise to put his strategic ideas into operational reality.

However, Halder enraged Hitler by his pessimism and habit of argument. In 1939 he was sure that by invading Poland the western Allies would strike in the west, something which did not in fact occur. In the winter of 1940, he was doubtful whether the western Allies could be overwhelmed in a lightning campaign, which in the event they were, thus confirming Hitler in his belief that the general staff was full of doubters. Halder annoyed Hitler by his laconic, icy logic and his refusal to be bullied by Hitler's emotional outbursts.

Although after the war Halder claimed that Hitler's interference had paralysed the army and ultimately led to its defeat, at the time he supported Hitler's military policy and substantially contributed to its success or failure. Halder played a very important

Below: A stiffly formal Halder greets Hitler while official cameramen record the scene. In private, the two men, who had little in common, found it hard to hide their mutual antagonism. After his fall from grace, Halder was on the fringes of the bomb plot in 1944, but was untouched by the subsequent retribution. After the war he worked with the US Army and his diaries highlighted his ambivalence to Nazism. Bottom: Heavy artillery crossing into Russia.

part in the planning for Operation Barbarossa, the invasion of the Soviet Union, and there is no doubt that he suppressed disagreeable facts that might have affected optimistic forecasts of a quick victory. Neither did Halder protest about the army's participation in the preparations for a racial war in the east.

In the first few weeks following the attack of 22 June 1941, Halder was very optimistic, believing, along with Hitler, that the campaign against the Soviet Union had already been won. But within two months, he was involved in a bitter dispute with Hitler and senior generals about operational objectives. He survived Hitler's dismissal of a number of his top generals on the Eastern Front in November 1941, but Halder soon found that his actual area of responsibilities was being reduced. Continual disagreements with Hitler over planning, command appointments, and, finally, the conduct of the battle of Stalingrad, led to his dismissal on 24 September 1942, with Hitler saying that he had been 'no longer equal to the psychic demands of the position'.

In his retirement, Halder was very much on the fringes of the July Plot, but on 22 July 1944 he was arrested, dismissed from the army and imprisoned in Dachau concentration camp. After the war Halder worked for the US Army and in 1949 wrote a best-selling pamphlet entitled *Hitler as War Lord*. His diaries as chief of the general staff were used in postwar trials and later became important historical documents. He died in Bavaria on 2 April 1972.

THE ELITE COMMANDERS

HARRIS

'Bomber' Harris

Between February 1942 and May 1945, Air Marshal Sir Arthur Harris – known to the public as 'Bomber' and to his men as 'Butch' – commanded one of the most sustained and controversial campaigns of the World War II. As Commander-in-Chief, RAF Bomber Command, he was responsible for conducting strategic bombing operations against Germany, ordering almost-nightly raids designed to destroy industrial centres and undermine civilian morale.

Arthur Travers Harris was born on 13 April 1892, the son of a civil servant based in India, and there was little in his early life to suggest future greatness. His education was patchy, forcing him to make his own way in the world; in February 1910 he travelled to Rhodesia, where he spent four years working as a planter, builder, transport boss and farm manager before joining the 1st Rhodesian Regiment as a

bugler at the outbreak of World War I. Arduous service in the campaign to capture German South West Africa left him determined to avoid marching into battle, and when he returned to England in late 1915 he joined the Royal Flying Corps as a pilot. After hasty training, he was sent to a home defence fighter squadron and then to the front line in France, and although he never managed to destroy an enemy aircraft in combat, it soon became apparent that he was a born leader of men. By November 1918 having commanded a variety of squadrons and begun to specialise in night flying, he was offered a

Left: Harris in the Bomber-Command interpretation room. Below: An Avro Lancaster is bombed up.

permanent commission in the newly formed RAF.

During the 1920s, Harris was groomed for higher command, serving as a bomber-squadron commander in India and Mesopotamia before being sent to the Army Staff College at Camberley for a two-year course. In 1929 he was appointed Senior Staff Officer to the Air Officer Commanding (AOC) Middle East and, four years later, he moved to the Air Ministry as a group captain, eventually becoming Deputy Director Plans in the Directorate of Operations and Intelligence. It was an important post at a time when Britain was beginning to emerge from her peacetime slumbers, and Harris was largely responsible for ensuring that strategic bombing became an integral part of the country's defence plans. Work on the creation of a bombing force, supervising the deployment of the first twin-engined monoplane bombers and initiating the development of their four-engined successors, gave him insight into the potential problems of his favoured strategy. Command of No. 4 Group and a tour of duty as AOC Palestine and Transjordan provided command experience.

THE 'AREA BOMBING DIRECTIVE'

Harris was, therefore, a natural choice for active leadership of part of the bomber force at the beginning of World War II in 1939, but when he took over No. 5 Group he faced a frustrating time. The government, wary of German response to a strategic campaign, restricted the use of Harris' Hampdens to leaflet-dropping and the sowing of sea mines, while the unexpected success of enemy air defences soon forced a shift from daylight to night operations, for which the RAF was not prepared. On 25 November 1940, Harris returned to the Air Ministry as Deputy Chief of the Air Staff, in which position he was responsible for rebuilding an effective bombing force, geared to a night-time campaign, but the problems were immense, not least the rather obvious one that few crews were able to find their precise industrial targets in the dark. By August 1941, when Harris was in Washington as head of an RAF liaison team, it was apparent that the strategic bombing of Germany was failing to achieve results – one report estimated that only about a third of all bombs were being dropped within five miles of their intended targets – and on 8 February 1942 the 'Area Bombing Directive' shifted the emphasis of the offensive to concentrate on entire cities rather

Above: Air Marshal Sir Arthur 'Bomber' Harris whose unparalleled knowledge of night bombing, and use of new developments in radar led to the creation of the Pathfinder Force. The Pathfinders, by marking the target, enabled waves of night bombers to implement the devastating 'Area Bombing Directive' – the bombing of entire German cities. Below: Cologne, 1944, after a visit from Harris' night bombers. The firestorm resulting from the intensive raids often did more damage than the exploding bombs and, as in the case of Dresden, resulted in the complete destruction of the city.

than the precise targets within them. It was this that Harris was ordered to put into effect as C-in-C Bomber Command a few days later.

He faced two problems. First, he needed to gain public backing for the continuation of the bombing campaign, and this he did by taking the enormous gamble of committing all his available aircraft to mount a publicity-seeking '1000 bomber' raid on Cologne on 30/31 May 1942. It had the desired effect, allowing Harris the time and political backing to tackle the second problem – the creation of an effective night-bomber force. It was a long haul, but one that was already under way with the deployment of four-engined aircraft such as the Stirling, Halifax and Lancaster and with the development of radar aids (Gee, H2S and Oboe) designed to take the bombers to their targets in the dark and, once there, to drop their bombs with a fair degree of accuracy. But new tactics were also needed to ensure a maximum effect, and under Harris' leadership such innovations as the Pathfinder Force, using experienced crews to spearhead the bomber stream and mark the route for the main force, were evolved.

Harris then tested his theory of air victory by mounting a series of sustained 'battles' – of the Ruhr (March-July 1943), Hamburg (July-November 1943) and Berlin (November 1943-March 1944) – but despite some dramatic successes (notably the fireraid on Hamburg in late-July 1943), bomber losses mounted and the results were difficult to gauge. A particularly disastrous raid on Nuremberg on 30/31 March 1944, in which 97 bombers were shot down, did nothing to convince Harris' critics and the decision to switch his command to tactical attacks in support of the Overlord invasion plan, although made some time before, seemed to reinforce the failure to achieve strategic success. But there can be no doubt that the bombers made a significant contribution to eventual Allied victory – between September 1944 and May 1945 they carried out a particularly damaging strategic campaign which included the destruction of Dresden – and although Harris' promise of complete air victory was not realised, his treatment at the end of the war, when he received no official reward for his efforts, was less than just. It was to lead to his resignation from the RAF in 1946 and a feeling of bitterness that was to persist to his death in 1984.

THE ELITE COMMANDERS

Commander of the First Army

'Hot dog Courtney, this will bust him wide open', was the memorable response of General Omar Bradley, commander of the US 12th Army Group in Europe, to news that elements of his First Army, under Lieutenant-General Courtney Hicks Hodges, had seized a bridge across the Rhine at Remagen on 7 March 1945. It was the latest in a long line of achievements by the First Army, yet the fact remains that Hodges himself is not widely remembered. A reticent man who avoided publicity, he has been enveloped in the shroud of history, overshadowed to a great extent by his fellow army commander in the 12th Army Group, George S. Patton.

Hodges was born in Perry, Georgia, on 5 January 1887. In 1904, having failed to gain entry to the US Military Academy at West Point (his grasp of mathematics was poor), he joined the army as a private soldier, serving three years in the ranks before being offered a commission. Active service in the Philippines and under General 'Black Jack' Pershing in Mexico led to rapid promotion, and in 1917 he travelled to France as a major in the 6th

Below: Lieutenant-General Courtney Hicks Hodges (1887-1966) led the US First Army which seized the Remagen bridge over the Rhine in March 1945. Below left: American and Russian troops celebrate during their historic meeting on the Elbe.

Infantry Regiment, 5th Division, American Expeditionary Force. In 1918 he commanded a battalion in the Meuse-Argonne offensive, earning a Distinguished Service Cross for courage under fire.

Once the war was over, Hodges was sent to Fort Benning Infantry School, where he came to the attention of George C. Marshall, the future Army Chief-of-Staff, and, while on a subsequent tour of the Philippines, he served alongside Dwight D. Eisenhower, then a lieutenant-colonel. Both were useful contacts. When America entered World War II in December 1941, Marshall called Hodges to Washington to act as his Chief of Infantry, and in 1943 he was appointed to succeed Lieutenant-General Walter Krueger as commander of the Third Army, then under training in the United States. In March 1944 Hodges transferred to the First Army, based in England, where he served as deputy commander

HODGES

84

Below: Two M10 tank-destroyers move through the Huertgen forest, 10 miles beyond Aachen, during the First Army's push into Germany in late 1944. The operation was cut short by the Germans' attack in the Ardennes in December, but, once the Battle of the Bulge was over, Hodges' men were able to renew their drive. After crossing the Rhine at Remagen, the First Army headed for the river Elbe where it met the advancing Soviet Red Army.

under Bradley, on the clear understanding that once the latter set up his army group in Europe after the D-day invasion, Hodges would assume the army command. This took place on 1 August 1944.

By then, Hodges was 57 and, despite his subsequent record, some historians have queried his suitability for command. His reticence seems to have made him a difficult man to work for and he did not always gain immediate respect, but this cannot alter the fact that his period of active command in Europe was successful.

When Hodges took over the First Army, the break-out from the Normandy lodgement area was already underway, with his three corps pushing south from the Cotentin peninsula and east towards the Seine. Once across the river, Hodges acted as link between the 21st Army Group in the north and the Third Army in the south, advancing on a wide front towards the German frontier. In the process, he faced two problems. On the one hand, his forces were stretched, covering a huge area from Holland almost down to the Saar; on the other, he was overshadowed by his publicity-seeking neighbours, Montgomery and Patton. Thus, during the strategic controversy over the merits of a single concentrated thrust, Hodges' opinions were ignored and Eisenhower was able to keep him short of supplies when Montgomery insisted on the assault through Holland towards the Ruhr.

By late September, First Army units were running out of fuel and, in order to protect Montgomery's flank, had been channelled towards the difficult country to the west of the Roer river on their left. As Hodges fed divisions into the horrific attritional battles around Aachen and the Huertgen forest, his defence in the Ardennes was thinned out. By mid-December, with the bulk of the First Army concentrated for a renewed thrust towards the Roer dams, the right flank was protected only by a weak corps.

Hodges was thus caught by surprise when the Germans mounted their Ardennes assault on 16 December, and for a time his headquarters faced considerable confusion. But he quickly asserted his authority, organising a defensive screen on the northern shoulder of the developing 'bulge' and absorbing the host of reinforcements committed to his area. On 20 December he accepted without question Eisenhower's decision to transfer the First Army to Montgomery's 21st Army Group, and began preparing a counter-attack. By the end of January 1945, the bulge had been eliminated.

NORTH TO THE RUHR

Returning to the 12th Army Group, the First Army's next task was a broad-front advance to the Rhine (Operation Lumberjack). Beginning in late February, the initial assault was concentrated on the left, towards Cologne and the Ruhr, but on 7 March the dramatic events at Remagen shifted the emphasis much further south. Hodges responded well, diverting all available forces to the bridgehead and displaying uncharacteristic ruthlessness when the local corps commander, Major-General John Millikin, seemed to be delaying the break-out on the east bank. On 18 March Millikin was sacked and, as elements of the First Army pushed north to the Ruhr, Hodges' reputation rose. Ten days later, Eisenhower allowed the 12th Army Group to lead the advance, ordering a broad sweep into central Germany for which the First Army was ideally placed. By late April Hodges had pushed as far as the Elbe, linking up with Russian troops from the east.

Despite promotion to full general on 15 April, Hodges did not remain in the army, choosing to spend his retirement in Georgia. He made little effort to attract publicity, with the result that much of his achievement went unnoticed. There is no doubt that, as an army commander, he had his weaknesses, but as Eisenhower wrote to Montgomery in December 1944, he could always be depended on to 'wage a good fight'. It was a fitting tribute.

THE ELITE COMMANDERS
HORROCKS

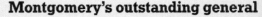

Montgomery's outstanding general

Lieutenant-General Sir Brian Horrocks was born on
September 1895 at the Indian hill station of Rannika
the son of a distinguished officer in the Royal Arm
Medical Corps. He joined the Royal Military College
Sandhurst, in 1913, and when war broke out wit
Germany the following year he was immediate
sent to the front. On 21 October 1914, at the battle
Armentières, he was wounded and taken prisone
Despite numerous attempts to escape, he remaine
in prison camps until the end of the war.

In April 1919, Horrocks volunteered to join Britis
forces in Vladivostok, supporting the White Russian
against the Bolsheviks in the Russian Civil Wa
Caught up in the disintegration of the White Russia
forces, he survived both typhus and further impri
onment before being repatriated to continue h
much interrupted British Army career.

Serving with the Middlesex Regiment, Horroc
made good progress in the peacetime army, ar
took the chance to display his fine sporting gifts –
even represented his country in the pentathlon at th
1924 Olympic Games. The outbreak of World War
found him in the post of senior instructor at the Sta
College, Camberley. On 13 May 1940, three da
after the start of the German blitzkrieg offensive
the west, he took command of 2nd Battalion, t
Middlesex Regiment at Louvain, Belgium, part
Montgomery's 3rd Division. His spell as a battali
commander lasted 17 days. As the British forces f
back in confusion towards Dunkirk, Horrocks w
promoted to command of a brigade, although h
authority was almost non-existent in the general retre

Having escaped back to England in the Dunki
evacuation, Horrocks continued his meteoric rise
high rank. By June 1941 he was an acting Majo
General, and on 20 March 1942 he was given co
mand of 9th Armoured Division, an extraordina
posting for an infantry officer. Then, on 14 August,
was ordered to North Africa to take over XIII Corp
part of the Eighth Army, with the rank of lieutena
general. To appoint as corps commander in a vi
sector a man who had a total combat experience
six weeks, spread over two wars was unorthodox,
say the least, but Montgomery, who had just assum
control of the Eighth Army, was prepared to exerci
his own very personal judgement in the choice
subordinates, regardless of their apparent qualifi
tions or suitability. Immediately after taking up
command in the desert, Horrocks had the unnervi
experience of a visit from Churchill himself. It did r
go well. Churchill told Montgomery: 'That ch
Horrocks is no good. Get rid of him.' But Montgome
did not.

In fact, Montgomery and Horrocks made an exc
lent team. Horrocks was an extremely modest m
(he once said, 'God never meant me to be an ar
commander'), and he was very impressed by Mo
gomery. He also shared Montgomery's taste
working up the morale of the troops through br
training routines, pep talks and personal appe
ances. As a result, the two men were never seriou
in conflict. As well as getting on with his command
Horrocks was soon popular with the troops.
enthusiastic, confident and optimistic outlo
transmitted itself to the ranks, where he was aff
tionately known as 'Jorrocks'.

Between 30 August and 7 September 1942, H
rocks conducted the superb defensive action kno
as the battle of Alam Halfa, which was a seri
defeat for Rommel's Panzerarmee Afrika. Althou

he had played little part in the conception of this defence, his execution of the plan was virtually faultless. Despite this success, however, XIII Corps was allotted a relatively minor role in the great offensive at Alamein that followed at the end of October, remaining at the south of the line as a decoy to draw Axis forces away from the area of the main Allied thrust in the north.

In December 1942, however, Horrocks was transferred to command of X Corps, Montgomery's armoured strike force, giving him the key role in the next year's fighting. On 20 March 1943 the Eighth Army attacked a strong Axis defensive position in Tunisia, the Mareth line. After a first attack near the coast had failed, Horrocks was ordered to send his corps in a 150-mile sweep southwards and to fight his way through a heavily defended gap in the mountains. With little time for proper preparation, Horrocks improvised the manoeuvre superbly and, with the help of effective air support, the forces under his command broke through in a week. The sequel was, however, less happy for Horrocks. In June, with victory in North Africa complete, he was hit by fire from a solitary German fighter launching a surprise attack on Bizerta. Seriously wounded, he was repatriated to England.

MARKET GARDEN

It took Horrocks over a year to recover, but on 2 August 1944, although still far from fit, he flew to France to take command of XXX Corps, once more under Montgomery. The first month of this new command brought spectacular success as XXX

Page 86.   Above: General Horrocks talks to the field commanders of the 51st Highland Division in the ruined town of Rees in northwest Germany.
Bottom: A tank crew repairs a track of their Churchill in a Normandy lane. This page.
Below left: A British Daimler armoured car fires the opening shots of the battle for Tripoli.
Background picture: Generals Montgomery (second from left) and Horrocks (third from left).

Corps spearheaded the drive across France and Belgium that brought the fall of Brussels in early September, but the events that followed were to haunt Horrocks for the rest of his life. First, he sent an armoured division to seize Antwerp, not realising that the port would be useless without control of the Scheldt penisula; meanwhile, 82,000 German troops escaped who could have been encircled had he by-passed Antwerp and cut off the peninsula. Then, XXX Corps was given responsibility for the land element of Market Garden, Montgomery's bold plan that would put an airborne army behind German lines in Holland. Despite their best efforts, XXX Corps failed to break through to the British paratroopers at Arnhem, and on 25 September Horrocks had to order the paras' withdrawal across the Rhine. Although he had had serious doubts about Montgomery's plan for Market Garden from the start, it was typical of Horrocks that he always held himself partly responsible for its failure.

In February 1945, Horrocks led XXX Corps through the grim battle of the Reichswald, operating as part of 1st Canadian Army, and in April commanded the taking of Bremen just before the German surrender. Knighted, he was finally invalided out of the army in 1949. He led a varied and successful life as a civilian, performing the ceremonial duties of Black Rod in the House of Lords, winning renown as a writer, broadcaster and TV presenter, and also becoming a company director. He died on 4 January 1985.

Horrocks was essentially a field commander, not a strategist, but his record was by any standards impressive. Eisenhower described him accurately as 'the outstanding British general under Montgomery'.

Astute tank commander

Hermann Hoth (1885-1971) became one of Germany's most successful armoured commanders of World War II, but was dismissed by Hitler in 1943 after a disagreement over strategy.

Following service in the Imperial Army during World War I, Hoth took up an appointment in the training department of the Ministry of War during the Weimar Republic. It was not long, however, before he returned to the army proper. He worked his way steadily upwards under the Nazi regime, and between 1935-38 commanded the 18th Division at Leignitz. By 1938 he had achieved a position as fiftieth in seniority on the Army List.

In 1939, Hoth took command of XV Army Corps and it was this formation that he led into Poland. Although most of his experience had been in infantry, Hoth took control of XV Panzer Corps during the preparations for the offensive in the West in 1940. Consisting of two panzer divisions – the 5th under Hartlieb and the 7th under Rommel – this corps achieved spectacular success and by the end of the campaign Hoth's command had been expanded into a Panzer Group. After the final surrender of France, Hitler made Hoth a colonel-general.

During Operation Barbarossa, Hoth commanded the 3rd Panzer Group, and achieved spectacular results during the opening phases of the offensive against the Soviet Union. By 15 July, he had pushed on to Smolensk and, together with Guderian, had encircled 500,000 enemy troops.

Hoth was convinced that the attack on Moscow through the centre of the front should be given priority over all other considerations; but Hitler's decision to send Guderian's forces south to help the southern group of armies led him to postpone the assault on the Soviet capital until the early autumn. In October, tanks reached to within 93 miles of Moscow, and the initial successes of this renewed offensive suggested that final victory was just around the corner; but Soviet reinforcements were now streaming into the line and the mud produced by the autumn rains was fatally slowing the German armour. By December, the Germans had ground to a halt.

In January 1942, Hoth was given command of the 4th Panzer Army, and was then sent south to the Voronezh front. German victories continued, but Hoth was unable to take the large numbers of prisoners and captured material that had marked the earlier offensives in the Soviet Union; the formations that he was facing retreated rapidly over the Don.

ASSAULT ON STALINGRAD

Hoth's command was a vital part of the summer offensive that aimed to destroy the Red Army in the southern Soviet Union, and take the Caucasus. Hoth's men were directed against Voroshilovsk in July and this objective was not taken until the end of the month. In support of Paulus's Sixth Army, Hoth's command then advanced against Tunutovo, Voroponovo and Pitomnik during late August and September 1942. Paulus could not match Hoth's success, however, and his failure to link up with Hoth's Army prevented encirclement of two Soviet armies.

The assault on Stalingrad, the centrepiece of this offensive, fell to the Sixth Army. Units of Hoth's panzer army were used to aid Paulus; but the Sixth Army, although it reached Stalingrad, was unable to clear the city of Red Army defenders. In November, the Soviets launched a counter-stroke, and the forces on the flanks of the Sixth Army were unable to halt a pincer movement. Hoth was ordered to relieve the encircled Paulus. On 12 December he advanced, but his units could cover only half of the 60 miles necessary. Hitler ordered Paulus to remain in Stalingrad, and the the Sixth Army was annihilated.

In the aftermath of Stalingrad, Hoth distinguished himself by his astute leadership of his formation between February and March 1943, when the Germans managed to restore their position in the Ukraine at the battle of Kharkov. The Soviet Sixth Army and Popov's Tank Corps were shattered in engagements at Krasnoarmeyskoe, Pavlograd and Barvenkovo. Soviet losses in these engagements reached 23,000 men killed, while they also sacrificed 1000 guns and 600 tanks.

Kharkov was a victory for superior mobility and more inspired leadership, against Soviet formations that threatened to break the whole German front. In terrible conditions, Hoth had manoeuvred his troops over vast distances to defeat the Soviet armour.

By the summer of 1943, the Wehrmacht was preparing for its last throw on the Eastern front – the offensive against the Soviet salient at Kursk in the central sector of the front. Hoth was given control of a vital area of this offensive, and his forces made the most progress of any of the German units. Unfortunately for him, German progress was then blocked and Hitler decided to call off the attacks.

Hoth, together with many other German commanders, realised after Kursk that the weight of Soviet material meant that the German armies could not hope to match the enemy in any further head-on confrontations; and that the only hope for the Wehrmacht in Russia lay in applying a mobile, flexible defence to 'roll with the punch' of Soviet offensives, and to make selected local counter-attacks where possible. Hitler was totally opposed to this more sophisticated approach; he wanted the German troops to hold on wherever they stood. Hoth's strategic suggestions were ignored by the Führer, and this most experienced of Hitler's armoured commanders, who had been in action constantly since 1941, was sent on extended leave in November 1943, after the fall of the city of Kiev to the Red Army. The propaganda value of the former capital of Russia was, for Hitler, far more important than the strategic flexibility proposed by Hoth. On 10 December, Hitler sacked Hoth, and the man who had registered successes in Poland, France and the Soviet Union, spent the rest of the war in retirement.

In 1948, Hoth was brought to trial at Nuremberg. Found guilty of war crimes and crimes against humanity, he was sentenced to 15 years imprisonment, of which he served six years.

Page 88, below: Hermann Hoth, a calm perceptive strategist and a contrast to some of the more flamboyant panzer leaders. Page 88, above: German mobile forces advance into the Soviet Union. Below: Hoth at the front in southern Russia.

THE ELITE COMMANDERS

Hitler's Mediterranean supremo

Field Marshal Albert Kesselring was born in Bavaria in 1885, trained for the artillery and served as an artillery officer in World War I, during which he revealed a considerable aptitude for planning and staff work. In 1933, however, he was sent to Hitler's still secret and illicit Luftwaffe, whose Chief of Staff he became in 1936. It is sometimes forgotten that the man whom Lord Alanbrooke regarded as the Allies' most formidable opponent in World War II, and whose name is most powerfully associated with what was essentially an infantry campaign, was and remained a Luftwaffe officer.

Transferred to operational command in 1937, Kesselring directed the bombing of Warsaw and Rotterdam, and of the retreating Allied troops before the Dunkirk evacuation. In 1940 his Luftflotte 2 (Air Fleet 2) was heavily involved in the bombing of airfields in

Field Marshal Albert Kesselring displayed great diplomatic prowess and charm that endeared him to Adolf Hitler and other Axis leaders such as Benito Mussolini of Italy. Below: 'Smiling Albert', as he became known to his colleagues. Right: In stark contrast, Kesselring (seated on the left), in a slightly more contemplative mood.

southern England during the Battle of Britain. In Jun of that year he became a field marshal. In 194 Luftflotte 2 took part in the offensive against Russia o the central front. When the Luftflotte was transferre to the Mediterranean theatre at the end of that yea Kesselring became Commander-in-Chief, Sout His considerable charm and diplomatic abilities ha already earned him the nickname of 'Smiling Alber In October 1942 he was given overall command of a German armed forces in the Mediterranean are except for those directly under Rommel's commar in North Africa. He was thus already in commar when the Allies landed in southern Italy in Septen ber 1943 and forced an Italian surrender.

Up until that point, German policy had been withdraw from southern Italy and hold the line in th north of the country. This policy was contrary Hitler's normal inclination to yield no ground witho fighting to the last man, and under pressure fro Kesselring, who recognised the strategic and po tical importance of holding a line south of Rom Hitler on 4 October issued the order to deny Rome the advancing Allies.

In defying the odds arrayed against him, Kesse ring had two major advantages. The first – perhap more perceptible in retrospect than at the time – w that the invasion of Italy was something of a com romise measure, agreed to by the Americans wi some reluctance; they were pressing for the openin of a second front in northern France, a front that w to be delayed until the summer of 1944. Lackir complete commitment, the Allies never gave the Italian operations the resources, or the detaile follow-up plans, that were needed for a decisi result. This was illustrated on two occasions – Salerno and later at Anzio – where landings we made with the intention of cutting off and annihilatir

KESSELRING

the retreating German armies. Neither succeeded, and in both cases the Allies were hard-pressed to break out of their beachheads. In retreating from Sicily, and later from the 'toe' of Italy, the Germans were able to make a planned withdrawal, taking heavy losses but keeping their cadres and their command structures virtually intact. The view with hindsight must be that Allied generalship in the Italian campaign left much to be desired.

Kesselring's other major advantage was that of terrain. Central and southern Italy offered him a narrow line of defence, and except at the coastal fringes the line ran over rough mountainous country that was a gift to any defending commander, especially if the attacking force was never given adequate resources for either amphibious outflanking operations or massive and sustained aerial bombardment. Kesselring took what nature had given him in the way of natural defences and added to them all that the Todt Organization could supply in the way of man-made obstacles. Where rivers ran at an angle from the mountainous spine of the country, the Germans would frequently flood the side of the river that faced the enemy, building deep dug-outs and machine-gun posts on their own side, while the mountains behind them offered sites for observation posts and artillery. Elsewhere, the natural defences were enhanced by pillboxes, bunkers and artillery emplacements reinforced with steel, railway sleepers or concrete. Belts of barbed wire, sometimes as deep as six feet, protected some of the weaker points in the line, along with anti-tank ditches and a wide variety of mines and booby traps. Where buildings appeared in the defensive line, they were either reinforced or demolished in order to provide an optimum field of fire. In such terrain, and against such defences, tanks could scarcely be used. The Italian campaign became of necessity an infantry campaign, and the appalling weather of the winter of 1943-4 ensured that for the attacking infantry in particular, it was a campaign of profound misery.

THE ITALIAN CAMPAIGN

Given the superiority of the forces the Allies had at their disposal, the Italian campaign could not be conducted by the Germans as other than a holding operation and a fighting retreat. Kesselring and his fighting generals, von Vietinghoff and von Senger und Etterlin, conducted the campaign with consummate skill, timing their withdrawals, fighting savage rearguard actions, and handling their reserves with remarkable dexterity. Above all, they fought their actions with flexibility, allowing field commanders a great deal of local initiative in what they recognised as an extremely fluid battlefield.

Following the Allied landings in the south, Kesselring withdrew first to the Winter and then to the massive Gustav Line, roughly 30 miles south of Rome and with the massif of Cassino, topped by its ancient monastery, as one of the key points towards its western end. For six months, the Allied commanders sent division after division to batter against these defences. Kesselring had given strict orders forbidding the occupation of the monastery itself by German troops, and made what propaganda he could out of the Allied bombardment – despite there being sound tactical reasons for leaving it unoccupied. When it was eventually demolished by a huge aerial attack, his troops simply moved into the ruins and added it to the defensive line. It was not until the massive Allied offensive of May 1944 that French troops under General Juin finally breached the Gustav Line.

The Germans then made a fighting retreat northwards, finally evacuating Rome on 3 June. The Americans, under General Mark Clark, marched triumphantly into the Eternal City on 5 June, but when the Normandy invasion took place the following day, Italy became even more of a subsidiary theatre. Within a matter of weeks, Clark was having to transfer some of his forces to the invasion of southern France. It had been decided that a massive Allied thrust up through Italy and into central Europe was undesirable. The Germans retired once again, this time to the Gothic Line in the north of the country between La Spezia in the west and Pesaro in the east, a line that the Allies did not breach until the Spring offensive of 1945, when the war was virtually over. By that time Kesselring himself had handed over the command to von Vietinghoff. In March 1945 he had been appointed Commander-in-Chief, West, in succession to von Rundstedt, although by that time the war was lost everywhere but in the mind of Hitler, and Kesselring surrendered all German forces in southern Europe to the Allies on 7 May 1945.

Kesselring's name will always be associated with one of the most fiercely fought campaigns of World War II, in which the fighting men of both sides showed almost superhuman courage and endurance. Although superiority both on the ground and in the air made the Allied victory inevitable, the generalship on the German side made that victory a long-delayed and very costly one.

THE ELITE
COMMANDERS

Background picture: German paratroopers fire on enemy positions from the cover of the ruins of the monastery at Monte Cassino. Bottom: Kesselring at his trial for war crimes, in the Cour de Justice, Venice. He was sentenced to death in 1947 for involvement in the shooting of 320 Italian prisoners (the so-called Ardeatine Caves massacre), but the sentence was commuted to life imprisonment. He was released in 1952.

Counter-insurgency commander

THE ELITE COMMANDERS

General Sir Frank Edward Kitson was born in 1926, the son of an admiral. It was a natural progression for him to pursue a career in the services – his grandfather had been an officer in the Indian Army and an uncle was awarded a posthumous VC in World War I.

Kitson was commissioned into the Rifle Brigade as a second lieutenant in 1946. His first posting was with the British Army on the Rhine (BAOR) where he remained until 1953. In that year, however, he received orders to move to Kenya where the Mau Mau insurgency was in full swing. The posting proved beneficial to both the man and the administration.

Kitson realised that the definition and destruction of the enemy were both aspects of the same process: that successful counter-insurgency relied upon the integration of intelligence-gathering and army command. The police and the army must work hand-in-glove. Such an approach was all very well in theory, but Kitson made it work in practice, in spite of certain difficulties with the Kenyan civil authorities. He also respected his enemy and similarly earned their respect, becoming highly successful at persuading Mau Mau members to change sides, and forming them into counter-gangs.

These counter-gangs, or 'pseudo-gangs' proved an invaluable method of obtaining information from the Kikuyu tribe (which was the main source of disaffection) and provided the white-run security forces with an insight into the aims and attitudes of the insurgents. The Mau Mau movement was motivated by a mixture of nationalism linked with social and land problems within the Kikuyu.

Greatly helped by Kitson's dedicated approach, the British campaign achieved spectacular success, and further developed the British approach to what Kitson himself was later to call 'low-intensity operations'. At the end of his tour in 1955, Kitson, now a major, was gazetted MC. He was soon engaged in counter-insurgency again, for in January 1957 he was

KITSON

Previous page, top: General Sir Frank Kitson, who became commander-in-chief of all UK land forces in 1982, the culmination of a career that took in many of Britain's most important campaigns of the modern period. Kitson first made his name in Kenya, during the Emergency there, and went on to become one of the world's experts on counter-insurgency. Previous page, below: Security forces investigate a hut during the campaign against the Kenyan Mau Mau insurgents. Below: British forces in Malaya with a captured guerrilla. Kitson played a prominent role in the mopping up of the communist insurgents there during the late 1950s.

assigned to the British security operation in Malaya.

When Kitson arrived in the peninsula, there were some 23 battalions deployed against a declining guerrilla force. The security forces had defeated all guerrilla offensives, but mopping up was proving slow and costly. Kitson noted that the failure of this large force finally to suppress the insurgents was almost certainly due to lack of good background intelligence. He believed that the practice of dropping para units into the dense jungles of Johore on large sweep operations could not trap the last die-hard guerrilla bands. He suggested that more effort be put into intelligence; and in particular that a great deal of low-grade information could be more effective in building up a picture of rebel movements than a few pieces of high-grade information. In practical terms, this meant that by examining such things as old camp sites, food distribution, forest paths and river crossings, the security forces could build up a picture of the living patterns of the guerrillas, thus making the pursuit of the insurgents much easier.

Kitson's intense intelligence campaign was once again successful and contributed a great deal to the haul of 8000 communists killed or wounded and the 2096 captured during the entire emergency. He received a second MC for his services, returned home in January 1958 and in June of that year joined the staff at the War Office. The deteriorating situation in Oman in 1958, with rebels occupying the Jebel Akhdar, presented Kitson with his first challenge in this new post. He devised a plan and was sent to South Arabia in October 1958; once elements of his plan were accepted, he was charged to help in its execution. Using SAS units, the rebels were isolated and their strongholds pinpointed; Kitson returned home in December 1958. The Jebel fell in January 1959.

In 1962, following a year as an instructor at the Royal Naval College Greenwich and six months at the Armed Forces Staff College in the US, Kitson became second in command of the 3rd Battalion of the Green Jackets and was posted to Cyprus. He remained there until 1964 when he returned to the Ministry of Defence. During his period there the Green Jacket Regiments were amalgamated into the Royal Green Jackets and in October 1967, Kitson became CO of the 1st Battalion. With this unit he returned to Cyprus amidst murmurings of renewed hostilities between Greek and Turk.

OXFORD AND IRELAND

Kitson returned to England in 1969 and took up a Defence Fellowship at Oxford until 1970. The report he produced after this period of reflection was published in 1971 under the title *Low-Intensity Operations*, and had an important role in codifying and making generally available his approach to the problem. He was then promoted commander 39 Infantry Brigade and sent to Northern Ireland, where he won a CBE before his promotion to Commandant of the School of Infantry at Warminster in 1972.

In 1974 Kitson left the School of Infantry and went on to the Royal College of Defence Studies in 1975. The following year he was promoted GOC 2nd Division (later 2nd Armoured Division), a position which he held until he became commandant of the Staff College in 1978. Two years later, in 1980, Kitson was elevated Deputy C-in-C of UK Land Forces (UKLF) and Inspector-General of the Territorial Army. In 1982 he became Colonel Commandant, the Royal Green Jackets.

Kitson was appointed C-in-C UKLF in July 1982. In this capacity he visited Beirut in 1983 to review the security arrangements of the British HQ of the peacekeeping force. He retired in June 1985.

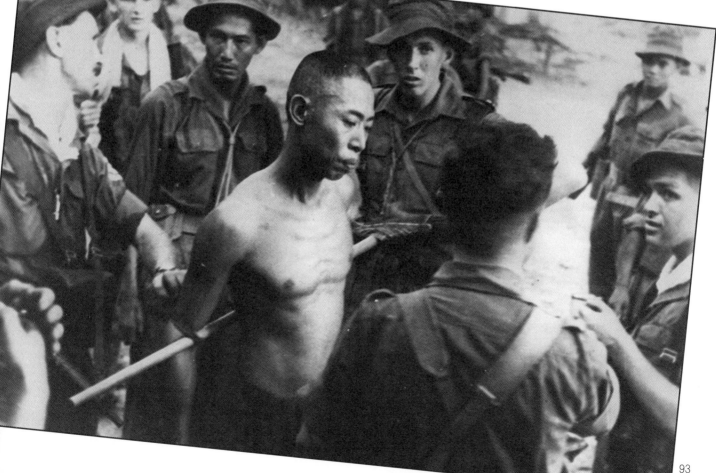

Masterful Free French Tactician

When the German Army unleashed its Blitzkrieg offensive on Western Europe in May 1940, Jacques Philippe de Hauteclocque, soon to become famous under the assumed name of Leclerc, was a captain serving with the French 4th Infantry Division. Born in 1902, scion of an aristocratic family with a long military tradition, he was a career officer with a romantic dedication to warfare and the honour of France. The abject behaviour of so many of his fellow French officers in the rout of late May and early June filled him with contempt. On 28 May he deserted from 4th Infantry to avoid surrender and, after being captured by the Germans and escaping again, he managed to join 2nd Armoured Group at Chantilly which was still fighting on. Wounded in a Stuka attack on 15 June, he was once more taken prisoner, but once more escaped. This time he headed for England, via Spain and Portugal, to answer General de Gaulle's call for volunteers to fight for Free France.

Arriving in London on 25 July, he was almost immediately sent with a few other officers to French Equatorial Africa in a bid to take over that part of the French Empire. It was at this time that he adopted the name Leclerc, to protect his family in France and to disguise his aristocratic origins which, he found, were a source of prejudice against him. Arriving in the French Cameroon, Leclerc quickly assembled a tiny force which, on 26 August, seized the capital, Duala, from the Vichy authorities.

With all of Equatorial Africa soon in Free French hands, Leclerc was transferred to command the forces in Chad, a vast desert territory whose northern border adjoined Libya, which was part of the Italian Empire. Leclerc immediately sought some means of going on the offensive against the Italians, despite the small under-equipped force of European and colonial troops at his disposal. It was fortunate that the British Long Range Desert Group (LRDG), operating out of Egypt, was also interested in attacking Italian positions in an area to the south of Libya known as the Fezzan. The LRDG and the Free French established a perfect understanding and, by the start of 1941, were ready to embark on combined raids into the Fezzan from bases in northern Chad. In

THE ELITE COMMANDERS

LECLERC

February, Leclerc committed 400 men, led by LRDG guides, to an advance against the stronghold of Kufra, 900km north of his main base at Faya. After three weeks of skirmishes and steady progress across terrain conventionally considered impassable, the force besieged Kufra on 20 February. Leclerc commanded the siege in person, and was present when the fort surrendered on 1 March. It was the occasion for a famous message to de Gaulle in which, in the 'Oath of Kufra', he pledged: 'We will not rest until the flag of France also flies over Paris and Strasbourg.'

Leclerc was now a 'brigadier-general and would soon be commander of all Free French Forces in Equatorial Africa. For almost two years, raids into the Fezzan continued, but Leclerc longed for a chance for bolder action. At last, in December 1942, with the Axis forces retreating across North Africa after the defeat at Alamein, his chance came. He planned an extraordinary 2500km drive north from Chad across the harshest desert in the world to link up with the Eighth Army on the Mediterranean coast. A force of 670 French and 4108 African troops was assembled with a bizarre collection of scratch vehicles, and on Christmas Day they set out on the epic journey. Leclerc's administrative duties did not allow him to accompany the force all the way, but he was constantly flying up to the front to join his men at crucial moments, and his tactical flair in encounters with the Italian forces in the area was superb. His columns split and manoeuvred in complex patterns of attack which confused and overwhelmed the enemy. Within three weeks the Fezzan was in French hands, and on 25 January 1943 Leclerc's Free French joined up with the Eighth Army.

Now Leclerc was determined to do some serious fighting. Ignoring de Gaulle's orders to hold the Fezzan for France, Leclerc went straight to Montgomery and asked to become part of Eighth Army. The British commander was impressed by this absurdly ragged French officer and his piratical troops. By early March, re-equipped with a few tanks and anti-tank guns, Force L, as it was now known, was playing a vital part in the battle for the Mareth Line.

LIBERATING PARIS

On the defeat of the Axis forces in North Africa, Leclerc was given the full equipment of a US armoured division and told to blend the French component of Force L and French North African troops – formerly loyal to Vichy – into the 2ᵉ Division Blindée (2nd Armoured Division – 2 DB). In April 1944 2 DB was transferred to join General Patton's Third Army in England, and on 31 July these French exiles returned to their native soil, to be thrown into the fighting in Normandy.

Like many Frenchmen, Leclerc was obsessed by the fate of Paris, and he had already despatched an unauthorised detachment towards the city when, on 23 August, he was officially ordered to liberate it. Showing great speed in manoeuvre, Leclerc drove his men forward from Argentan, about 100 miles west of the capital, to enter Paris on the evening of the 24th. The following day, Leclerc accepted the German surrender of the French capital.

This was Leclerc's most famous hour, but his most spectacular action was still to come. The armoured division continued to take part in the eastward advance of the Third Army, and in mid-November was facing strongly prepared German positions in the Vosges mountains. On the other side of the Vosges lay the Alsatian city of Strasbourg, an impor-

Page 94, top: General Jacques Philippe Leclerc in Tunisia in May 1943. Bottom: Leclerc, the officer on the left, inspecting forward artillery positions in Tunisia 1943 after leading his men on the epic journey north across the Sahara from Chad.
This page below: Leclerc in his beloved Paris shortly before accepting the German surrender of the city on 25 August 1944.

tant symbolic goal for a French patriot. The Germans believed the only way through the Vosges for armour was the Saverne gap, but Leclerc discovered side roads he believed could be used. Despite orders not to advance, on the night of 21/22 November he sent his tanks through the undefended mountain roads and the following day overwhelmed the startled enemy on the plain beyond, cutting off the German forces in the Saverne gap. Still ignoring orders to consolidate, on 23 November Leclerc's armour pushed on into Strasbourg itself, to the astonishment of German officers caught relaxing in cafes and restaurants. The resistance of the enemy Leclerc had by-passed on the way was soon mopped up.

After the Strasbourg exploit, Leclerc was ordered to join General de Lattre de Tassigny's French First Army, but he refused. The events of 1940 had left Leclerc with a distrust of the French Army, and he insisted on fighting instead under British or American command. He got his way, returning to Patton's Third Army. After a spell on the south Atlantic coast, 2 DB ended the war with a wild dash across Germany to become the first Allied troops to reach Hitler's 'Eagle's Nest' at Berchtesgaden.

After the war, Leclerc was posted first to French Indochina and then to French North Africa where, on 28 November 1947, he was killed in an air crash. Always keen to lead from the front, with a total disregard for personal safety, Leclerc had proved himself a master of modern mobile warfare.

LEMAY

Inspired bomber commander

Above right: Curtis
Emerson LeMay with his
customary cigar, talking to
the press at a NATO
Exercise at Camp
Volucean, near Paris. He
had been urging Congress
to appropriate 320 million
dollars more than the
administration had
requested for the long
range RS-70 bomber. He
told the press, 'I will use
the most effective
weapons systems that will
do the job.' Top: Boeing
B-29 Superfortress
bombers en route to
targets in Japan.

Curtis Emerson LeMay was born on 15 November 1906 in Columbus, Ohio. He studied civil engineering at Ohio State University. However, his real interests at college were the Reserve Officers' Training Corps (ROTC) and, in particular, flying. LeMay had been fascinated by aircraft since childhood and had first flown in 1924 when he had paid five dollars for a 10-minute flight with a barnstormer pilot. LeMay achieved his ambition in 1928 when he was commissioned into the US Air Corps. Originally, LeMay trained as a pursuit (fighter) pilot, but his interest in bombers grew, and it was as a strategic bombardment commander that he was to achieve fame.

In 1936, LeMay was posted to the 49th Squadron as operations officer, and in the years preceding the entry of the US into World War II he made several long-distance flights to South America in the aircraft with which he was to become so intimately involved – the B-17 Flying Fortress. After a time as a squadron commander in the 34th Bombardment Group, in

1941 LeMay was transferred to the Atlantic Ferr[y] Organisation (ATFERO). However, with the Ger[-] man declaration of war on the US in December 1941 LeMay was soon back with bombers. In 1942 he wa[s] sent to England to command the 305th Bomb Group with the rank of colonel.

The earliest raids on Nazi-occupied Europe b[y] the US Army Air Force (as the Air Corps had bee[n] renamed) were not wholly successful. Unlike th[e] RAF, which had abandoned precision dayligh[t] bombing in favour of 'area' or 'carpet' bombing b[y] night, the USAAF clung to the concept of [a] self-defending bomber force capable of penetra[t-] ing enemy air space by day to bomb industria[l] targets accurately. On early missions against th[e] U-boat pens in France in 1942, B-17s had employe[d] a loose formation of flights of three planes in a ['V'] formation, each squadron (of two flights) operatin[g] separately. This formation allowed each B-17 t[o] manoeuvre into an advantageous position for bomb[-] ing, but left the bombers extremely vulnerable [to] attack by enemy fighters. LeMay according[ly] experimented with various formations designed [to] maximise the defensive firepower of the bombe[r] force for, until the arrival of the long-range P-5[1] Mustang in December 1943, the Allies could n[ot] provide fighter cover deep into Germany. The 305th practised the new tactics in England with LeMa[y] standing in the upper turret of a B-17, personal[ly] placing each aircraft in its correct station. LeMay['s] tactics ultimately consisted of staggered three[-] plane elements (sticks) within the squadron, an[d] staggered squadrons within a 'combat box' of [18] B-17s. Such a formation could bring 162 heav[y] machine guns to bear on fighters attacking from an[y] angle of approach in the rear; the optimum defen[-] sive position was two or three combat box[es]

'stacked' in echelon. Slightly modified, LeMay's tactics were adopted by the entire Eighth Army Air Force.

If each plane had been obliged to manoeuvre into position before bombing, the bombing procedure would have become immensely complicated. LeMay solved this problem by placing his elite bombardiers in the leading planes. When the lead bombardier dropped his bombs, the rest of the stick simply followed suit. Again, LeMay's innovations became standard operating procedure for the Eighth Army Air Force. Using these tactics, LeMay flew a number of missions into enemy territory, including the notorious raid on Regensburg, deep in southern Germany, on 17 August 1943. On that occasion, LeMay's 4th Bombardment Wing (which he had taken over in May 1943) lost 24 aircraft out of 146. Undoubtedly, without LeMay's innovative tactics, the losses would have been even higher.

In March 1944 LeMay was transferred to the Far East theatre and there he organised the B-29 Superfortress raids on Japan – a year earlier he had been promoted to general at the age of only 37. In January 1945 LeMay was faced with his greatest challenge yet. Newly appointed to command 21st Bomber Command, LeMay was forced to modify drastically the tactics in use by the B-29 crews. LeMay ordered that the B-29s were stripped of their defensive armament, thus greatly improving their payload. He also initiated intensive retraining for radar operators as a preliminary to switching from daylight to night attacks, during the latter of which the bombs were to be aimed largely by radar. Finally, LeMay decided that the B-29s were to be deployed in low-level attacks at around 5000-9000ft, gambling that the manually operated Japanese anti-aircraft guns would be slow to react to low-flying planes.

NEW TACTICS

On 9 March 1945 LeMay's new tactics were used for the first time. The gamble paid off; 12 pathfinder planes guided a force of over 300 B-29s to Tokyo, each plane loaded with incendiaries. The raid was a complete success; only 14 out of 325 bombers were lost, 100,000 Japanese died, and 250,000 buildings were burnt to the ground in an area of 16 square miles. Over the next few months such raids reduced most of Japan's cities to rubble, the coup de grâce being delivered by B-29s, under LeMay's overall command, dropping atomic bombs on Hiroshima and Nagasaki in August 1945.

LeMay's postwar career was equally distinguished. As head of Strategic Air Command (SAC), from 1948 to 1957, he revitalised the US deterrent force and made a significant contribution to the maintenance of peace by doing so. He became successively Deputy Chief of Staff then Chief of Staff of the USAF 1957-1964, retiring in 1965. LeMay then began to dabble in politics. As the running mate of the fiercely anti-communist George C. Wallace in the 1968 Presidential Election, LeMay created a sensation by advocating the use of nuclear weapons to end the stalemate in Vietnam.

LeMay's claim to the status of an elite commander rests, first, on his genius as a tactician of bombing, and second, as an inspired leader of men. His outwardly cold manner earned him the nickname of 'Iron Ass' from the men of the 305th, but they were always proud of LeMay's connection with them and adopted the title of the 'Can Do' group.

THE ELITE COMMANDERS

Above: A B-29 Superfortress commander makes a final inspection of his crew before they take off from Guam to bomb Japan. Right: Vice-Chief of Staff, General Curtis LeMay at the controls of a KC-135 Jet Tanker, the aircraft in which he set a world record. He flew 6350 miles, at a speed of 484mph, to demonstrate the long reach of US airpower.

Dedicated Commander of the Chinese People's Liberation Army

On 12 September 1971, an aircraft carrying Marshal Lin Piao, Minister of National Defence of the Chinese People's Republic and heir apparent to Mao Tse-tung as Chairman of the Chinese Communist Party, crashed in Mongolia, killing all on board. Initially presumed to be an accident, rumours quickly spread that this was an assassination, ordered by Mao to prevent Lin's defection to the Soviet Union. The truth may never be known.

Lin Piao was born on 5 December 1907 in a village on the north bank of the Yangtze river in Hupeh province, the son of a purser on a Yangtze river-boat. After a rudimentary education in local schools, he travelled to Shanghai in 1925, where he joined the Communist Youth League. This enabled him to gain entry to the Whampoa military academy, then under the command of the Nationalist (Kuomintang) leader, Chiang Kai-shek. Appointed a lieutenant in Yeh T'ing's Independent Regiment of the Fourth Army in 1926, Lin took part in the Northern Expedition of that year, quickly gaining a reputation for inspired military leadership. However, when Chiang tried to purge his army of communist elements in 1927, Lin was among the officers who led the so-called Nanchang Uprising, breaking away from the Kuomintang and joining up with guerrilla forces in Hunan under Mao Tse-tung to form the Fourth Red Army.

By 1928, Lin was commanding a regiment in the Red Army, fighting Kuomintang forces to the south of Mao's main base in the Chingkang mountains. He proved to be so effective, particularly in the defeat of Kuomintang units at the battle of Ta-po-ti in February 1929, that promotion was rapid: by 1930 Lin was commanding the entire Fourth Army in its operations against the first of Chiang Kai-shek's attempted 'Extermination Campaigns', and three years later, in command of the First Army Corps, he successfully defended Kiangsi province, grinding down the Kuomintang with a combination of guerrilla and conventional tactics.

But the communists could not survive indefinitely against the superior numbers and weapons of their enemy, and in October 1934 Mao ordered the breakout from the Chingkang base known as the 'Long March'. Lin's battle-hardened units spearheaded the move, fighting endless engagements in defence of the main column. Casualties were heavy, but when Mao and the survivors reached the remote northwestern province of Shensi in October 1935, Lin had emerged as perhaps the most effective fighter on the communist side. Unfortunately, his health had suffered and, as the new 'safe base' was set up, he was given the less active post of president of the Red Army Academy.

His rest period was curtailed in 1937, when Japan threatened the communist area. Lin took command of the 115th Division of the Eighth Route Army and,

LIN PIAO

Above right: The stoutest walls could not keep the communists back. Below right: Marshal Lin Piao clutching the 'little red book' of Chairman Mao's quotations.

THE ELITE COMMANDERS

using his familiar mix of guerrilla and conventional tactics, advanced to meet the enemy across the Yellow river. At first he was successful, ambushing a Japanese force in the P'ing-hsing Pass, but overwhelming numbers soon caused him to pull back and to devote his energies to harassing attacks on enemy supply lines. In 1938, Lin was wounded in action so seriously that he had to travel to the Soviet Union for medical treatment.

Lin did not see action again until August 1945, when the Japanese surrender heralded a resumption of civil war between the communists and Kuomintang. In that month, he was ordered to lead up to 250,000 men into Manchuria, to infiltrate the cities and seize control once the invading Soviets had withdrawn. Once again, he enjoyed some success to begin with, but Chiang Kai-shek, aware of the danger, committed crack troops to oppose him. Withdrawing to the north of the Sungari river, Lin used guerrilla tactics to seize rural areas and to weaken Kuomintang resolve, preparatory to a fresh offensive in February 1948. By then, Chiang's forces were

Below left: Chinese communists armed with a French Chatellerault modele 24/29 machine-gun. Below: Comrades-in-arms: (left foreground) Lin Piao, (right foreground) Premier Chou En-Lai and (centre background) Ch'en Po-Ta, all holding Mao's red book.

overstretched and weak. By November the city of Shenyang had fallen to the communists and Manchuria – the industrial heartland of China – was in their hands.

Lin did not stop there: by late December he had pushed south to Kalgan and, in January 1949, he led his triumphant troops into Peking, receiving the surrender of a demoralised Kuomintang garrison without a fight. Mopping-up operations absorbed Lin's army until October, when the advance continued as far as Canton and Kwangsi province. By then, Lin had been elected a member of the Central People's Government and, as Chairman of the Central-South Military and Administrative Committee, was in overall charge of some 175 million Chinese in the populous provinces of Hupeh, Hunan, Kiangsi, Kwangtung and Kwangsi. He seemed set for a political career, playing a key role in the creation of the new People's Republic.

INTO POLITICS

But his health let him down. Despite his appointment to a variety of important committees in the early 1950s, he suffered badly from tuberculosis and was forced to take a back seat until at least 1958. By then he was a member of the ruling Politburo and a Marshal of the People's Liberation Army (PLA), but it was not until 1959, when he replaced P'eng Te-huai as Minister of National Defence, that his active career recommenced. P'eng had been retired in disgrace, having advocated closer ties with the Soviet Union and the creation of a professional PLA, equipped with all the latest weapons, and Lin was chosen to replace him chiefly because he echoed Mao's belief that revolutionary zeal should take precedence. As Lin concentrated on strengthening political control over the PLA, his standing in the Party hierarchy increased until, in 1965, he was appointed senior vice-premier. A year later, as the Cultural Revolution began, he was named as Mao's chosen successor but, as the energies released by Mao's call for fresh ideological commitment threatened to get out of hand, the PLA began to assume unprecedented control. By 1971 Mao may have realised that Lin was becoming too powerful: if so, his attempted escape to the Soviet Union and subsequent death may be understandable.

Victor in Poland, France, Greece and the Soviet Union

Siegmund Wilhelm List was born at Oberkirch, Bavaria in 1880. He saw service in Eastern Europe during World War 1, especially in the Balkans. After the war he continued in the army under the Weimar Republic, and by 1933 had achieved a senior post as Chief of Army Training. He then took over the 4th Division, (based at Dresden) with the rank of lieutenant-general, and in 1935 took up command of the IV Army Corps (under von Bock); in 1936 he was promoted full general of infantry.

List survived Hitler's purge of the high command in 1938. His support for Hitler was well known, and by 1939 he held a potentially difficult and responsible command in Austria. List then became the senior commander (with the rank of colonel-general) under von Rundstedt's Army Group South in the invasion of Poland in September 1939.

THE INVASION OF POLAND

List's command in the Polish campaign was the Fourteenth Army, which consisted of six infantry, one mountain, one light and two panzer divisions. Although his training had been in the old Prussian Army, and although he was classified as an 'infantry' general, List showed the superb level of professional competence that so many other German commanders manifested, and deployed his armour in such a manner as to cut through the Polish forces facing him, in what became known as the 'Blitzkrieg' manner, and pushed far east, eventually linking up with Guderian's panzers to the east of Warsaw.

In 1940, List was given command of the Twelfth Army facing the Western Allies, part of Army Group 'A', again under von Rundstedt. This army had a crucial role to play in the breaking of the Allied line across the Meuse, and once again List showed the most professional grasp of the essentials of the new style of warfare that the German Army had developed, and was promoted to Field Marshal.

List's success in Poland and France was followed by what was perhaps his greatest campaign – that of the Balkans in 1941. As German and Soviet ambitions came increasingly into conflict during the last months of 1940 and early 1941, List performed important negotiations in the Balkans and concluded an agreement with the Bulgarian authorities whereby German troops had free passage across Bulgarian soil. This gave Germany increased leverage in an area which had importance for various reasons: namely, the strategic situation of the Romanian oil-fields, the presence of British troops in Greece, the continuing uncertainty about the future policy of Turkey and the growing mutual hostility of the two great totalitarian powers of Europe.

Having secured this diplomatic advantage, List was then tasked with taking over a great part of the invasion of Greece and Yugoslavia. The conquest of Greece by List's Twelfth Army was one of the most complete victories ever won by the German Army,

Below: List with some of his mountain troops after the great success in the Balkans in spring 1941. The conquest of Greece was one of the most complete victories of the whole war.

and List's 15 divisions (four of them armoured) swept through often difficult terrain to occupy Athens by 27 April. The British and Commonwealth formations in the country were forced to pull back to Crete, and then that island fell to an audacious airborne attack.

The victor in the Balkans was then appointed Commander Armed Forces Southeast, with his headquarters in Salonika. List returned to more active service in 1942, when the great summer

campaign in the southern Soviet Union was launched. He was given command of Army Group 'A', a formation created out of Army Group South. His job was to conduct the arm of the offensive leading towards the Caucasus, and his first objective was Rostov, which fell on 25 July.

Following this success, List's command was tasked to encircle and destroy the retreating Soviet forces and take the entire eastern coast of the Black Sea. This was to be followed by occupation of the Baku area. List was uncertain that these aims could be achieved. The problems of the Sixth Army to his north reinforced this view. Initially, however, List's troops gained ground and managed to establish bridgeheads across the Kuban river and pushed on to the Maykop oilfields. They continued to advance south from these objectives but were not successful in forcing battle upon enemy units that fell back before them. By 10 August, List's panzer formations had reached the foot of the Caucasus range and by 14 August Krasnodar had been taken: List's men had covered 200 miles in 16 days. List then deployed General Ruoff's forces to take the Black Sea Ports.

Novorossiysk fell quickly but the logistics system now began to fail. By the end of August, Army Group 'A' could not advance much beyond the Terek river nor take further important oilfields. Called to meet Hitler, personally, List explained that the lack of resources made victory impossible. This cool, professional appraisal did not suit Hitler, who removed List from command for the rest of the war.

At the Nuremberg trials, List was sentenced to life imprisonment for war crimes committed in the Balkans and Greece. He was pardoned in December 1952, and died in 1971. Ostensibly an infantryman, List had proved excellent in the direction of armoured and mountain troops. He had also displayed a gift for diplomacy, particularly in his handling of his Balkan command. Although he had been one of Hitler's favoured generals, his professionalism did not allow him to continue along a suicidal course – and in this List compared favourably with many, more complaisant, members of the High Command.

Right: Siegmund Wilhelm List, a superbly professional commander. Below: List (on left), recently created a field marshal, at a ceremony in Vienna in 1940.

'I shall return'

Douglas MacArthur (1880-1964) was one of the half-dozen outstanding military personalities of World War II. He played a critical part in the Korean War, where his leadership of the UN forces added to the lustre of his military reputation.

MacArthur came from a military family; his father had won the Medal of Honor during the Civil War, and later became the senior officer in the US Army. MacArthur (junior) passed out top at West Point in 1903, and from there his career rapidly took off. He served as an aide first to his father and then to Theodore Roosevelt.

From 1919 to 1922, MacArthur was superintendent of West Point, where he tried to modernise the institution; from 1930 to 1935 he was Chief-of-Staff of the Army. In this post, normally the peak of any serving officer's career, his political opinions caused unfavourable comment in some quarters. A conservative right-winger by upbringing and conviction, he refused to believe that social unrest might be caused by the Depression, preferring to see communist conspiracy as a motive force.

In 1935, MacArthur accepted an offer to go to the Philippines as military adviser to the government, and in 1937 he resigned from the US Army to concentrate on his work in the Philippines – he had become a field marshal in the virtually non-existent Filipino Army in 1936. In July 1941, he was recalled to take over the US Army in the Far East.

MacArthur had persuaded the US government that the Philippines was defensible in the event of Japanese attack, but the weight of the Japanese assaults (Japanese forces landed in the Philippines in December 1941) compelled the Filipino and US units on Luzon to pull back to positions on the Bataan Peninsula. MacArthur had handled the withdrawal to Bataan very skilfully, but there was little hope for the forces beleaguered there, as Japanese naval and air units by then ruled the Pacific. MacArthur himself was ordered to return to safety in Australia (something he did with reluctance) and when he reached Australia, he made his famous comment: 'I came through and I shall return'.

In April 1942, MacArthur was created commander of the southwest Pacific area. while Admiral Chester Nimitz commanded US forces in the central Pacific. MacArthur's command was vast, and he had to cope with many problems. The Japanese were bent on expansion while the US Pacific Fleet had still not recovered from Pearl Harbor; there were only 25,000 US troops available to him when he took over, and the strategy of 'Germany first', meant that he would have to fight hard within the US governing apparatus to divert resources to the Pacific theatre.

The battles of the Coral Sea and Midway during the early summer of 1942 effectively ended Japanese dreams of victory, and the question was then, by what means, and how quickly, could the US force the Japanese to surrender.

During 1943, MacArthur's main tasks were the reconquest of the Solomons chain, and the defeat of Japanese forces in New Guinea. He demanded extra resources to accomplish this, but was refused. MacArthur had put into practice a system known as 'island-hopping', whereby his forces by-passed

MacARTHUR

Below: A historic moment as General MacArthur signs the Japanese document of surrender aboard the USS *Missouri* on 2 September, 1945. Below: The 2nd Battalion, 165th Infantry wades ashore at Makin Atoll in the Gilbert Islands, some of the thousands of men involved in the US campaign in the south Pacific. Launched in August 1943, this campaign saw some of the most bitterly-fought actions of World War II.

many Japanese strongholds, taking just a few key points from which US naval and air power could effectively isolate the enemy garrisons that had not been reduced. MacArthur's grasp of the potential of air and naval power was as sophisticated as that of any other commander of World War II.

While the US counter-offensive in the Pacific gathered momentum, MacArthur was insistent that the liberation of the Philippines must be a priority. The Navy, in the person of Nimitz, believed that the most economical way of defeating Japan would be to take island-hopping to its logical conclusion, and abandon the attack on Japanese garrisons in the Philippines as an irrelevance, concentrating instead on a direct approach to the Japanese homeland via Formosa. MacArthur, however, managed to win the day at a final conference on strategy, in July 1944. His arguments were accepted; the Philippines would be as effective a base for the assault on Japan as Formosa, and the moral commitment to free the Filipinos could not be abandoned.

JAPAN SURRENDERS

In October 1944, the island of Leyte in the Philippines was attacked by US amphibious forces, and the main island Luzon, was under attack by January 1945. By the end of February, the Japanese had been effectively defeated and a Filipino government could be installed.

In April 1945, MacArthur was appointed commander of all US ground troops in the Pacific, and on 2 September, aboard the USS *Missouri* in Tokyo Bay, he was the main Allied signatory of the document accepting the surrender of Japan. He had come from the dark days on Bataan to preside over total victory; in the following years he virtually ruled Japan as Supreme Commander of Allied forces there.

These achievements would have been more than enough to ensure a permanent place in the history books, but there was more to come. In 1950, the North Koreans invaded South Korea, and MacArthur was put in command of the US and UN forces that moved in to support the South's army. While the US units held a defensive perimeter in the far south, around Pusan, MacArthur built up his strength in Japan, and prepared an audacious amphibious landing near Seoul, at the port of Inchon.

The Inchon landings of September 1950 were decisive; the North Korean Army was caught extended, and forced into headlong retreat back over the border of the 38th Parallel. From then on, however, MacArthur made several serious errors.

To begin with, he supported the South Korean leader, Synghman Ree, in his requests to carry the war into the North. Then, when the war was being fought north of the 38th Parallel, he discounted the possibility of Chinese intervention – and thus exposed the UN forces to the defeat of late 1950 that sent them tumbling back south. Once China had entered the war, MacArthur talked openly about using the atomic bomb on Chinese territory, and made statements that the US government found difficult to accept. MacArthur was also prepared to communicate directly with opposition politicians in the US to try to get his way over government policy in Korea.

In the end, President Harry Truman had had enough. He relieved MacArthur of his command in March 1951. The great general returned to the United States and was greeted with a tickertape welcome. His active career was ended, but he had set standards in every sphere of the military profession that would be very difficult to equal.

THE ELITE COMMANDERS

Left: General Douglas MacArthur fulfils his famous prediction, 'I came through and I shall return,' as he visits Leyte in the Philippines after the American invasion of 1944. Below: MacArthur was made commander of US and United Nations forces when the United States entered the Korean War in 1950, but was recalled in 1951 after violating a White House order. MacArthur, on his first return to the US since the end of World War II, was greeted with a tickertape welcome.

THE ELITE
COMMANDERS
MANNERHEIM

Embodiment of Finnish nationalism

Carl Gustaf Emil Mannerheim (1867-1951) has been dubbed 'the George Washington of modern Finland' and indeed, during a highly successful career as a soldier and statesman that spanned nearly 60 years, he not only secured the independence of his native country but was called upon to defend that independence in agonising wars.

Ironically, in the light of subsequent events, Mannerheim's military career began in the army of Tsarist Russia where he was to serve for 30 years. Born in Finland, which was then a grand duchy under Russian control, Mannerheim attended the Nikolaevski Cavalry School in St Petersburg. After passing out he served a year in Poland as a subaltern in the 15th Alexandreski Dragoons but soon transferred to the elite Chevalier Guards where he rose to the rank of captain. In February 1904 he left for the Far East to serve as Lieutenant-Colonel in the Nezhinski Hussars during the Russo-Japanese war (1904-05). In 1914 he was appointed major-general of the crack Brigade of Cavalry of the Guard of Warsaw.

During World War I Mannerheim fought several successful actions against the Austrians and Germans on the Eastern Front, during which he was awarded the Cross of St George, and was promoted to Lieutenant-General. In 1917, as Russia began to collapse in the throes of Revolution, Mannerheim returned to Finland, having experienced several narrow escapes from the Bolsheviks.

In early January 1918, Lenin recognised the independence of Finland but there were still 40,000 Russian troops in Finland supported by a Red Guard, organised by the Finnish left, who saw the future of Finland as linked with that of the new Soviet Union. To 'liberate' the country and defend Finland's future independence, Mannerheim was immediately appointed commander of a 'White' Civil Guard, tasked with expelling communist Russian forces from Finnish soil. Desperately short of war materials, troops and supplies, Mannerheim applied himself to the fighting of a bloody and confused civil war with imagination and energy, making the fullest use of whatever materials were available. With the aid of a force of 12,000 German troops and Finnish Jägers trained in the German Army, he claimed victory over the 'Reds' and by mid-1918 Finland was cleared of Soviet troops.

At the age of 50, with three wars behind him, Mannerheim resigned from military command to be elected Regent of Finland in December. In the elections held in the following July he was defeated in the contest for the presidency of the new republic and retired into private life.

In 1931, hoever, Mannerheim re-emerged into the military sphere and was appointed chairman of the

Above: Mannerheim in his early student days in Finland before he moved to the Russian cavalry school in St Petersburg. Below: Mannerheim meets Hitler, his co-belligerent in the war against the Soviet Union, during a German official visit to Finland in 1942 to mark the occasion of Mannerheim's 75th birthday. Overleaf: Mannerheim, Marshal of Finland.

Finnish Defence Council. In this role, faced with reluctance on the part of the Finnish government to finance military expansion, he undertook the construction of a line of defensive positions across the Karelian isthmus in southern Finland to guard against any future Soviet aspirations in this direction. The so-called 'Mannerheim Line', although not a solid wall of defence like the Maginot or Siegfried Lines, consisted of a series of defensive emplacements and earthworks making the very best use of ground in the rugged terrain and wooded areas.

The construction of the line was to prove a wise precaution for in December 1939 the Soviets launched a massive offensive into the Karelian isthmus. In the ensuing 'Winter War' Mannerheim's comparatively small army of 300,000 troops, 80 per cent of whom were called-up reservists, fought a grim and heroic struggle against an invading army of nearly a million men. Familiar with the fearfully low temperatures, well-disciplined and imaginatively led, the Finnish troops employed highly mobile guerrilla tactics. Clad in white smocks for camouflage against the snow – the Russian troops soon came to know them as the 'white death' – they swooped in on skis to attack Russian units and their merciless sniping inflicted heavy casualties on the poorly organised Russian soldiers.

Unable to combat Mannerheim's mobile strategy with any effect, the Russians replied with an all-out offensive against the Mannerheim Line. For two weeks wave after wave of cannon-fodder assault troops were thrown into the teeth of a resolute Finnish defence with little regard for casualties. On 12 March exhausted and stunned by the massive losses (an estimated 25,000 Finnish troops and 200,000 Russians were killed in the three-month war) Finland sued for peace and under the terms of the armistice lost considerable areas to Russia in the north-east of the country and in the Karelian isthmus.

Despite the territorial losses, the Winter War was

a success for Mannerheim. Under his command the Finns had capitalised on every tactical advantage relying on flexibility and mobility and the swift and efficient deployment of units and supplies while plagued by massive shortages. It was this versatility and the ability to improvise militarily at all levels that saved Finland from total defeat.

From March 1940 to the following summer Finland enjoyed peace. In June 1941, however, having allowed German troops rights of transit between German-occupied Norway and Germany in 1940, Finland once again came up against the Soviet Union. Hitler had launched his offensive in the east – Operation Barbarossa – and German troops were pouring into Finnish Lapland. Mannerheim saw the successful German offensive as an opportunity to regain the areas lost in 1940; Finland declared war and the 'War of Continuation' commenced.

Mannerheim, now aged 74, again took up the reigns of command and went on to the offensive. He was careful, however, to preserve Finnish independence of command from the Germans. By the end of August 1941 the areas lost in the Winter War had been reclaimed and in the following months further gains were made in eastern Karelia. But as the tide turned against Germany on the Eastern Front and Stalin was preparing a massive offensive against Finland, the Finns sued for peace again in 1944. With Mannerheim as president a less than favourable armistice was signed with the Soviet Union. Finland, however, had avoided becoming a Soviet-German battlefield.

With the war in Europe at an end in 1945, Mannerheim continued as President until 1946 when, at the age of nearly 80 and suffering poor health, he retired to Switzerland to record in writing the events of his remarkable career in his *Memoirs*. He died in Switzerland in 1951.

MANSTEIN

Master strategist on both Western and Eastern Fronts

Fritz Erich von Manstein (1887-1973) was a commander considered by many to have been the finest general of World War II. The originality and flexibility of his strategy may be favourably compared with that of almost any other military leader of the modern period.

The son of an artillery officer, Eduard von Lewinski, Manstein adopted the name of a favourite uncle who was a successful soldier. He was commissioned into the 3rd Regiment of Foot Guards in 1906, and first saw active service in World War I. Seriously wounded in November 1914, he ended the war in a staff position. His reputation as a staff officer grew during the 1920s and he was made head of the Operations Department of the General Staff in 1935.

A member of the more conservative wing of the German officer corps, Manstein found himself temporarily out of favour when the Army Commander-in-Chief, von Fritsch, was dismissed in 1938. By the outbreak of World War II, however, he was once again in a senior position as Chief of Staff to von Rundstedt, commander of Army Group South during the Polish campaign. He followed von Rundstedt to the Western Front in October 1939, and devised the strategy for an offensive through the seemingly impassable Ardennes that formed the basis of German victory in May 1940. During the offensive in the West, Manstein commanded XXXVIII Corps.

Manstein again held a field command during Operation Barbarossa, the invasion of the Soviet Union in June 1941. His LVI Panzer Corps advanced

Left: Field Marshal Erich von Manstein. Below: Manstein's troops in action in Russia.

THE ELITE COMMANDERS

on Leningrad, but in September he was promoted and moved to the southern front. His Eleventh Army pushed into the Crimea, and after the winter lull, cleared the Crimea of the Red Army. In a masterly demonstration of siege warfare, Manstein took the fortress of Sevastopol in July 1942, and was promoted to Field Marshal.

SAVIOUR IN THE SOUTH

Impressed by this string of successes, and by his ability to conduct both mobile and positional battles, Hitler moved Manstein north again, to try to take Leningrad, which was holding out against everything the Germans could throw at it. A Soviet offensive took up all Manstein's energies, however, and by the time his forces were ready to take the initiative themselves, disaster in the south had changed everyone's preoccupations. The Soviet offensive of November 1942 had cut off the German Sixth Army at Stalingrad, and threatened to destroy all the German armies in the area.

Manstein was given command of the troops in the southern sector (although Hitler insisted on giving direct orders to the Sixth Army itself). Although he could not save the men beleaguered in Stalingrad, he mounted a brilliant recovery operation to save the armies that had moved into the Caucasus, and stabilised the German lines during February, when, in appalling weather, operating over vast distances

and heavily outnumbered, he inflicted a severe defeat on the Soviet forces around Kharkov. The victory at Kharkov was a model of how to use space and superior manoeuvrability to defeat an enemy who has the advantage of numbers.

Manstein's next major operation was during the German offensive against the Soviet salient at Kursk, the final attempt by the Wehrmacht to regain the initiative on the Eastern Front. Manstein himself would have preferred a defensive strategy, and realised that time had almost run out for the Germans; he urged that any offensive be mounted as quickly as possible, because every day the Soviet defences were becoming stronger. He was very pessimistic when Operation 'Citadel' as the offensive was code-named, was put off until July, and although he prosecuted the battle with his usual flair, the Russian defences held out.

German defeat at Kursk was followed by the Soviet summer offensive. In trying to stem this great tide of men and material, Manstein again showed himself a consummate master of the battlefield, but Hitler refused him the freedom of manoeuvre that he needed, and although he managed to save many of his forces in a withdrawal to the Dnieper, his relations with the Führer were by now very bad. Hitler refused to accept Manstein's advice about the best way of meeting the Soviet winter offensive of 1944, and in March 1944 Manstein was dismissed.

Manstein's achievements were enormous. He had devised the strategy that brought victory in the West, had won stunning victories in mobile and siege warfare during the high summer of the Wehrmacht on the Eastern Front, had saved the southern group of armies in the winter of 1942-43, had come close to success at Kursk, and had led fighting retreats thereafter. Manstein was known to have behaved with great propriety on the Eastern Front and there was an outcry when he was sentenced to 12 years' imprisonment for war crimes. In the event, he served only four years before being released.

Below and below left: Manstein inspecting his troops on the Eastern Front. The vast spaces of the Soviet Union gave Manstein the opportunity to implement his great gifts as a strategist who knew how to use space in defence and attack; but in his conduct of operations such as the siege of Sevastopol he showed an equal mastery of the classic manoeuvres of positional warfare.

THE ELITE COMMANDERS

The People's Leader

Mao Tse-tung, arguably the most successful and influential revolutionary leader of the 20th century, was born in the village of Shaoshan, in the Chinese province of Hunan, on 26 December 1893. The eldest son of a 'middle-ranking' peasant, fortunate enough to own a small plot of land, he received a rudimentary education at the village school which opened his mind to the world of books and political ideas. An active supporter of Sun Yat-sen's Kuomingtang (Nationalist) Party during the upheavals of 1911-12, Mao went on to train as a teacher before travelling to Peking in 1918. While working as an assistant librarian at the University, he came into contact with Marxists and, in July 1921, represented Hunan at the founding conference of the Chinese Communist Party (CCP).

The CCP was modelled on the recently successful Soviet pattern of urban revolt, but from an early stage Mao realised that, in a predominantly rural China, political power could be gained only through the actions of the peasant masses. He therefore returned to Hunan, setting up 'cells' of support for the CCP among local farmers, and when, in 1927, an attempted Soviet-style uprising failed, he led his new followers ot the inaccessible Chingkang mountains, away from the wrath of the Kuomingtang (KMT), by now under the more militaristic leadership of Chiang Kai-shek. Once in the mountains, Mao began to recognise a new reality: if 'safe bases' of CCP activity could be created in remote areas, containing deeply

Left: Chairman Mao, leader of revolutionary China. Below: Mao Tse-Tung with his troops in Shensi, 1947. Below left: Many of Mao's beliefs are encapsulated in his 'little red book'.

MAO TSE TUNG

committed peasants who were prepared to offer food, shelter and recruits to the revolutionary activists, a solid organisation of revolt would emerge. It was the beginning of a remarkable set of 'theories' of revolutionary war which were to ensure Mao's place in the history of the 20th century.

Mao's aim was to exploit the discontent of peasant masses caught in the turmoil of a country split between the KMT and repressive local warlords, using the organisation and leadership of the CCP to create an overwhelming force which would eventually seize political power. Beginning quite literally from nothing, Mao used his training as a teacher to gain support, offering education as an escape route from the drudgery of peasant life and promising the establishment of a new social order based upon justice and a redistribution of land. As peasants responded to his call, he set up 'safe base areas' in which an alternative society emerged, with its own forms of taxation, justice and social order, and as soon as such bases were created in one region, specially chosen leaders moved on to repeat the process elsewhere – a development likened by Mao to ink spots on blotting paper, each spreading inexorably to join up with others until the whole of the paper was covered. But neither the warlords nor the KMT were likely to allow this to happen unchecked, and Mao was forced to think about defence. As the people lacked arms, ammunition and military expertise, yet enjoyed the priceless advantages of local knowledge and popular support, guerrilla techniques were the obvious choice. Using hit-and-run tactics, enemy outposts could be attacked, equipment captured and local success enjoyed. Eventually, as the guerrillas gained in strength and the enemy, weakened and demoralised, declined, a third phase of revolutionary war could be entered, in which Mao's followers would assume the organisation of a regular army, defeating their enemies in open battle preparatory to a takeover of political power.

THE ROAD TO VICTORY

The fact that this pattern of revolution worked in China between 1927 and 1949 should not disguise the realities of Mao's position as a 'theorist'. Many of his ideas – sound though they were – tended to be retrospective, reflecting the often harsh experiences of the Red Army and its guerrilla supporters as they fought to defeat the KMT. The road to communist victory was certainly far from smooth. By the early 1930s the Chingkang base (renamed the Kiangsi Soviet in November 1931) was powerful enough to attract the attention of Chiang Kai-shek, and although his attempts to wipe the base out failed between 1931 and 1933, his 'extermination campaign' of 1934 made deep inroads into the mountain area. By October 1934 the Kiangsi Soviet seemed doomed, forcing Mao to order a strategic withdrawal to avoid complete annihilation. Leaving a small rear-guard to delay the KMT forces, he led an estimated 100,000 followers on the epic 'Long March', breaking through the enemy encirclement and moving across mountains, deserts and swamps some 6000 miles to the comparative safety of Shensi province in the remote northwest of the country. Chiang Kai-shek, prevented by his generals from conducting a pursuit because of the growing threat from Japan, had eventually to negotiate a truce with the CCP, creating a United Front against the Japanese invaders in 1937. Between then and 1945, the brunt of the fighting against Japan was borne by the KMT, with Mao devoting his energies to guerrilla warfare and the consolidation of peasant support, so that once the Japanese menace had been destroyed, the CCP was far stronger than its rivals inside China. Moving into the 'open warfare' phase in 1945, Mao's Red Army took on and defeated the KMT in a civil war which, in October 1949, led to the declaration of the People's Republic in Peking, with Mao at its head. It was a remarkable achievement.

Mao acted as president of the republic until 1959, but from then until his death in 1976 he remained effective leader of China, guiding a once-fragmented country towards the ultimate goal of superpower status. In addition, his theories were copied and adapted in countries as far afield as Vietnam, Malaya, the Philippines and Cuba, and although they did not always succeed as they had done in China, their impact cannot be denied. Revolutionaries looked to Mao for inspiration, recognising the central truth of his thinking – 'With the common people of the whole country mobilised, we shall create a vast sea of humanity and drown the enemy in it'.

Below: Chairman Mao inspects the tanks of the People's Liberation Army, only seven months before the defeat of the KMT in October 1949. While history remembers Mao primarily as a theorist, he also possessed a superb grasp of military strategy. One of his greatest assets was undoubtedly his ability to maintain strict control over his generals and troops while at the same time earning their respect. In total contrast, Mao's opponents in the civil war lacked such discipline and were plagued by internal dissension which contributed to their eventual defeat. Below right: Mao at Yenan after the 'long march' which took he and his followers 6000 miles across mountains and deserts to avoid being completely wiped out by the KMT.

THE ELITE COMMANDERS

Proud, committed para commander

Armies involved in the delicate and difficult task of counter-insurgency always run the risk of becoming involved in politics. Because their opponents are aiming for a political goal – the assumption of power in the affected state – the government response must also be political, providing the people with incentives to remain loyal and using tthe army merely to control the security situation. But if the army ever believes that it can defeat the insurgents on its own and is being prevented from doing so by government restraint, it may be tempted to step in to alter the government to one more amenable to its views. This is what happened with the French Army in Algeria (1954-62); in the process a number of professional and courageous officers were drawn inexorably into the political arena, often with tragic results. One of those officers was Jacques Massu.

Massu, born in 1908, was dedicated to the army. After training at St Cyr in the late 1920s, he saw extensive service in French West Africa, quickly gaining a reputation for physical toughness and command ability. He was not involved in the debacle of 1940, when the French forces collapsed under the pressure of Blitzkrieg, but he was deeply shocked by the capitulation and, as a result, proved a willing supporter of Charles de Gaulle. In 1943, Massu accompanied General Leclerc on his epic march

MASSU

from Lake Chad to join Allied forces in Tripoli, seeing service thereafter in North Africa and Northwest Europe. Immediately after the war, he helped to raise the first of the French parachute units, imbuing them with a toughness and professionalism that soon put them in the forefront of counter-insurgency campaigns. After service in Indochina, Massu returned to France to create the 10th Parachute Division, an elite formation that was soon ready for action and raring to go.

In February 1956, the division was sent to Algeria, where it soon proved its worth against insurgents of the Front de Libération Nationale (FLN) in rural areas. After only nine months, however, the paras were withdrawn to spearhead the Anglo-French assault on Port Said. Massu led his men in the successful attack on Port Fuad, at the northern tip of the disputed Suez Canal, and he shared their disgust at the ceasfire imposed less than 24 hours later. It was the beginning of a feeling that politicians were letting them down.

By January 1957, the division was back in Algeria, just as the FLN was increasing the pressure with a

series of bomb attacks against civilian targets. The government response was to commit Massu's paras to Algiers with full police powers and little political restraint. In purely military terms, the outcome was impressive. Para units, led by officers dedicated to the heavily politicised doctrine of *guerre révolutionnaire*, showed their ruthlessness as early as 28 January, when they broke an FLN-inspired general strike among the Moslem population, and this was followed by extensive patrols in the Casbah, traditionally a 'no-go' area for the French. Suspects were rounded up, interrogated and even tortured, until a very clear picture of the FLN networks in the city had been built up. This enabled key leaders such as Ben M'hidi, Saadi Yacef and 'Ali la Pointe' to be isolated and either captured or killed. By the time of the paras' withdrawal in October, Algiers was quiet.

DIVISION WITH DE GAULLE

But the political ramifications of Massu's methods were disastrous. As reports of torture and the disappearance of up to 3000 suspects leaked out, hitherto uncommitted Moslems were alienated and, more importantly, French public opinion (particularly on the political Left) began to condemn the role of the army in Algeria. Massu himself was convinced that torture was justified, especially in a situation where terrorist outrages were commonplace, but the damage had been done. As successive French governments tried to impose restraint, Massu and his officers became convinced that if their methods were used throughout Algeria the FLN would soon be destroyed. They began to resent decisions made in Paris and to believe that a strong political leader, sympathetic to the army, was essential. De Gaulle fitted the bill exactly.

The results of such thinking were tragically predictable. In May 1958, as the army drew closer to the policies of the *pieds noir* (French settlers in Algeria), Massu helped to establish a 'Committee of Public Safety' in Algiers and to plan a paradrop on Paris to overthrow the newly formed government of Pierre Pflimlin. As a preliminary, elements of the 10th Para Division seized control of Corsica, but this proved sufficient to gain their political objectives. On 27 May de Gaulle agreed to form a government.

Any hopes that Massu may have had about de Gaulle were soon dashed as it became obvious that he was interested in a political rather than a military solution to the problem of Algeria. A deep division

between the two men quickly emerged, despite Massu's promotion to command of the entire Algiers area in the aftermath of the 1958 affair. The situation came to a head in January 1960, when Massu openly criticised government policy in an ill-considered newspaper interview. He was recalled to France and given the obviously inferior command of the garrison at Metz, and for a time it looked as if his career was over. But he clearly learnt from his mistakes. In April 1961, when elements of the army in Algiers attempted another 'putsch', he refused to lend his support, and this display of loyalty ensured his return to the mainstream of the army. Seven years later, by which time he was commanding French troops in Germany, Massu responded positively to appeals from de Gaulle to support the government as it faced the students and workers of Paris. Soon afterwards, he retired from the army, spending his time writing about the Algerian War and justifying his actions during the Battle of Algiers. It was a conflict that had nearly cost him his reputation.

Page 110. Left: Troops of 3 RPC spot check Algerian civilians in the streets of Algiers, possibly to be interrogated at a later date. Right: General Jacques Massu, upright, steadfast and resilient para officer.

This page. Below: Massu enjoys a brief moment of quiet in Algeria in 1957. Right: A member of Bigeard's paras of 3 RPC, armed with a 9mm M-49 sub-machine gun, on watch on a rooftop of the Casbah. Above: General Massu being decorated in 1957 by Prime Minister Bourges-Maunoury for his outstanding service in Algeria.

THE ELITE COMMANDERS

Master of naval aviation

Marc Andrew Mitscher (1887-1947) has a good claim to being considered the most successful naval aviation commander of all time. He participated in the most decisive battles in naval aviation history (Midway, the Philippine Sea and Leyte Gulf), always on the winning side, and the raids of his fast carrier forces in the Pacific brought a new dimension to naval strategy.

Mitscher graduated from the US naval academy in 1910 and in 1915 underwent flight training. By 1918 he was commander of the Naval Air Station at Rockaway, and in 1919 became responsible for the Pacific Fleet's Air Wing at San Diego. In 1926 he joined the Navy's first aircraft carrier (USS *Langley*). In 1939, Mitscher became Assistant Chief of the Bureau of Aeronautics, and then, in October 1941, took over the newly launched aircraft carrier USS *Hornet*, a post he held when the Japanese attacked the US fleet at Pearl Harbor in December 1941.

The Hornet was soon involved in some of the most important action of the whole Pacific War. In April 1942, it was the carrier which launched the aircraft of the 'Doolittle raid' – a morale-boosting attack on the Japanese mainland. The Doolittle raid did no actual damage to the Japanese war effort, but it did lead to

Below right: Marc Mitscher discussing plans for operations against the Japanese fleet. Mitscher's audacious incursions into areas of the Pacific that the Japanese nominally controlled were the product of meticulous planning, an impeccable logistics network that enabled his carriers to roam as far as they wished, and a weight of air power that no Japanese base or fleet could match. Below: A stricken Japanese plane crashes into the sea near an American carrier during the battle of the Philippine Sea, a shot photographed from the deck of another carrier where Grumman Hellcats are waiting to be prepared for action.

the decision of the Japanese High Command to try to destroy the US Pacific Fleet at the battle of Midway.

Midway was the turning point of the Pacific War. In it, four Japanese carriers were sunk for the loss of one US carrier; and Mitscher's *Hornet*, heavily engaged in the battle, was one of the two surviving US carriers that gave the US Navy the dominance it now enjoyed. After Midway, Mitscher was promoted to rear-admiral and, late in 1942, took up a posting in the Solomons, where the air and naval battles were reaching a climax. In April 1943 he was appointed commander of all air forces in the Solomons, and P-38 Lightnings of his command ambushed and shot down the plane carrying Admiral Yamamoto.

The peak of Mitscher's career came, however, in 1944. As commander of Carrier Division Three (later renamed the Fast Carrier Task Force or TF 58) he controlled a striking force more powerful than anything seen before in naval warfare. His fleet, which sometimes included up to 17 aircraft carriers, ranged deep within what the Japanese had hoped would be a secure defensive perimeter, swamping all opposition with its weight of air power. At the battle of the Philippine Sea in June 1944, he destroyed the remnants of Japanese naval aviation, and won renown and admiration for his boldness.

Mitscher's carriers took part in the battle of Leyte Gulf in October 1944; and then provided the cover for the landings on Iwo Jima and Okinawa early in 1945. In these last battles, the US Navy had to develop new defensive techniques to counter the strikes by Japanese kamikaze aircraft, a role in which naval aviation was once again prominent.

Mitscher became commander-in-chief of the US Atlantic Fleet in September 1946, but died early the next year. His achievement in naval aviation is likely to remain unequalled.

MITSCHER

THE ELITE COMMANDERS

MONTGOMERY

BERNARD LAW MONTGOMERY, Viscount Montgomery of Alamein, was born on 17 November 1887 and died on 23 March 1976. He became the most successful British commander of World War II, and, indeed, of the whole 20th Century.

There is no doubting the scale of his achievement. By the time war broke out in 1939, he had already been noticed as an officer of outstanding ability, and his command of the 3rd Division during the campaign of 1940 was recognised as exemplary. After the evacuation of Dunkirk he was promoted to corps command and was in charge of important stretches of the south coast of England during the next two years.

From his assumption of command of the Eighth Army in August 1942, however, Montgomery moved onto a new plane of command, and the level of success he met with was quite remarkable. He checked the final offensive of the Afrika Korps at the Battle of Alam Halfa (31 August-6 September 1942), and then prepared his forces for the first decisive British land victory of World War II, at El Alamein (23 October-4 November 1942). After Alamein, he led his men in an inexorable advance across North Africa, defeating an attempt to check his progress at the Battle of Medenine (6 March 1943), and smashing the German defences barring his way into Tunisia at

In 1942, Montgomery realised that he needed to make himself a readily-identifiable personality to the troops under his command. He did so by wearing unorthodox headgear – first the rather unflattering Australian slouch hat (below) and then the more successful beret (above).

the Battle of Mareth (21-27 March 1943); and he then took part in the final advance that trapped over 600,000 German and Axis troops around the city of Tunis itself and cleared North Africa of Axis forces. Next, he commanded the Eighth Army in the successful invasion of Sicily (10 July 1943) and took it across the Straits of Messina on 3 September 1943 to advance up the toe of Italy to relieve the hard-pressed forces that had landed further north at Salerno. The Eighth then pushed north up the east side of the Italian peninsula.

D-DAY AND AFTER

On 2 January 1944, Montgomery returned to the United Kingdom, where he was given the task of commanding the Anglo-American ground forces that were to land in Normandy the following summer. His contribution to the preparation of the plans for the landing, and to the training of the troops that were to take part, was acknowledged in all quarters to be immense. By the time that the D-Day landings took place on 6 June, he was respected throughout the ranks of all the Allied forces involved. During the fighting for Normandy itself, after the initial landings, Montgomery managed the problems of maintaining an offensive against a resourceful, determined foe in difficult terrain with great understanding of the respective weaknesses and strengths of both the Germans and his own forces; and when the breakout from the bridgehead was eventually achieved, advance was rapid. Allied forces reached Paris on 25 August.

After General Dwight D Eisenhower assumed supreme command of all the Allied forces in Europe, in September 1944, Montgomery's 21st Army Group, consisting of the British 2nd and Canadian 1st Armies, attempted to push into northern Germany across the Rhine in the Arnhem operation (17-25 September 1944). This was not as successful as had been anticipated, but during the late autumn, the problems of supply were ironed out, and the Channel ports opened to shipping. Then, in December, during the German counter-offensive in the Ardennes, Montgomery was called upon to take over all those forces, including the American units, to the north of the salient that the 'Battle of the Bulge' had opened up.

In February 1945, Montgomery's Army Group cleared areas of the west bank of the Rhine, and then, on 23 March, crossed the Rhine itself in one of the great set-piece operations of World War II. British and Canadian forces moved steadily across northern Germany, and Montgomery had the great satisfaction of being the first Allied commander to be approached by the German government and high command for surrender terms: when Field Marshal Keitel sent a delegation to his headquarters on 3 May 1945.

The solid achievement upon which Montgomery's reputation as a military commander must rest is, therefore, immense and unquestionable. His strengths as a commander were many and various. First and foremost, perhaps, was his ruthless professionalism – a comparatively rare attribute in an army such as the one in which he served for much of his life.

If Montgomery was given a task he could work out whether it was possible; and if it was possible, just what was the best way of achieving it. If it was impossible, he would be adamant. He knew that he could deliver the goods if allowed to go about things his own way; and only once in his career as a commander – at Arnhem in 1944 – did he really fail to do so. Secondly, there was his ability to inspire his troops. In this respect, Montgomery was also a master, and his achievement here is doubly impressive in that he was a rather uncharismatic figure and not possessed of the physical or personal attributes that normally make an individual immediately publicly successful. He had decided, however, to impose himself as a personality upon the Eighth Army, and set about devising schemes and approaches – such as the wearing of unconventional headgear (an Australian hat and then a tanker's beret with two badges) to give him a popular image. Montgomery made his troops feel important as individuals and he also told them what the basic objective was. On occasion this would be chillingly simple – a matter of 'killing Germans'.

POISE AND PLANNING

The ability to describe matters clearly to those under him was only a reflection of what was, perhaps, his greatest attribute: the firmness yet flexibility of his planning. Where necessary, he was capable of forcing his army remorselessly to follow his scheme – as at Alamein itself – but he always knew when more flexibility was called for. At Mareth, for example, he switched the main axis of attack when the frontal assaults on the German positions were held up.

Montgomery was not without weaknesses, which have been pounced on by his critics. He was not a great intuitive commander when it came to running a fluid battle – as the relatively slow pursuit after Alamein in 1942 and the failure at Arnhem in 1944 demonstrate. Nor was he a comfortable subordinate or ally – especially where the superior did not command his professional respect. This latter aspect has, however, been somewhat overplayed by his detractors. After all, war is not supposed to be a pleasant social occasion where civility is a prime re-

quisite, and in his dispute with the US generals, he rarely pushed the argument to the point where a real rupture was likely.

Assessing Montgomery in absolute terms as a general is always difficult, because the material advantages he possessed from 1942-45 can be used to suggest that he had an easy task. But compared with his contemporaries among the Allied generals in the Mediterranean and European theatres during the same period – Patton, Bradley, Eisenhower, Alexander, Clark, Leese or Dempsey for example – he comes out very near the top as a battlefield commander, leader of men and manager of the complexities of modern war.

Right: Montgomery addressing troops of the Eighth Army in Sicily in 1943. His ability to get on with his troops was crucial to his success. He used many striking effects to let the men in his armies know that they were going to be well looked after – for example, he would ask one of a number of soldiers gathered around his jeep what was his most important possession. 'My rifle, Sir,' would be the inevitable reply. 'No it's not, it's your life, and I'm going to make sure that you don't lose it,' Montgomery would retort. Below: Montgomery with three of his senior subordinates during the battle for Normandy, July 1944. From left, Miles Dempsey, George Patton and Omar Bradley.

THE ELITE COMMANDERS

Commander of British land forces in the Falklands

Major-General John Jeremy Moore (1928-) was commissioned into the Royal Marines in 1947 and began a career that was to make him the most highly decorated officer in the regiment. His first posting took him to Malaya where he was appointed as a troop commander in 40 Commando. When he arrived in Malaya, the Emergency was in full swing. Moore quickly distinguished himself and during his command earned the first of his two Military Crosses. Following the Malayan posting Moore saw service with 40 Commando in Malta and then the Suez Canal Zone before returning to the United Kingdom.

Below inset: Major-General Jeremy Moore, victor in the Falklands and the most decorated Marine officer. Below: Some of the troops under Moore's command go ashore in the Falklands in 1982.

He was then appointed as an instructor at the NCO's training school, a job he held for 18 months, and in which his experiences in Malaya proved highly valuable. Following this, Moore was posted to Cyprus during the Emergency there, as adjutant to 45 Commando.

Once more returning to Britain, he was posted to the Royal Military Academy Sandhurst for three years. In his role as instructor, Moore was responsible for the selection and training of officer cadets prior to commissioning.

In 1962 he returned to a more active role with a posting as adjutant to 42 Commando in the Far East. Within a few months he took command of L Company, 42 Commando, based in Brunei. Shortly after, he won his second Military Cross in a dramatic amphibious assault against a force of 350 rebels who were holding British hostages at Limbang. Moore commandeered two riverboats and led his marines in a dawn attack against the rebel base. Five marines died in the assault but his men killed or captured 100 insurgents and rescued all the hostages unharmed.

In 1963 Moore took part in British operations during the confrontation with Indonesia. During this period, he proved to have an excellent grasp of the methods needed to win the 'hearts and minds' of the frontier tribes. In 1971 Moore was promoted to the

MOORE

rank of Lieutenant-Colonel and took up his new post as commanding officer of 42 Commando. With him he brought over 20 years of experience in counter-insurgency techniques which were to prove of great value in his next posting – to Northern Ireland. Moore applied his experience throughout Operation Motorman in 1972 when the British forces moved into the Republican 'no-go' areas of Belfast. Following the success of his command, Moore was awarded the OBE in 1973.

He was then moved on and took up his appointment as Commanding Officer of the Royal Marines Depot Regiment at Lympstone in Devon. Then he became Commandant of the Royal Marines School of Music and, following promotion to colonel in 1975, attended the Royal College of Defence Studies.

In 1977 Moore was promoted to brigadier and given command of 3 Commando, a post he was to hold for two years. Much of this time was spent training in amphibious and Arctic warfare in the Norwegian training areas – a training he employed to great effect in the Falklands War. In August 1979, Moore was appointed Major-General Royal Marines Commando Forces and when the British Task Force was assembled in April 1982, he assumed command of Land Forces Falkland Islands.

Despite the huge logistic problems facing the British forces Moore demonstrated a clear understanding of his men's capabilities and the tasks facing them. Working closely with Task Force commander

Rear-Admiral Sandy Woodward and with Colonel Pennicott RA, Moore employed the extra firepower and flexibility of Naval Gunfire Support which proved crucial to land operations and helped to reduce casualties by ensuring that the Argentine forces kept their heads down. His three pronged assault toward Stanley was spectacularly successful in the use it made of his troops' physical prowess. In the most important assault of the war, that of 2 Para at Wireless Ridge, Moore recognised the effectiveness of light tanks and employed their substantial firepower in support – almost certainly clinching the battle for the British land forces.

Triumph of the diplomat

The British victory was that of a man who was both strategist and diplomat. He was capable of motivating even the most reluctant of men through his sympathetic understanding of the tasks facing them. He did not shirk from responsibility and his reputation, which had gone well before him, for leadership, loyalty and courage was a substantial boost to the morale of the British troops.

Following the conclusion of his duties in the Falklands, the man who went to war with a copy of Shakespeare's sonnets in his pocket ('I couldn't fit the complete works into my gear, but the sonnets do well, they give you ease of mind, you know') was made a Knight Commander of the Bath. After a short period in an advisory capacity on defence, Jeremy Moore retired, assured of a place in history.

Below: Jeremy Moore (left) and Rear-Admiral 'Sandy' Woodward, overall commander of the British Task Force that set out for the South Atlantic in 1982 and took back the Falkland Islands from the Argentinian armed forces.

THE ELITE COMMANDERS

Royal Sea Lord

When war broke out in September 1939 Lord Louis Mountbatten was 39 and had just taken command of HMS *Kelly*, leader of the newly formed 5th Destroyer Flotilla. He had already been recognised as an officer of outstanding ability and intelligence, having been promoted to captain at the unusually early age of 37. He was also a great-grandson of Queen Victoria, a cousin of King George VI, the son of a former First Sea Lord, and a relative of most of the royal families of Europe.

The career of HMS *Kelly* was eventful. In the first six months of her war service she came near to capsizing, was struck by a mine, and collided with another destroyer. In May 1940 she was crippled by a German torpedo and would have been lost if Mountbatten had not exercised outstanding seamanship in bringing her back to safety after a 91-hour tow. A year later, assisting a doomed attempt to prevent the German invasion of Crete, she was attacked by Junkers dive-bombers and went down with all guns firing.

The weight of professional naval opinion is that Mountbatten was not a first-class naval commander, and that at least some of *Kelly's* misfortunes were attributable to his recklessness. But on the other hand there is no doubting his courage or his capacity to inspire devotion, amounting to love, in the men who served under him. The pains he took to know his men individually stemmed partly from a truly generous nature, partly from a capacity for hard work and for the mastery of detail that was to characterize everything he did.

After the loss of *Kelly* Mountbatten was offered the command of the aircraft-carrier HMS *Illustrious*, but Churchill had other plans for this young officer whose qualities of dash and imagination appealed to his own romantic nature. While on a visit to the United States, he was summoned back to London to take up the post of Adviser, Combined Operations. In March 1942 he became Chief of Combined Operations, with the acting ranks of Vice-Admiral, Lieutenant-General and Air Marshal, sitting with the other three Chiefs

Below: HMS Kelly, the destroyer captained by Louis Mountbatten, seen here after being torpedoed by a German E-boat. The vessel would certainly have been lost if it were not for the grit and determination shown by Mountbatten in bringing her back to shore. Below right: Lord Louis Mountbatten proudly displaying his medals.

of Staff as an equal member. Throughout his care he had to cope with the difficulty of commanding m who were his seniors by 10 or 20 years.

The responsibility of Combined Operations was provide the training and technical advice for ampl bious operations from small raids on the coast occupied Europe to the ultimate invasion. There is doubt that Mountbatten worked furiously at prepa ing the plans and organising the trained personn for combined operations, and his importation of t scientists was to pay off in the planning for D-day

As far as small raids on the continent were co cerned COHQ's record was one of modest succes The tragic failure was the raid on Dieppe of 19 Augu 1942, when nearly 70 per cent of the Canadian troo who were landed became casualties.

Mountbatten must carry some of the blame Dieppe, along with Montgomery and others, in th he continued to press for the operation even when was aware that several of his own stipulations fo had not been met: he had wanted two flank landi rather than a frontal assault, and had been ov ruled; there was no prior air bombardment and support from heavy naval guns; the brave but ine perienced Canadians had been substituted for t trained amphibious troops he had called for in t original plan.

In August 1943 Mountbatten was appoint

MOUNTBATTEN

Supreme Commander, South East Asia, comprising Burma, Malaya, Siam, Indo-China and the adjacent parts of China and India. In this newly-defined theatre, a demoralised British 14th Army was barely holding the line against the Japanese in Burma. Aside from Mountbatten's conflict with his American deputy, General 'Vinegar Joe' Stilwell (and quite often with his own commanders-in-chief), he was faced with a fundamental difference in policy between the Americans and the British. The former wished to support the Chinese in the north, the latter were perceived as wishing to recover Burma on their way to restoring their own and the French and Dutch colonies in the region.

The worst problem of all was that, while the struggle in Europe continued, the resources necessary for a full-scale assault on the enemy simply could not be spared. Mountbatten did what he could, and it was considerable. Faced with the initial problems he identified as the three M's – malaria, monsoon and morale – he made considerable strides in fighting all three. His refusal to accept the conventional view that it was impossible to fight during the monsoon season paid off completely in General Slim's victory at Imphal in 1944.

What Mountbatten might have done in South East Asia was never fully brought to the test, for the simple reason that the resources were never made available for his more ambitious amphibious operations. By the time it was possible to mount Operation Zipper, the seaborne invasion of Malaya, the Japanese had already surrendered. Nonetheless, given the obstacles in his path, Mountbatten's record in that theatre was one of success, later earning him the title, 'Mountbatten of Burma'.

After the war Mountbatten was to become the last Viceroy of India, Commander-in-Chief Allied Forces, Mediterranean, First Sea Lord (his lifelong ambition) and Chief of the Defence Staff. He was to play a variety of major parts in public life until well into his seventies. He was murdered by an IRA bomber on 27 August 1979.

His military career was long and controversial, in

many ways not unlike that of his one-time master, Winston Churchill. In both cases, after one has admitted many mistakes, one recognises the quality called greatness, linked with a deep response to the men and women serving under them.

Above: Mountbatten inspecting the troops in Burma. Right: Keeping a watchful eye on the fleet while aboard HMS *Glasgow*.

119

THE ELITE COMMANDERS

Pacific conqueror

Chester William Nimitz (1885-1966) had the distinction of commanding the Central Pacific area of US operations during World War II; he was the first holder of the US Navy's highest rank (fleet admiral) to which he was promoted in December 1944, and it was his flagship, the USS *Missouri*, on which the surrender of Japan was formally confirmed on 2 September 1945.

Nimitz was born at Fredericksburg in Texas. He graduated from the US Naval Academy at Annapolis in 1905, and by the entry of the US into World War I in 1917 was chief of staff to the commander of the US Atlantic submarine force.

In 1939, Nimitz was made chief of the Bureau of Navigation, but in the aftermath of the surprise Japanese attack on Pearl Harbor in December 1941, he was made commander of the US Pacific Fleet – a critical posting. The battleships of the fleet had all been put out of action; and although the fleet's aircraft carriers had been absent from Pearl Harbor during the attack, at this stage, few would have believed that they could have provided an adequate challenge to the larger Japanese carrier forces.

In spite of the grievous blows already dealt to his units, Nimitz did, however, enjoy certain distinct advantages in formulating his strategy. First of all, it was clear that Japanese plans did not (at first at least) include any intention to pursue the US fleet to destruction; the Imperial Navy was more concerned to cover the campaigns to conquer the oil and mineral-rich areas of southeast Asia. And secondly, the US cryptographers had cracked the Japanese naval codes, giving Nimitz a unique opportunity to anticipate his enemy's movements and assemble his vessels at precisely the right point.

The main intention of US strategy during the early months of 1942 was to maintain communications with

Above: The carrier USS *Intrepid* took part in operations against the Marshalls and participated in the battle for Leyte Gulf. Left: Chester Nimitz, commander of the US Pacific Fleet.

NIMITZ

Bottom: The Essex-class carrier USS *Franklin*, part of Nimitz's Pacific Fleet. The *Franklin* came in for its fair share of battle damage during the war: it was hit twice by kamikazes and successfully bombed on a further two occasions. Below: Admiral Nimitz at his desk. In the Pacific, Nimitz proved himself to be a brilliant organiser as well as a sound strategist. For his contribution to the war, he received decorations from the US and 11 other countries. He was also honoured with the distinction of having the modern American nuclear-powered aircraft carrier USS *Nimitz* named after him.

Australia – and it was quite clear that Japanese intentions were to disrupt this vital link. The first major naval confrontation between the US and Japanese fleets came in May, when Nimitz despatched two of his carriers to halt a Japanese plan to land troops on the southern coast of New Guinea – a plan that the US codebreakers had discovered. In a confused series of engagements, the Battle of Coral Sea was, in tactical terms, a marginal US victory in that the Japanese invasion plans were abandoned.

THE BATTLE OF MIDWAY

The codebreakers' greatest success, however, was the discovery of the Japanese plans, formulated by Admiral Yamamoto, to lure the still weak US Pacific Fleet into an action near Midway Island in June 1942, to put the Americans out of action for a considerable time. Yamamoto had constructed a complex scheme which involved the concentration of dispersed forces; Nimitz put his much smaller carrier fleet (just two vessels, soon made up to three when the damaged *Yorktown* was made seaworthy in record time) at a point north of Midway to prevent the Japanese concentrating. This was a decision fraught with risk, but one in the aggressive naval tradition of inviting a major confrontation. US naval aircraft were, in general, inferior to Japanese machines; the Japanese had the confidence borne of six months of success. Nevertheless, under Raymond Spruance, the US units won a decisive victory, sinking four Japanese carriers for the loss of the *Yorktown*.

Midway was a fatal check to the Japanese. Henceforth they were on the defensive. For Nimitz's next move was to launch the amphibious assault on the island of Guadalcanal. The fighting for Guadalcanal was a seesaw struggle, lasting throughout the second half of 1942. In a series of naval engagements, the Japanese showed their mettle, and their superiority in night-fighting at sea, but were eventually defeated. By the end of 1942, the future of the Pacific War was clearly dependent upon where, and how, the US wished to launch its next offensive.

Control of the war in the Pacific was divided by the US into two areas: the Pacific Ocean (or Central Pacific area) under Nimitz, and the Southwest Pacific area under general Douglas MacArthur. Both of these areas included massive concentrations of naval, air and land forces. During 1943 and early 1944, the US high command was involved in a long strategic debate about the best way to defeat Japan. MacArthur was convinced that there should be a steady advance towards the Philippines, and thence to the Japanese home islands; Nimitz, on the other hand, was the representative of the 'navy' view that an advance due west from Hawaii, taking the Gilbert, Marshall and Mariana island chains, and then taking Formosa, as a base for the final offensive on Japan, was the logical method.

In the event, both axes of advance were developed. While MacArthur moved north from Australia, Nimitz's forces took the key points in the Gilberts in November 1943, had occupied the Marshalls in February 1944 and in June 1944 destroyed Japanese naval aviation at the Battle of the Philippine Sea, during the move against the Marianas. Now, however, MacArthur's views prevailed and the Philippines themselves were invaded late in 1944. The ring was tightening inexorably on the Japanese: the capture of Iwo Jima in March 1945 and Okinawa in June was the prelude to invasion – but the use of the atomic bomb made this final operation unnecessary.

Nimitz had had to make the crucial decision to risk all at the Battle of Midway in June 1942. After that, however, his main task was to ensure that victory was assured as rapidly and efficiently as possible. In this task he proved an excellent strategist and organiser. He presided over the construction of an immense supply fleet that underpinned all US naval operations. At the same time, he imposed a remorseless squeeze upon Japanese communications, using, in particular, a submarine campaign that must rank as the most successful in history.

After the war, Nimitz served for two years as chief of naval operations. His contribution to US victory in World War II was immense. He had taken over when prospects looked extremely bleak, and had seen his country through to total success, having directed the most powerful set of fleets ever seen with a secure grasp that can hardly be criticised. He was not an admiral who directed from sea; indeed, he spent most of the war on land, on Hawaii. But he understood perfectly what he had to do – and how to do it.

THE ELITE COMMANDERS

O'CONNOR

Aggressive Desert leader

When General Sir Richard Nugent O'Connor died in 1981, he was mourned as the 'lost leader of the Desert War'. It was an apt description, for of all the Allied generals who fought in North Africa between 1940 and 1943 he enjoyed the most spectacular success, only to be forgotten as he suffered the humiliation of capture soon afterwards. In a campaign which lasted less than 10 weeks in late 1940 and early 1941, his Western Desert Force of only 36,000 men advanced nearly 500 miles into Libya and destroyed an Italian army more than four times its size. Moreover, it did so by making full use of the mobility and flexibility of armour – a method of warfare in which few British commanders of World War II were adept.

O'Connor was born in 1889 and, at the age of 20, was commissioned from Sandhurst into the 2nd Battalion, Cameronians (Scottish Rifles). During World War I he saw extensive active service on both the Western and Italian fronts, winning two DSOs, an MC and the Italian Silver Medal for Valour. Peace-time soldiering was more mundane, but it was soon apparent that he was earmarked for higher command: by the mid-1930s he had been both a student and instructor at Staff College and had gained invaluable experience in a wide range of military posts. A small, wiry man, often likened to a terrier, O'Connor soon acquired a reputation for high professionalism and command efficiency.

In 1936 he was sent to the Middle East, where he commanded a brigade in the Arab Revolt before becoming military governor of Jerusalem. It was while in the latter post that he was chosen, in early June 1940, to command the Western Desert Force, a hastily-assembled formation centred on the 7th Armoured Division, which had been created to guard the borders of Egypt against possible Italian attack. O'Connor wasted no time in preparing his units for action, and when news was received on 11 June that Italy had declared war on Britain and France, he authorised cross-border raids into Libya to seize the initiative. When the Italian Tenth Army,

122

commanded by Marshal Rodolpho Graziani, finally began a laborious march into Egypt on 13 September, the British already held the upper hand: after only three days, the Italians ground to a halt and dug in around Sidi Barrani. Receiving permission from the C-in-C Middle East, General Sir Archibald Wavell to mount a short sharp 'raid', O'Connor went on to the offensive in December.

A STRATEGY FOR VICTORY

His strategy was simple but effective. While the infantry of 'Selby Force' diverted Italian attention to the east, the men of the 4th Indian Division, closely supported by 57 Infantry ('I') tanks of the Royal Tank Regiment, broke into the main camp at Nibeiwa, shielding a thrust through the centre of the enemy positions by the medium and light tanks of 7th Armoured Division. As the latter broke through to the coast, Italian resistance began to crack: by 0830 on 9 December, Nibeiwa had fallen and, 24 hours later, Sidi Barrani was back in British hands, 38,000 Italian prisoners had been taken and the Tenth Army was in retreat. It was a remarkable victory.

But O'Connor did not stop there. Dispatching elements of 7th Armoured Division through the desert to cut the coast road behind the retreating enemy column, he sent the Indians in close pursuit, chasing Graziani across the border and investing the port of Bardia. On 3 January 1941, newly-arrived infantrymen of the 6th Australian Division, supported by the 'I' tanks, artillery and naval gunfire, breached the Italian defences and by mid-afternoon the port had been captured, along with a further 40,000 dispirited men. By now, the British were running desperately short of supplies – in the end, they survived by using captured Italian stockpiles – but the opportunity for decisive victory could not be ignored. On 21 January the key port of Tobruk fell to the Australians and, as Graziani pulled back along the coast road to Benghazi, he was given no respite. On 4 February O'Connor released 7th Armoured Division across the base of the Cyrenaica 'bulge' in a classic outflanking move, aiming to cut the enemy's line of retreat at Beda Fomm. The going was hard, but on the 7th, as the head of the Italian column came into view, the tanks were waiting. By the end of the day,

Page 122 below: Lieutenant-General (later General) Richard Nugent O'Connor pictured at a ceremony in Nijmegen in May 1946. O'Connor's genius for exploiting the flexibility and mobility of armour lent an almost incredible air to his victories in the Western Desert and resulted (below right) in his bagging 78,000 Italian prisoners in a matter of weeks, in December/ January 1940/41, as his Western Desert Force thrust towards the sea, to put the Italian Tenth Army on the run. Page 122 above: Allied troops advance through abandoned Italian defences for the attack on Tobruk and (this page below) Allied troops await the signal to attack as Tobruk falls victim, on 21 January 1941, to the unstoppable O'Connor war-machine.

caught between the hammer of the Australians and the anvil of 7th Armoured Division, the remaining Italian forces surrendered.

Unfortunately, O'Connor could not exploit his victory to the full, being ordered to divert part of his force to the ill-fated campaign in Greece, and the subsequent lull allowed the Germans to deploy the first elements of Rommel's Afrika Korps to Libya. When they attacked on 31 March, British defences were weak and it was while conducting a forward reconnaissance of his scattered units on 6 April that O'Connor was captured. He was to spend over two years in Italian prisoner of war camps, but refused to give up. After three attempted escapes, he finally reached Allied lines during the confusion of the Italian surrender in late 1943, arriving back in Britain in time to be offered command of VIII Corps for the forthcoming invasion of Europe. Accepting with alacrity, he led his three divisions (15th Scottish, 43rd Wessex and 11th Armoured) in the confused and bitter fighting around Caen in June and July 1944, but despite his skill, he could not achieve the breakthrough so desperately needed.

By November it was obvious that he was tired, forcing Montgomery, a personal friend, to relieve him of his command. He was sent to India to serve once more under Wavell and, after a term as Adjutant General in London in 1946-47, he retired. His desert victory was apparently forgotten, but to students of armoured warfare it became a classic.

THE ELITE COMMANDERS

Aggressive naval commander

Jisaburo Ozawa (1886-1966) was one of the leading Japanese naval commanders of World War II, and exemplified the offensive, attacking spirit that had given the Japanese navy such impressive victories since the days of the Russo-Japanese War of 1904-05. He was involved in one of the most interesting episodes of World War II when he took part in a Japanese raid into the Indian Ocean, which could have ended in Japanese forces linking directly with those of Nazi Germany; and he controlled important Japanese naval forces during two of the greatest battles of World War II – those of the Philippine Sea and Leyte Gulf. It was his personal misfortune that major command was only his when overwhelming US forces made Japanese defeat inevitable.

Ozawa graduated from the Japanese naval academy in 1909, soon after the conclusion of the Russo-Japanese War. The crushing naval victories of this war, culminating in the battle of Tsushima in which the Russian fleet was all but annihilated, raised the status of the navy and gave the attacking theories of Admiral Togo great importance.

Ozawa rose gradually within the Japanese navy, and by 1936 had become a rear-admiral. As a vice-admiral in 1940, he became president of the Naval Academy, but in October 1941 was given an active command, and was involved in the early tide of Japanese victories that swept over Southeast Asia in the wake of the surprise attack on the US fleet at Pearl Harbor in December.

Ozawa commanded forces in Vice-Admiral Nagumo's Carrier Fleet. After the successful action against Allied vessels in the battle of the Java Sea, and the raid south that gave the Japanese possession of the strategically vital point of Rabaul in New Britain, Ozawa was given control of one wing of an ambitious plan to strike a new surprise blow against the British in spring 1942. While Vice-Admiral Kondo led a carrier force towards Ceylon, Ozawa led a light carrier and cruiser force into the Bay of Bengal, to prey on merchant shipping.

The Japanese intention was to exploit Allied weakness, and to extend their air and naval superiority into the Indian Ocean. The British formed the so-called Western Fleet under Sir James Somerville to try to frustrate this scheme; but Kondo and Ozawa swept aside any resistance. Ozawa's forces sank 23 merchant vessels in the first 10 days of April, while Kondo's carriers posed such a threat to Somerville's vessels that the British admiral had to begin withdrawing his fleet to East Africa.

Had the Japanese followed up this initial success by pursuing Somerville, the results could have been disastrous for the Allies. India might have been cut off, and Japanese naval forces could have threatened Egypt from the south while Rommel pushed from the west. The whole history of World War II would have been altered. In the event, however, the Japanese turned back, and missed a great opportunity. They never threatened the Indian Ocean again.

In November 1942, Ozawa was given a senior command when he replaced Nagumo in charge of the Third Fleet (later renamed the Mobile Fleet), which contained most of Japan's aircraft carriers. He had assumed his post at a difficult time, however,

Right: Commander Jisaburo Ozawa, whose Third Fleet, composed mainly of carriers (below), was thrown into battle in June 1944 against the might of the US Fifth Fleet and an advance that threatened the Japanese homeland itself. Ozawa's fleet, vastly outnumbered, suffered a dreadful defeat from which Japanese naval aviation was unable to recover during the remainder of the war.

OZAWA

when the initiative was swinging inexorably to the Americans. In spite of stout Japanese naval actions in the Solomons, within a year US material superiority was such that Japanese defensive planning was outmoded. Ozawa had two main tasks: to maintain his fleet in being as a threat to the Americans, and to help devise a strategy by which, if the Japanese Navy was to be defeated, it should at least inflict maximum damage on the Americans – a strategy of sacrifice.

Ozawa was the commander to whom the Japanese looked to take on Admiral Spruance's powerful US Fifth Fleet that was threatening the Mariana Islands in summer 1944. The Marianas were a key point in the Japanese defensive perimeter, and would bring B-29 Superfortresses within range of Japan itself, as well as threatening the Philippines.

Ozawa's forces were vastly inferior to those of Spruance – he had only nine carriers to the US 15, and 430 aircraft to the US 891. But Ozawa hoped to offset these weaknesses with land-based aircraft flying from the Marianas themselves. In June, Ozawa's vessels were split into two groups. One group, under Vice-Admiral Kurita, was to act as a decoy, while the other, under Ozawa himself, was to surprise Spruance's carriers once their aircraft were engaged against Kurita's fleet.

Spruance found the location of Ozawa's two main bodies, however, before the Japanese attacks even began, and the result was a massacre of Japanese naval aviation, in a series of engagements that US

Below left: Ozawa's warships, in line ahead, during operations in the Indian Ocean. Bottom: A Japanese destroyer is blown apart by a hit from a US B-25. On 22 October 1944, General Douglas MacArthur and the US Sixth Army landed on the island of Leyte in the Philippines. The Japanese responded by launching Operation Sho I, which required Ozawa to draw off Halsey's Third Fleet from the scene of operations on Leyte, while a force under Kurita and a force under Shima steamed through the San Bernardino and Surigao Straits to engage the Americans in Leyte Gulf. The operation, however, was not a success and, while Ozawa's force carried out its task, the Japanese losses were enormous: four carriers, three battleships, six cruisers and 14 destroyers.

navy pilots named the 'Great Marianas Turkey Shoot'. Japanese naval aviation would never recover from this catastrophe.

THE BATTLE OF LEYTE GULF

Ozawa's next crucial command came in October 1944, when the Japanese navy made a vain attempt to block the US landings in the Philippines. At the Battle of Leyte Gulf, Ozawa commanded the northern, decoy fleet that was designed to draw off the main US Third Fleet under Admiral Halsey. His units carried out their mission, but the predatory fleets that were expected to seek out the US transports and landing craft failed in their task. Ozawa's carrier force was destroyed in carrying out its part of the plan. In November 1944, Ozawa was appointed Vice-Chief of the Naval General Staff; and late in May 1945, he assumed control of the entire Combined Fleet, after the US had seized control of Okinawa. However, there was little that any naval commander could have done at this stage, in the face of total US superiority. Without such necessities as oil, without any trained aircrew and with the idea of the kamikaze the only answer to US might, Japan was doomed.

Ozawa was a skilled naval leader: historian Samuel Eliot Morison, in his classic work on the Pacific War, has seen in him, 'a scientific brain and a flair for trying new expedients, as well as a seaman's innate sense of what can be accomplished with ships'. By the time Ozawa reached the highest commands, however, US naval aviation had tipped the scale against the Japanese, and the crushing weight of US superiority left the Japanese fleet with little hope of redressing the balance. Nevertheless, in defeat, Ozawa carried out his duties well, maintaining the naval tradition he had inherited. As he told his men just before the battle of the Philippine Sea, 'It is hoped that the forces will exert their utmost and achieve as magnificent results as in the battle of Tsushima.'

THE ELITE COMMANDERS

Projecting a tough and ruthless image, 'Old Blood and Guts' was always a controversial figure

GEORGE SMITH PATTON JNR (1885-1945) led some of the most stunning offensives mounted by the Allies during the last two years of World War II, and will always be associated with great sweeps by large armoured forces. He drove his men and machines on with the belief that speed and movement were the keys to success. He and Field Marshal Bernard Montgomery had a mutual antipathy that they found difficult to hide, but although their methods of waging war were very different, they both had a common belief in the need to present a strong personality to their troops; just as Montgomery carefully cultivated his public image, so Patton too made sure that the men he commanded saw the side of him that he wanted to project.

From an early age, Patton had wanted to be a soldier and when he graduated from West Point in 1909 he chose to go into the cavalry. In November 1917, he became one of the first American officers to be given command of tanks, and recognised the new weapon as perfectly suited to his character and approach to warfare. He was badly wounded in the Meuse-Argonne offensive, and the war ended before he could get back into active combat, but he had already shown his flair for directing units equipped with the new weapon.

In the interwar years, tanks were assigned to the infantry. Patton returned to the horse cavalry but he studied the works of the prophets of armoured warfare – Liddell Hart and Fuller – and was ready for his new command when he became first a brigade commander, and then divisional general of the 2nd Armored Division in 1940. He trained his men enthusiastically, preaching the virtues of speed, dash, and the indirect approach – 'Catch the enemy by the nose and then kick him in the pants' was one of his favourite sayings.

Left: George S. Patton, during his period as commander of the US Third Army. Brought over to France after the Normandy landings had established a firm foothold on mainland Europe, Patton's men led the breakthrough at Avranches that opened up France to sweeping Allied advance.

Below: M4 Shermans of Patton's command spearhead the drive into Germany. Although inferior to the best German machines, the Sherman was a fast, reliable tank with a useful 75mm gun.

PATTON

In July 1942, Patton was appointed to the command of the Western Task Force during Operation Torch, the Allied invasion of French North Africa, and rapidly showed his genius for coping with the problems of the battlefield by forcing his men inland in spite of heavy congestion on the landing beaches.

During the invasion of Sicily in July 1943, Patton again showed great dash and elan as he led the American forces of his Seventh Army in a long loop around the north of the island, to enter Palermo just before Montgomery's Commonwealth forces, which had become bogged down by defences in the plains on the more direct route to the city.

Although the Sicilian campaign established Patton as a great leader of men and a general with an eye for the opening that could transform a campaign, his career was put in jeopardy by some of his actions towards soldiers under his command. On two occasions he slapped weary and shell-shocked soldiers, and although he apologised, the story leaked to the press. Patton always made a point of giving his soldiers the impression that he was a tough, ruthless warrior, and practised his 'war face' in front of a mirror. His nickname, 'Old Blood and Guts' was a tribute to the bellicose image he had created.

A tough leader, who got results, was just what the American press wanted in 1943 – but the penalties of popular fame rebounded after the incident of the slapped soldiers. In spite of Eisenhower's reluctance, Patton had to keep a low profile for a time to allow the storm of public outrage to die down.

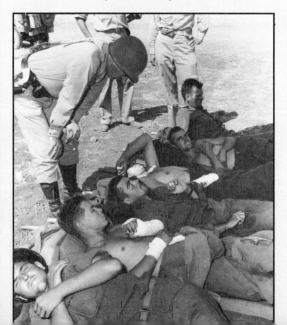

Even in obscurity, however, Patton was able to play a useful role for the Allies. He was appointed to a diversionary command in East Anglia, part of the great deception plan to convince the Germans that the invasion of Europe would be aimed at the Pas de Calais across the Channel from Dover, rather than further west, in Normandy.

Patton's command, the Third Army, did become operational in August 1944, when it was chosen to head the Allied breakout from the Normandy bridgehead. As part of General Omar Bradley's Twelfth Army Group, Patton's men swept through the gap in the German lines at Avranches. Patton realised that he now had the opportunity that he had been waiting for all his life. He pushed his armour in great sweeps to surround German forces, and never let the enemy rest. The rapid exploitation of Hitler's refusal to allow the German forces in northern France to pull back was largely due to the energy of Patton's command.

During the advance northeast, after the Normandy victory, Patton made no secret of the fact that he believed that his axis of advance should be given number one priority. He had no sympathy with Britain's Field Marshal Montgomery, whom he considered a pedestrian leader, unfit to direct a rapid advance that might exploit German weakness. Patton angrily demanded extra supplies from Eisenhower, even when the Supreme Commander had made it clear that Montgomery's Army Group was to have first call on valuable fuel, and Old Blood and Guts even commented approvingly when members of his staff were said to have stolen petrol allocated to another formation.

'Sweat saves blood'

As the Allied offensive came to a halt late in 1944, Patton's Third Army was in the central sector of the Allied line. He made a significant contribution to the containment of the German attack in the Ardennes when he wheeled three divisions towards the enemy incursion, and relieved the besieged town of Bastogne within three days.

The final serious German threat having been defeated, Patton led his men across the Rhine into Germany and Czechoslovakia (he was forbidden to take the Czech capital, Prague, which was allocated to the Red Army), and then moved into Austria.

Following the German surrender, Patton wanted to be transferred to the Pacific Theatre, but had to content himself with the military governorship of Bavaria. This was not to his liking, and he created embarrassment when he advocated using capable ex-Nazis to help in reconstruction work, and claimed that the Russians would have to be attacked if Eastern Europe was to be freed. He died after a car crash near Mannheim in December 1945.

Patton was a character who provoked strong feelings – British generals found his carrying of pearl-handled revolvers and his outspoken style hard to take, while US servicemen saw him as a positive figure whose belief that 'sweat saves blood' made his pushing them so hard quite acceptable.

There can be no doubting Patton's aptitude for armoured warfare. He felt very strongly that the way to make war was to keep driving forward, and that opportunities had to be taken with the minimum of preparation if great victories were to be won. This might seem a reckless doctrine; but in Patton's hands 'Attack, always attack' proved a highly successful formula, and secured his reputation as one of the greatest modern commanders.

Above: 'Old Blood and Guts' in typically defiant pose. Patton practised his 'war face' in front of a mirror and made the cultivation of a tough public image one of his priorities. Above left: Patton in victory. Promoted to four-star general, Patton steers a launch across Lake Adder in Austria soon after the final German surrender. Unusually, his more common pearl-handled pistol has been replaced by a standard-issue M1911A1 with general's stars fixed to the butt.

Left: Patton meets some wounded US servicemen in Sicily in 1943. Although he was an inspiring leader of men, Patton's rage at two shell-shocked soldiers in Sicily provoked a public incident that put him under a cloud for a time.

THE ELITE COMMANDERS

Exemplary staff officer

On 30 January 1943, Hitler promoted General Friedrich Paulus, the commander of the encircled German Sixth Army at Stalingrad, to the rank of Field-Marshal, on the assumption that this would stiffen his resolve, and in the belief that no German field-marshal had ever capitulated on the field of battle. The next day, Paulus formally capitulated to the Soviets and accompanied some 90,000 of his troops into captivity. Hitler was furious when he learnt the news, and poured scorn on Paulus for not taking his own life, predicting that he and other generals would allow themselves to be used for Soviet propaganda.

Friedrich Wilhelm Ernst Paulus was born in 1890 and came from a family of middle-class civil servants in Hesse-Nassau. He was educated at the Wilhelms-Gymnasium in Kassel, and hoped to join the navy. In the event, despite his relatively humble background, he was commissioned into Infantry Regiment No. 111, the 3rd Baden Regiment in 1911. In the following year he married the daughter of an immensely wealthy Romanian family which helped his military career. During World War I Paulus served for the most part as a regimental officer, then as a staff officer. He soon gained a reputation as a conscientious worker who was readily adaptable and could get on with his superiors. Paulus gained experience serving on the staff of the Alpine Corps in 1917, and ended the war as a captain. During the period of revolutionary turmoil in Germany in 1919 he served in the Freikorps in the east, and then in

PAULUS

Below: General Friedrich Paulus at Stalingrad, November 1942. After a bloody attritional battle to capture the city, Paulus was forced to surrender as the Soviet counter-offensive encircled his Sixth Army.
Page 129, above: Two Germans survey the captured ruins of Stalingrad that cost the lives of 200,000 of their fellow soldiers.
Below: Field-Marshal Paulus is taken for interrogation by his Soviet captors. Hitler had promoted Paulus to field-marshal in January 1943 in the fanatical hope that it would spur him on to fight to the death. With his Sixth Army trapped and starving, however, the promotion could only delay the inevitable decision to surrender and Paulus became the first German officer of that rank to capitulate.

1920 he was appointed adjutant of the 14th Infantry Regiment in the Reichsheer.

In the 1920's Paulus gained a reputation for meticulous staff work and gradually gained promotion through a series of staff appointments. In 1934, as a lieutenant-colonel, Paulus took command of Motor Transport Section No. 3, which became the prototype of many of the later panzer units. A decisive promotion for Paulus came in 1935 with his appointment as a full colonel to chief of staff of the newly formed Mechanised Forces headquarters in Berlin. Paulus was, therefore, in at the beginning of the formation of the panzers and worked closely with many officers who were to hold high rank during World War II. Paulus generally supported Nazi policies, and regarded Hitler as a great leader who was saving Germany and expanding the army.

In August 1939 Paulus was promoted to major-general and was appointed chief of staff of the Sixth Army commanded by General Reichenau. During the period 1939-40, the Sixth Army played a leading part in the success of German military operations in Poland and the West. Reichenau was highly appreciative of the superb staff work undertaken by Paulus, and this helped in his promotion to the rank of lieutenant-general and appointment as deputy chief of the Army General Staff, under Franz Halder. Thus, in the summer of 1940, Paulus was effectively the third senior member of the army high command after Brauchitsch and Halder. Paulus found that his main task was to plan the operational aspects of Operation Barbarossa, the invasion of the Soviet Union. However, he found himself caught up in the deep divergence of opinion between Hitler, Brauchitsch and Halder over the objectives of Barbarossa.

For the first six months of the war on the Eastern Front, Paulus continued to serve as Halder's deputy, attending conferences with Hitler, and being sent on confidential missions to the army group headquarters. Although he began to have misgivings about the nature of German strategy in August 1941, he still retained an overall optimism that Germany could win a decisive victory against the Soviet Union. Following the disasters outside Moscow in December 1941, and as part of Hitler's re-shuffle of command appointments, Paulus was promoted full general and took up command of the Sixth Army. This caused some comment as Paulus had never commanded any formation above a regiment, and most of his subordinate generals were senior to him in the army. But Paulus gradually won their respect and successfully commanded the Sixth Army in the fierce, defensive fighting of early 1942 around Kharkov.

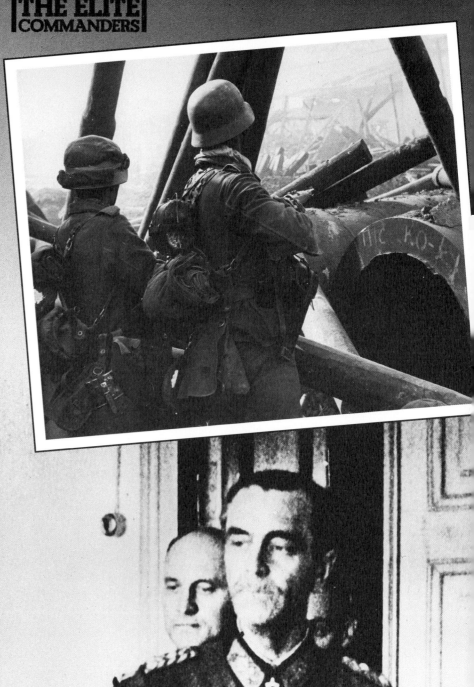

STALINGRAD

For the summer offensive of 1942, the Sixth Army formed part of the German spearhead in the south, and continued the advance towards the symbolically important town of Stalingrad on the river Volga. Paulus was aware that the further the Sixth Army advanced, the longer and more vulnerable became its lines of communication, and that its flanks were guarded by a motley collection of foreign troops. On 23 August the Sixth Army reached the northern suburbs of Stalingrad and thus began the brutal attritional battle for the city that was to rival that of Verdun in 1916.

For the next three months the Sixth Army slowly fought its way through to the centre of Stalingrad, with Paulus becoming increasingly aware of his vulnerable flanks. On 19 November the Soviets began a major offensive against those flanks which broke through weak Romanian and Italian divisions, and within a few days the Sixth Army was in danger of being encircled. Paulus was convinced that he had to break out to the southwest, but Hitler ordered him to stand fast, and await relief by a ground offensive while the Luftwaffe supplied him by air. In the event, the ground offensive failed and the Luftwaffe was unable to supply the Sixth Army with anything like its daily consumption of food or ammunition. By Christmas 1942, Paulus knew that it was only a matter of a few weeks before he would be forced to surrender. Worn down by the burdens of command and sick with dysentery, Paulus, the loyal staff officer, was in no position to take independent action. Hitler refused to allow any attempt to break out, and in the last few days before the capitulation he hoped that Paulus would commit suicide with his soldiers.

At first, in captivity, Paulus would not associate himself with any of the Soviet sponsored anti-Nazi organisations, but when he learnt of the bomb plot against Hitler in July 1944 and the subsequent execution of many old friends he joined the 'Free Germany' Committee and made broadcasts to Germany. After the war he was eventually released and chose to live in Dresden in East Germany where he died in 1957.

THE ELITE COMMANDERS

Architect of Hitler's Navy

Grossadmiral (Admiral of the Fleet) Erich Raeder (1876-1960) controlled German naval power for the first half of World War II and was largely responsible for the build-up of German naval strength that enabled the Nazi regime to present a powerful challenge to the larger Allied navies in this period; but he was, in the end, unable to cope with the contradictory demands that Hitler made on the navy.

Raeder was essentially an officer of the old school. He had entered the Imperial German Navy in 1894, and during World War I served under Admiral Hipper. In 1928, Raeder became chief of naval staff, and in 1935, Hitler appointed him commander-in-chief of the entire Navy. Under his energetic command, the ship-building programme was accelerated. In order to get round the naval provisions of the Versailles Treaty, Raeder had already set in motion the building of 'pocket battleships' – vessels that packed the armament of a battleship within the restricted size of a heavy cruiser – but after 1935, when Hitler formally denounced those provisions and signed the Anglo-German Naval Treaty, a new phase of shipbuilding began. Raeder was to preside over the construction of a U-boat fleet and the planning of new battleships.

Early in 1939, Raeder's ambitious 'Z Plan' was accepted by Hitler. This was a scheme to reach naval parity with Britain by 1945, provided that peace was maintained until then. Unfortunately for Raeder's plans, war broke out far sooner than he had expected.

When war did break out, Raeder showed a keen grasp of strategy. He had been a late convert to the idea of raiding on commercial vessels, but saw that Germany had little alternative; outright confrontation with the British fleet would have been suicidal, and the early clashes – such as the sinking of the *Admiral Graf Spee* after a cruise in the South Atlantic – soon demonstrated this fact. Raeder could see that German expansion north into Scandinavia would give him great advantages in a war on Britain's trade routes, and in October 1939 he noted: 'We must find out if there is any possibility of obtaining bases in Norway ... This would radically improve our

RAEDER

strategic situation.'

The invasion of Norway, which took place in April 1940, was to result in heavy losses for the German Navy, however. The British and French forces that went to the aid of the Norwegians were defeated, but in the process, several important German vessels were lost, and in the Battle of Narvik British destroyers proved that they were well able to account for similar German vessels.

Raeder's sound grasp of strategic principles is illustrated by the fact that he ordered his staff to consider the problems and possibilities involved in an invasion of the British Isles during the spring of 1940, although Hitler proved unwilling to consider

Left: Grossadmiral (Admiral of the Fleet) Erich Raeder, commander-in-chief of the German Navy from 1935 until 1943. Above: The heavy cruiser *Prinz Eugen*, a vessel of his small but powerful surface fleet.

the difficulties involved until July. Late in July, the army at last produced an ambitious plan for landings in southern England, which Raeder condemned as unworkable; his staff had already spent two months working on the logistics of transporting the necessary number of troops across the Channel in the face of air and naval attack by British forces. His pessimism was given further weight by the losses that the German fleet suffered when trying to locate minefields off the British coast. By the autumn, the Luftwaffe had failed to achieve mastery of the skies, and Hitler called off the invasion.

THE U-BOAT OFFENSIVE

In spite of the failure of the bid to invade Britain, the German conquest of France had gained bases on the French Atlantic seaboard that were to enable Raeder to launch effective warfare on the British merchant marine – an offensive that might well have strangled Britain. In spite of the fact that U-boat production actually fell early in 1940 (Göring's Luftwaffe was staking a major claim in the allocation of resources), U-boats became a major threat to British supply lines. Surface vessels also brought pressure on the British sea lanes, either in the form of disguised merchant raiders (of which six sailed into the high seas in 1940) or of regular naval units. For example, in October 1940 *Admiral Scheer*, a pocket battleship, broke out into the Atlantic and began a cruise of destruction that ended only when it returned to port in March 1941.

After the sinking of the *Bismarck* by the Royal Navy in May 1941, the German naval effort came to be increasingly concentrated in the U-boat arm, which was now closely controlled by Admiral Dönitz. The last great success that Raeder's surface vessels enjoyed was the 'Channel dash', the bold movement of the three vessels (*Scharnhorst*, *Gneisenau* and *Prinz Eugen*) north from Brest through the English Channel in broad daylight on 11 February 1942. The main function of the surface fleet was now to threaten the Arctic convoys sent by Britain to aid the Soviet Union. *Tirpitz*, sister ship of the *Bismarck*, was

Below: Grossadmiral Erich Raeder inspects what proved to be the most potent weapon of his arsenal, the U-boat. Bottom: *Prinz Eugen* in the celebrated 'Channel dash' of February 1942. The bold manoeuvre gave Raeder three warships for use against Allied shipping in the Arctic.

moored in Norwegian waters, and she was the basis of a threat which also included U-boats and aircraft operating from Norway.

Convoy PQ17 was largely destroyed as a result of this triple threat in July 1942. But in December, two British cruisers, and a destroyer flotilla escorting another convoy, beat off an attack by superior German surface vessels (including the pocket battleship *Lützow* and the heavy cruiser *Admiral Hipper*) with some ease. This demonstration of the impotence of his surface fleet enraged Hitler. He became extremely insulting to Raeder, and informed him that all heavy naval units would have their guns removed for use on land. Raeder resigned

in the face of this scheme, unable to persuade Hitler that the very existence of vessels such as *Tirpitz* in Norwegian waters forced the British to deploy many of their major naval units in a defensive role against the threat they represented. Although he took up an honorary inspectorate, Raeder played no further major part in naval strategy. Ironically, his successor, Dönitz, managed to persuade Hitler to abandon his insane plan. At the Nuremberg trials, Raeder was given a life sentence, but he was released in 1955.

THE ELITE
COMMANDERS
RICHTHOFEN

Architect of Blitzkrieg

Baron Wolfram von Richthofen (1895-1945) was a younger cousin of Manfred von Richthofen of 'flying circus' fame, and served for some time in that squadron during World War I. He rejoined the armed forces in 1923, and his great opportunity came in 1936, when he was appointed Chief of Staff to Sperrle in the famous Condor Legion, the German air force unit that served on the Fascist side in the Spanish Civil War. The successes of this force gave officers of the Luftwaffe active service experience that they put to good use when World War II broke out.

During the invasion of Poland in September 1939, von Richthofen commanded VIII Fliegerkorps, and the aggression and perseverance of his Stuka squadrons contributed mightily to the speed of German victory. This formation was again of great importance in 1940, during the invasion of France, and yet again in 1941 when perhaps the most complete of all the Blitzkriegs – that against Yugoslavia and Greece – was launched. Between the successes in France and the Balkans, however, the all-conquering Stukas

Left: Baron Wolfram von Richthofen, one of the Luftwaffe officers who pioneered the close-support tactics that gave the German armed forces such an advantage during the first three years of World War II. Interestingly, von Richthofen had at one time been convinced that close support of ground forces by aircraft was impossible and as late as 1936 he believed that such operations were impractical. Nevertheless, during the Spanish Civil War, von Richthofen realised that aircraft could be used in close coordination with armoured units, and put his new ideas into operation with great effect in the Polish and French campaigns, during which the Ju 87 Stuka (seen above) proved his central weapon. Von Richthofen was a forthright, uncompromising man who did not hesitate to criticise Army commanders when he thought they were operating ineffectively: in particular he was very scathing about the Army High Command during the battle of Stalingrad in 1942-43.

had suffered a serious check, when they proved vulnerable to the British Hurricanes and Spitfires during the Battle of Britain.

In June 1941, VIII Fliegerkorps proved its worth once more during Operation Barbarossa, the invasion of the Soviet Union, and on many occasions, such as at Kalinin in October, von Richthofen's Stukas rescued Army units that were in danger of being overrun. In 1942, von Richthofen's aircraft first helped Manstein to overrun the Crimea (flying over 1000 sorties per day against the defences of Sevastopol), and then moved to support Bock's Army Group South against the Don Basin.

FROM STALINGRAD TO SARDINIA

When the German Sixth Army was cut off at Stalingrad, von Richthofen was given the task of resupplying it from the air. From the start, however, he made it clear that the 500 tons of supplies per day that were needed was an impossible target, and he became extremely dissatisfied with Hitler and Göring when they refused to accept his advice.

In 1943, von Richthofen, now a Field Marshal, was moved to the Mediterranean theatre. Here, he made a serious error of judgement, when he guessed that the Allies would attempt to invade Sardinia. He concentrated his fighters for the defence of that island, and was thus unable to present more than a minimal defence to the Allied invasion of Sicily in July.

Von Richthofen underwent severe brain surgery in 1944, and died in 1945. He will always be remembered as an aggressive, flamboyant commander who pioneered the techniques of close support that are still regarded as a central role of modern air forces.

|THE ELITE|
|COMMANDERS|
RIDGWAY

Superb combat commander and victor in Korea

Matthew Bunker Ridgway, born in 1895, was commissioned into the US infantry from West Point in 1917. He failed to see active service during World War I and spent the 1920s and early 1930s in normal postings in the United States and the Philippines, but thereafter his career began to blossom. After attendance at the Command and General Staff College and the Army War College, he was assigned to the War Plans Division of the War Department General Staff as a lieutenant-colonel in 1939, just before war broke out in Europe. When America entered that war two years later, Ridgway was hurriedly promoted to brigadier-general and appointed assistant commander, under Major-General Omar Bradley, of the 82nd Infantry Division. In June 1942 Bradley moved on, leaving Ridgway to command the division at the moment of its conversion to the airborne role.

He proved to be an ideal man for the job of training and leading the new division, with its mix of parachute and glider-borne units, but his first taste of action was beset with problems. On 10 July 1943 the 82nd, committed to spearhead the invasion of Sicily, suffered heavy casualties as the laden transports approached the drop-zone at night over the heads of an invasion fleet wary of any air activity. Ridgway had already expressed grave doubts about the operation and he was proved right as only a quarter of his force

Above: The dispirited retreat of the UN forces in Korea in December 1950, under the threat of massed Chinese attacks. Matthew Ridgway (right) rectified the low morale and combat-weariness of the UN forces soon after his assumption of command late in December, and he devised tactics that countered the fluid offensive methods of the Chinese forces.

landed safely: the rest were killed by 'friendly' anti-aircraft fire, deposited elsewhere by nervous transport pilots or returned to their bases in North Africa. Despite the fact that Ridgway, through personal leadership, managed to hold the drop-zone until relieved by ground forces, it was a cruel baptism of fire: if it had not been for a more successful drop at Salerno two months later, America's airborne elite might well have been disbanded.

Ridgway's next task – that of leading his division to help secure the western fringe of the Normandy

Above: Ridgway as
commander airborne forces
during World War II. His
leadership of the 82nd
Airborne Division in Sicily,
Italy and France was marked
by great resolution in the face
of difficulties in all theatres,
and he ended the war in
charge of XVII Airborne
Corps, leading it during the
Battle of the Bulge and the
invasion of Germany. Above
right: Men of Ridgway's 82nd
Airborne in Normandy, 8 June
1944. Below: Ridgway, as
Chief of Staff of the US Army,
at a press conference.

invasion beaches in June 1944 – was little easier than Sicily. Late on 5 June the 82nd followed its sister-unit, the 101st Airborne, across the Channel from bases in England to seize positions on both sides of the Merderet river, behind what was soon to be Utah beach. Ridgway jumped with the main assault wave, only to experience familiar problems. His division was badly scattered, casualties were heavy and contact with the invasion fleet was lost when gliders carrying the heavy radios landed in marshes along the river. For two days, Ridgway operated in a vacuum, not even sure that the invasion had taken place but once again he was successful.

On 15 August Ridgway was promoted to command the newly-formed US XVIII Airborne Corps and within a month he was committing his two available divisions (the 82nd and 101st) to Operation Market Garden in Holland. Their objectives – the bridges at Eindhoven and Nijmegen – were seized in a hard-fought action, but even under Ridgway's personal command, the Americans could not break through to relieve their British counterparts at Arnhem. Two

months later the divisions were back in action, this time as ground forces rushed to plug the widening gap in US lines in the Ardennes. The 101st, detached from Ridgway's command, defended Bastogne against the German onslaught, while the 82nd, joined by various non-airborne units, held the northern shoulder of the 'bulge' before counter-attacking.

Manufacturing the 'meatgrinder'

Withdrawn for a much-needed refit, XVIII Corps resumed its airborne composition in February and, a month later, took part in General Montgomery's crossing of the Rhine at Wesel. Ridgway, despite a wounded arm, was prominent wherever the fighting was hard, and his corps pushed into the Ruhr before advancing north to the Danish border as the war came to a close. It seemed a fitting culmination to a remarkable career.

But Ridgway still had one more war to fight, for in December 1950 he was called upon to assume command of the US Eighth Army, battling to survive against a Chinese onslaught in Korea. He held the post for only 15 weeks before replacing the discredited General MacArthur as Supreme Commander, but in that time he transformed what had been a demoralised army, riddled with 'bug-out fever', into a professional, effective force, capable of preventing a communist victory. Ridgway was particularly insistent upon the troops under his command making the maximum possible use of their technical superiority, especially in artillery, to punish the more primitive armies they were ranged against. This approach, known crudely but accurately as the 'meatgrinder', caused frightful casualties among the communist forces.

Many commentators regard Ridgway's success in Korea as his greatest achievement. It was rewarded in 1952 by his appointment as NATO Supreme Commander; and then, one year later, by promotion to US Army Chief of Staff. He resigned from this post in 1955 after a disagreement with President Eisenhower over peacetime Army strengths, but by then his reputation as a vigorous, brave and efficient combat leader at all levels of command was assured.

THE ELITE COMMANDERS

Advocate of mobile war

Konstantin Rokossovsky (1896-1968) has been described, with some justification, as one of the most able and successful Soviet commanders of World War II. One of the few generals to survive the debacle of 1941 with his reputation still intact, he went on to command increasingly large and complex formations in most of the major battles on the Eastern Front, from Stalingrad to Berlin. By May 1945 he was being hailed as a key member of Marshal Zhukov's command 'team'.

Yet only seven years earlier Rokossovsky, arrested during Stalin's purge of the officer class, had been on trial for his life, accused of participation in an 'anti-Soviet conspiracy'. In Stalin's eyes, he was suspect on two counts: he had been born in Poland and had served in the Czarist Army in World War I. Admittedly, he had transferred to the Red Guard at the time of the 1917 Revolution and had fought with the cavalry during the Civil War (1919-21), but since then he had compounded his 'errors' by advocating mobile, mechanised war, contrary to the Leninist tradition of a mass workers' army. Officers had been shot for less and Rokossovsky was lucky to survive. In May 1940, when the Red Army was reorganised, he was released and rehabilitated, even being promoted to major-general and given command of the 19th Mechanised Corps near Kiev, but relations between him and Stalin were always strained.

When the Germans attacked Russia in June 1941, Rokossovsky's corps was rapidly overwhelmed by the pace and power of Blitzkrieg. However, he fought creditably, falling back towards Smolensk and, at one point, assuming temporary command of the remnants of two armies. He was rewarded in

Below right: General K.K. Rokossovsky, surrounded by members of his staff, issues orders during Operation Bagration, the Red Army's drive to the Vistula in mid-1944. Born in Poland, he survived Stalin's purges of the late 1930s and was recalled to active service in May 1940. After playing a distinguished part in the defeat of the German Sixth Army at Stalingrad, Rokossovsky's Central Front bore the brunt of the fighting in the Kursk salient during the summer of 1943. Below left: Crouched in a muddy trench, Soviet infantry wait out a preliminary bombardment before going over to the offensive.

early October, when he received permanent command of the Sixteenth Army, with orders to hold the key defensive positions around Volokolamsk, on the approaches to Moscow. The fighting was hard but a defence line was consolidated. In January 1942, the Sixteenth Army was shifted south to defend Sukinichi, and it was here that Rokossovsky was wounded, narrowly escaping death.

He returned to duty in July 1942, being given command of the Bryansk Front (army group) in the Stalingrad sector, where the German advance was threatening to break through on the river Volga. Two months later, Rokossovsky's command was reorganised into the Don Front, and it was this formation that he led in successful attacks from the northeast which completed the encirclement of German forces and contributed to the destruction of General Paulus' Sixth Army. By mid-December Rokossovsky, in concert with General Vatutin's South-West Front on his right, had shattered defence lines held by the Romanians and Italians to the north of the city of Stalingrad and had started the long haul of liberation westwards. On 4 February 1943 the commands were reorganised again, with Rokossovsky taking over the new Central Front, driving towards the city of Kursk. By April, the advance had been halted by a lack of supplies, with Central Front forces occupying the northern sector of the Kursk salient. Rokossovsky dug in and waited.

A LONG, HARD ROAD

The German counter-attack at Kursk (Operation Citadel) opened on 5 July 1943 and Rokossovsky's units bore the brunt of the action in the northern sector. Days of bitter fighting followed, but Rokossovsky kept his nerve, saving his armour until his

Continued overleaf

ROKOSSOVSKY

Continued from back cover

infantry had blunted the panzer advance. In the tank battles that ensued, the cream of the German armour was destroyed. Pausing merely to regroup, Rokossovsky organised a pursuit of the shattered remnants: by late November lead elements of his command had reached the Dniester river, poised for an attack into the Ukraine. Poor weather and supply problems delayed the next offensive, but Rokossovsky's reputation as an effective commander had been made.

In early 1944, in yet another reorganisation, Rokossovsky emerged as commander of the Belorussian Front, tasked with mounting attacks in the southeastern sector during the forthcoming Operation Bagration. His first objective was the town of Bobruisk and, at a planning conference on 22/23 May, he advocated a two-prong attack, taking the town from north and south in an encircling move. Stalin disagreed, favouring a frontal asault, and Rokossovsky was twice sent away to 'think things over'. Nevertheless, he persisted: at the third submission of his proposals, Stalin was forced to agree. Fortunately the plan worked – Bobruisk fell on 29 June – but the lack of consensus between Rokossovsky and his supreme commander was obvious.

Once Bobruisk had been taken, the Belorussian Front forged ahead, aiming for the river Vistula and the gates of Warsaw. As the Soviets approached, the Polish Home Army, convinced that they were about to be 'liberated', rose in revolt. Rokossovsky was apparently taken by surprise, with his forces committed to north and south of the city at the end of very stretched supply lines, but he made no attempt to prevent the Germans' ruthless repression of the Polish resistance fighters. Indeed, at one point he

THE ELITE COMMANDERS

Above: A formal portrait of Rokossovsky taken during the early stages of the Great Patriotic War. Below right: Soviet assault troops supported by a KV-85 heavy tank clear a German-held village in Belorussia. Bottom: Parading the fruits of victory in Moscow's Red Square.

even pulled his units back from the Vistula and it was not until early 1945, by which time he had assumed command of the northern sector of the Belorussian Front (renamed the 2nd Belorussian Front), that Rokossovksy could resume his advance. With Marshal Zhukov to his left, he pushed towards the Baltic coast, cutting off German forces in East Prussia. Danzig fell on 30 March and, as Rokossovksy's units moved along the coast, preparations began for the final battles of the war.

The 2nd Belorussian Front was not directly involved in the capture of Berlin – that was left to forces under Zhukov further south – but Rokossovsky's advances along the Baltic coast ensured that the main assault did not need to worry about outflanking moves from the north. By 5 May Rokossovsky had reached Wismar, linking up with British forces from the west. It was the end of a long, hard road, expertly navigated by an effective commander. But relations with Stalin were still poor and Rokossovsky's subsequent appointment to command forces in Poland was interpreted by some as a 'snub'.

ROMMEL

Leader of the Afrika Korps and master of mobile warfare

Field Marshal Erwin Rommel (1891-1944) was one of the greatest generals of World War II, and his inspired leadership of armoured and mobile formations made him a legend in his lifetime – even among his enemies.

During World War I, Rommel had received the highest decoration possible in Imperial Germany, the 'Pour le mérite', for his personal bravery during the Caporetto offensive against Italy. In the interwar period he taught at infantry schools, and attracted the attention of Adolf Hitler because he subscribed to ideas of mobile warfare. When war came in 1939, Rommel was commander of Hitler's personal headquarters. After the defeat of Poland, Hitler granted his request to be given the command of a panzer division.

The division that Rommel took over was 7th Panzer. As part of Army Group A, it was allotted an important part in the strategy that had been devised to break through the Allied defences in the Ardennes in May 1940. Rommel pushed his men and machines to the limit during the drive to the Channel. He did not rest when darkness fell: during the night of 16/17 May his tanks covered 40km, crossing the Franco-Belgian frontier and reaching Le Cateau.

After the defeat of France, Rommel was recognised as an outstanding exponent of 'Blitzkrieg', but his orders when he took up his next major command were to remain on the defensive. This command was of the German forces that had been sent to North Africa to shore up the tottering armies of their Italian ally, recently badly defeated by the British.

In spite of his orders, Rommel decided to take the offensive. This first series of attacks, launched on 31 March 1941, achieved its basic aim of forcing the British back into Egypt, but Rommel was unable to complete his success by capturing the important port of Tobruk, and settled down for a siege.

The first British attempt to relieve Tobruk was Operation Battleaxe of June 1941. During the fighting of this period, Rommel showed his genius as a leader, when he took his tanks in a gigantic 'right hook' around the south of the British positions to force the British army to withdraw back into Egypt. The next series of battles was fought in November, when General Claude Auchinleck ordered the newly named British Eighth Army against the German positions during Operation Crusader. This time, the Allies had more success. Auchinleck refused to allow his units to withdraw in the face of another of Rommel's drives east, and bludgeoned the Axis forces into abandoning their positions.

The success of the Crusader offensive raises several questions about Rommel's approach. He had abandoned contact with the main part of his army during the flanking manoeuvre that ultimately failed, and the aftermath of the defeat was an increase in tension between the German general and his Italian allies. Rommel never made any secret of his contempt for the Italian generals under whose command he was nominally placed, and he frequently refused to obey orders, or to take their interests into account.

Although a master of the battlefield, and able to inspire his men to great feats, Rommel was less sure

THE ELITE COMMANDERS

Page 138, top: Rommel, with his Knights Cross with swords and oak leaves at his throat. Page 138, bottom: Rommel (on right) leading from the front in North Africa. Above: The successful commander of 7th Panzer takes part in the victory parade in Paris, 1940. Note the 'Pour le mérite' above the Knights Cross at his throat. Right: Rommel shares a meal in a command car, North Africa 1942. Below: Baton in hand, Field Marshal Rommel inspects the defences of the Atlantic Wall in 1944.

of the place of this battlefield within the wider theatre. This was a serious weakness in an area as complex as the Mediterranean.

The first six months of 1942 saw Rommel recover from the setback of the Crusader battles and take the offensive again. The first attacks of 1942, beginning on 21 January, were carried out against the strict instructions of the Italians, and were even kept secret from the German high command. But the initial offensive drove the British back across the 'bulge' of Cyrenaica, and the reluctant Italians were bound to move up troops in support. Then, in May, Rommel proposed a new attack, to take Tobruk and drive the British back into Egypt. This was agreed to, but only as a limited offensive, part of a general strategy of isolating Malta, the thorn in the side of the Axis supply lines across the Mediterranean sea.

The initial victories in this new offensive were stunning, however. The Gazala battles defeated the Eighth Army and then Tobruk fell at last to the Axis forces. Rommel decided to push on to Alexandria, hoping to defeat the British totally in North Africa. He managed to reach the El Alamein position, but there, stiffening British resistance forced him to a halt.

Rommel's men were now at the end of a long and tenuous logistics chain: material from Italy was subject to air and submarine attack from Malta. Rommel knew that the inexorable British build-up made his long-term chances slim; and so he made one last desperate attack, at the battle of Alam El Halfa. This consisted of another of his famous 'right hooks' around the south of the British positions, but failed in its objectives. Under its new commander, Lieutenant-General Bernard Law Montgomery, the Eighth Army stood firm.

As the autumn wore on, the Allies in turn prepared their counter-offensive, opened by the Battle of Alamein in October/November 1942. Rommel had supervised the construction of a very effective de-

fensive position, and although numerically superior, the British forces found it hard to break through; but eventually they did so, and the Afrika Korps began a long retreat. Meanwhile, an Anglo-American Army had landed in French North Africa and began advancing on Tunisia. The Axis forces in North Africa were inevitably squeezed to death, but nevertheless, Rommel fought an inspired retreat as he pulled back, eluding all Montgomery's attempts to trap the remnants of his army, and inflicting a bloody nose on American forces in Tunisia at Kasserine. He left

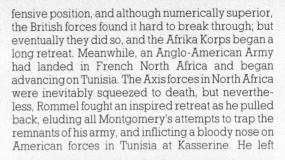

Africa before the final Axis defeat of May 1943.

In January 1944, Rommel was given command of Army Group B, in France, preparing to meet the expected Allied landings in northwest Europe. His strategy was to resist as close to the shoreline as possible, and he put an enormous effort into improving the beach defences. After the Normandy landings, however, Rommel clearly realised that Germany could not hope to avoid defeat, and advised Hitler that surrender terms must be agreed. Rommel's disillusion with the Führer had grown to such an extent that he was prepared to give some support to the plotters who were trying to assassinate the German leader. The aftermath of the failed bomb plot of 20 July led to revelations of the Field Marshal's involvement, and Rommel, who had been seriously wounded on 17 July when his staff car was attacked by Allied fighter bombers, was given the option of standing trial, or taking poison. He chose the latter.

Rommel's name will always be synonymous with mobility and dash in warfare. The open spaces of the desert gave him a great opportunity to employ his gifts, an opportunity he took with both hands. But he could also conduct tenacious and skilful defence, as he showed at and after Alamein, and during the first days of the Normandy landings. What marks out Rommel above all, perhaps, is that his ability to withstand the strains of directing a battle was matched by his ability to inspire his men, and by a concern for the moral standards to be observed on the battlefield – towards prisoners and civilians especially. This combination is rare in any epoch.

Rundstedt

The man who enjoyed the highest commands throughout World War II

When the British military historian Basil Liddell Hart assessed German generalship during World War II in his book *The Other Side of the Hill*, he afforded fulsome praise to Field Marshal Gerd von Rundstedt (1875-1953), describing him as 'a gentleman to the core' and a leader of rare distinction. The succession of high command appointments held by von Rundstedt and his close involvement in many of the key campaigns of the war certainly suggest that this is a viable view, but it is interesting to note that such adulation is not widely shared by Liddell Hart's counterparts in modern Germany. To them, von Rundstedt epitomises two aspects of 20th-century German generalship – the militarism of the 'old Germany' and the meek acceptance by the army of Hitler's rise to power – that are difficult to forgive.

This divergence of views makes any balanced assessment of von Rundstedt difficult. There is no doubt that the modern German condemnation contains an element of truth. Von Rundstedt, born in Prussia on 12 December 1875, did represent the old order: he came from a military family and was educated specifically for an army career. Equally significantly, his qualities as a military leader were largely untapped before the rise of Nazism – he fought throughout World War I as an infantry and staff officer, yet was still only a major in 1918. His inclusion in the postwar Reichswehr seems to have owed more to his administrative than his fighting skills, but once Hitler had come to power in 1933, von Rundstedt's rise was assured.

VICTORY IN POLAND

At best, von Rundstedt was a 'naive' officer, firm in his belief that a soldier's first duty lies in loyalty to his political masters, regardless of the excesses carried out in their name. As early as August 1934, he accepted without question the new oath of allegiance which tied the army to Hitler personally rather than to the state, and 10 years later he seems to have seen nothing morally wrong in presiding over a Court of Honour designed to strip 'disloyal' officers of their ranks and condemn them to the tender mercies of a People's Court.

But there is also truth in Liddell Hart's judgement, for von Rundstedt's military abilities cannot be denied. Despite his background and infantry bias, he was not slow to appreciate the new potential of the tank and during the interwar period supported those officers who developed the early models of Blitzkrieg. When von Rundstedt was appointed in 1939 to take command of Army Group South in the Polish campaign, he proved quite capable of translating the new ideas into strategic victory. Tasked to advance east across the San River, he dispatched

Left: Gerd von Rundstedt (standing, right) with *Reichswehrminister* von Schleicher, during the 1930s.

autumn – but once again, by allowing the panzers to move freely, he succeeded, reaching Rostov by late November. In the process, however, he suffered a heart attack, and, on 1 December, relinquished his command. Three months later, he was appointed Commander-in-Chief West and given responsibility for the defence of France and the Low Countries against an Allied invasion, a post he was to retain until July 1944. During that time he advocated a mobile defence, keeping the bulk of his armour in central France ready to strike at beach-heads wherever they might appear, and it was the failure of this approach in June 1944, when Allied airpower prevented movement towards the Normandy lodgement, that led to his dismissal. By September, however, he had been reappointed, acting as C-in-C West through the Ardennes offensive of December and during the retreat to the Rhine.

Relieved for the last time in March 1945, von Rundstedt was taken prisoner by the Western Allies in May and prepared for trial as a 'war criminal'. His reputation, age and ill-health spared him that humiliation: released in 1949, he died on 24 February 1953 at the end of a militarily brilliant but politically questionable career.

THE ELITE COMMANDERS

Left and above: Von Rundstedt inspects men of the Hitlerjugend Division during the preparations to defend the Atlantic coast against Allied invasion. Below: Von Rundstedt inspects the Leibstandarte Division in Paris, 1943.

elements of his Tenth Army to encircle and destroy Polish forces on the Bzura. It was a major contribution to German success and one that guaranteed von Rundstedt's future employment.

Less than a month later, in October 1939, he was transferred to the west, taking over Army Group A in readiness for the forthcoming invasion of France. Located in the centre of the German line, it was the panzers of Army Group A that pushed out of the Ardennes in May 1940 and swiftly reached the Channel coast, cutting the Anglo-French armies in two. In recognition of this achievement, von Rundstedt was promoted to field marshal on 19 June.

He was then transferred back to the east and, on 22 June 1941, he commanded Army Group South in the invasion of Russia. His task was not easy – he was expected to secure the whole of the Ukraine before

THE ELITE COMMANDERS

Headstrong and ruthless Israeli commander

Born in Palestine in 1928, Ariel 'Arik' Sharon gained early military experience in the Haganah armed forces, taking part in the guerrilla war against the British which paved the way for the creation of the State of Israel. At the outbreak of the War of Independence in 1948, Sharon was a platoon commander in the Alexandroni Brigade of the newly formed Israeli Defence Forces (IDF). In 1953 it was decided to create an elite formation, Unit 101 (which later became 202 Parachute Brigade), to mount retaliatory raids against Palestinian *fedayeen* and Sharon seemed a natural choice to lead the new formation.

On 29 October 1956, it was a para battalion belonging to this brigade that jumped to the east of the Mitla Pass in Sinai, well behind Egyptian lines. By late on the 30th, Sharon had led the rest of the brigade in a ground assault to link up with the paras, leaving the Egyptian defenders split up and confused. But Sharon refused to rest there. Granted permission to send a patrol into the pass, he chose to expand the nature of the operation without consulting his superiors. The results were disastrous. A combat team of armour and half-tracks advanced into an Egyptian ambush and, in a confused and vicious firefight lasting seven hours, 38 Israeli paras died. It was an unnecessary battle and Sharon came in for substantial criticism.

But such independence of action does not seem to have affected his career. By June 1967, as Israel prepared for another war, Sharon was one of three armoured-division commanders poised to re-enter Sinai, reluctantly evacuated under international pressure 10 years earlier. Sharon's specific task was

SHARON

to operate on the left of a three-pronged advance, destroying Egyptian positions around Um Katef, close to the Israeli border. On 5 June, he sent his units foward in a frontal assault, but the going was hard. Um Katef was well defended by artillery, armour and infantry, forcing Sharon to pause and rethink. What followed was arguably his most brilliant battle. Infiltrating armour around the Egyptian flanks, over apparently impassable sand-dunes, he brought in heliborne paras to complete the encirclement. Under cover of darkness, his forces then turned inwards against Um Katef, dealing the defenders a series of blows from which they could not recover. Within 24 hours, he had cleared Um Katef and was sending units west towards the Suez Canal and south towards Sharm el Sheikh.

Once the Six-Day War was over, Sharon's reputation ensured him further promotion, and by the early 1970s he was General Officer Commanding Southern (Sinai) Command. But in July 1973 he left the regular army to enter the Israeli *Knesset* (Parliament), joining with others to form the hard-line *Likud* Party. However, he remained on the reserve, and when the Egyptians and Syrians mounted their surprise attacks across the Suez Canal and onto the Golan Heights respectively on 6 October, he was

Left: Major-General Ariel 'Arik' Sharon, whose sometimes rash decisions have tinged his military career with controversy and criticism.

THE ELITE
COMMANDERS

called upon to command an armoured division rushing to battle in Sinai. When he arrived, he found himself in a bizarre position, being expected to serve under Major-General Shmuel Gonen, his erstwhile deputy in Southern Command.

On 8 October, Gonen ordered a counter-attack against Egyptian bridgeheads on the east bank of the Canal, holding Sharon's division in reserve to act as reinforcement if the main attacking force encountered opposition. At first, all seemed to go well, enabling Sharon to set off to the south for his own counter-attack near the Great Bitter Lake, but almost immediately, the main force fell victim to Sagger anti-tank missile ambushes. Gonen hurriedly recalled Sharon, who faced the difficult task of turning his entire division round on desert roads. His confidence in Gonen evaporated and he began to take an independent line, switching his radios off to avoid contact with his superiors and conducting unplanned raids into Egyptian lines. Gonen immediately requested Sharon's dismissal, but the Israeli Cabinet, aware of his political contacts, refused and they sent General Bar Lev to act as mediator: within 48 hours, he too was requesting Sharon's dismissal.

PEACE FOR GALILEE

The main bone of contention concerned the mounting of an Israeli crossing of the Canal, for neither Gonen nor Bar Lev was prepared to authorise such a move while the bulk of the enemy armour remained intact. When this was committed to battle in Sinai and badly mauled – not least by Sharon – on 14 October, the crossing was given the go-ahead. Elements of Sharon's division – a para brigade backed by armour – pushed through to prepared positions at Deversoir, north of the Great Bitter Lake, while the rest of the division concentrated on creating a corridor along which the bridging equipment could travel. As the paras crossed in rubber boats, a complex battle developed around Chinese Farm on the east bank and it was not until 18 October that Israeli forces could begin to cross in strength.

Sharon returned to politics after the 1973 War, serving in a number of ministerial posts under Menachem Begin. By 1982, he was Minister of Defence and it was in this capacity that he planned and executed Operation Peace for Galilee, Israel's drive into southern Lebanon, in early June. Intent on the destruction of the Palestine Liberation Organisation (PLO), Sharon pushed his forces to the gates of Beirut in an operation which soon proved a political embarrassment, especially when Christian Militia allies of the Israelis massacred Palestinian refugees in the camps at Sabra and Chatila. In the subsequent furore, Sharon was forced to resign, although he did remain in the Cabinet, surviving the crisis – as he had survived so many – to emerge in September 1984 as Minister of Trade and Industry in the new coalition government led by Shimon Peres. As a soldier, Sharon's bravery, resolution and almost uncanny 'feel' for battle cannot be denied, but throughout his career he has been headstrong and rather rash. It is a potent mixture.

Above left: Sharon discusses battlefield strategy with his commanders, at his southern headquarters in Gorodish, during the Yom Kippur war of 1973. Left: Israeli Defence Forces M113 armoured personnel carriers await embarkation.

THE ELITE COMMANDERS

The man who masterminded the Egyptian assault across the Suez Canal

Lieutenant-General Saad Mohamed el-Husseini el-Shazli was the most successful Egyptian commander of modern times, although the political and military environment in which he operated severely limited his eventual achievements.

Shazli was born on 1 April 1922. He first studied agriculture at Cairo University, but in 1939 moved on to military college, passing out as a lieutenant in 1940. It was not until 1948 that Shazli had his first taste of action when, as a platoon commander, he took part in the Arab war against the newly declared state of Israel. The humiliation of the Arab forces must have affected him deeply.

Under the new radical Egyptian regime of President Gamal Abdel Nasser from 1954, Shazli's career flourished. Nasser regarded Shazli as an extremely able officer, and Shazli inevitably shared in most Egyptians' appreciation of Nasser's efforts to restore national pride. From 1956 to 1958, Shazli commanded a parachute battalion, and in 1960 he was sent to the strife-torn Congo as head of Egypt's contingent of the United Nations' intervention force.

After a brief period as defence attaché to Britain Shazli was soon back in action. In 1962, Egyptian troops were sent to the Yemen on the Arabian peninsula to back the Republican side in a civil war. As a brigade commander, Shazli distinguished himself, most notably in the offensive which captured the

Royalist stronghold of Marib. When war with Israel threatened once more in 1967, it was natural that Shazli should be given an important command.

Task Force Shazli, as his armoured group was known in 1967, was stationed on the southern flank of the Sinai front. with the aim of cutting the Israeli line north of Elat. But the subsequent conflict was another disaster for the Egyptians. Shazli found little opportunity to exploit his military skills in the general debacle, although he emerged with his reputation relatively unscathed through his accomplishment of a partially successful withdrawal.

In the aftermath of the 1967 War, Shazli was appointed commander of special forces (rangers and paratroopers), a key post as Egypt attempted to maintain pressure on the Israeli forces in the Sinai through commando raids across the Suez Canal. Then, in 1971, Shazli reached the peak of his military career, being appointed chief of staff of the Egyptian

SHAZLI

Below: Soviet armour on parade in Egypt. As a general, Shazli always enjoyed the benefit of considerable quantities of Soviet war material, but the relationship with the Soviets was often stormy, and President Sadat expelled Soviet advisers from Egypt in the early 1970s. Right: Shazli as a major-general. Rank is denoted by the crossed sabres and eagle worn on the shoulder boards.

THE ELITE COMMANDERS

Below: Troops under Shazli's command in Israeli positions on the east bank of the Suez Canal. The crossing of the Canal and the defeat of the initial Israeli counter-attacks during the Yom Kippur War were the high spots of Shazli's military career. This success was achieved by meticulous planning. Below right: Shazli, now a lieutenant-general (crossed sabres, star and eagle worn on the shoulder boards) addresses a press conference.

armed forces. It was in this capacity that he supervised the planning and preparations for the Egyptian Army's greatest success – the 1973 crossing of the Suez Canal.

Shazli's background of service with commando units undoubtedly helped him achieve the flexibility and imagination which marked out this operation as so different from the general run of Egyptian military efforts. His openess to fresh ideas is clearly shown by the unexpected use of high-pressure hoses to breach the sand obstacles on the east side of the Canal, while his capacity for meticulous attention to detail was revealed in the extensive training of the troops involved and the excellent organisation to cope with logistic problems under any eventuality.

The crossing, on 6 October 1973, was in fact achieved far more easily than Shazli expected. The assault was deliberately launched on the widest front possible so that the Israelis would be uncertain where to deliver their initial counter-attacks. In fact, for the first week the Israeli response was far less strong than expected.

From 13 October onwards, however, the Israelis recovered the initiative. Shazli soon found himself involved in bitter controversy with his political superiors. Making a realistic assessment of the situation, he had opposed the Egyptian Minister of War, General Ahmed Ismail Ali, when, in an excess of optimism, he ordered the Egyptians onto the offensive from their bridgehead – in direct contradiction to Shazli's original plan to seize and then hold a narrow strip along the east bank.

When the Israelis boldly established their own bridgehead on the west bank, it was dismissed by Ismail as of only local significance, but Shazli clearly perceived its true importance. He insisted that substantial armoured forces should recross the Suez to smash the bridgehead, but was overruled by Ismail on the direct orders of Egyptian President Anwar Sadat. Had Shazli's proposal been instituted, much might have been saved, yet in the face of limited opposition, the Israeli bridgehead assumed increasing importance. Instead, the Egyptian 25th Armoured Brigade was ordered to strangle the Israeli corridor in a pincer movement with the 21st Armoured Division. Shazli noted that the 25th would probably be wiped out if the plan went ahead. It was.

On 18 October the Israeli forces broke out of their bridgehead, and Sadat was forced to seek a ceasefire. For Shazli, the reversal was a personal disaster. He had done his best, but the strain was too much. He collapsed from exhaustion and was relieved of his post. Shazli's outspoken condemnation of Sadat's handling of the war led to his effective exile from the military field. After a number of diplomatic postings, he withdrew into opposition in exile.

THE ELITE COMMANDERS

SLIM

The victor in Burma

William Joseph Slim (1891-1970) – universally and affectionately known as 'Bill' – was one of the great British generals of World War II. Although he served in neither Europe nor the Western Desert, his unique combination of strategic insight, tactical flair and personal charisma was put to good use in Burma, where he not only helped to save an army in 1942 but also contributed to its recovery and led it to victory three years later.

Slim was born in Bristol on 6 August 1891 and grew up in Birmingham, where he was among the first to volunteer for the army at the outbreak of World War I in 1914. Commissioned into the 9th (Service) Battalion, Royal Warwickshire Regiment, he saw action at Gallipoli in 1915, receiving the first of a number of wounds as well as an insight into the chaos of a badly organised campaign.

Transferring to the 6th Gurkha Rifles as a regular officer in 1918, Slim spent the interwar years learning his profession, attending the Staff College at Quetta before serving for a time as an instructor in its British equivalent at Camberley. By then it was obvious that he was an extremely able officer, destined for high command. At the outbreak of war in 1939 he was given command of the 10th Indian Infantry Brigade, which he prepared for active service before leading it in the defence of Sudan against Italian attack in 1940. Subsequent service in Eritrea, Iraq and Syria confirmed Slim's abilities as a commander.

This was just as well, for in March 1942 he was pitched into the chaos of Burma, where the British Empire forces were reeling under Japanese attack. Appointed to command 17th Indian and 1st Burma Divisions (together known as 'Burcorps'), Slim faced enormous problems: the troops were demoralised by the recent Japanese seizure of Rangoon, the

Page 146 above: William Joseph Slim at the flag-raising ceremony after the recapture of Fort Dufferin in Burma, March 1945. Slim's reconquest of Burma after the defeat of the Japanese offensive of 1944 was his crowning achievement. Page 146 below: Men and machines of the 62nd Armoured Brigade under Slim's command move forward towards Meiktila. Above: Slim (second from left), with one of his most famous subordinates, Chindit leader Orde Wingate (third from left).

terrain was inhospitable, the enemy seemingly invincible and the command chain confused. Nevertheless, he quickly imposed his authority, sharing the hardships of his men and doing all he could to improve their conditions and fighting skills. When Burcorps was ordered to pull back to the Indian border in April, he conducted a dangerous and lengthy withdrawal, most of it in close contact with the enemy, covering nearly 1600km across rivers, through jungles and along tracks which threatened to become impassable in the imminent monsoon.

It was to be another two years before the British could mount a successful counter-offensive, but Slim did not stand idle. Transferred to command XV Corps in eastern India, he devoted his energies to an analysis of the recent defeat, and his conclusions, stressing the importance of improved morale, guaranteed supplies and tactical flexibility, acted as a firm base for future action. In March 1943 he was sent into the Arakan to extricate IV Corps from a failed offensive and seven months later he took over the newly-named Fourteenth Army, responsible for the defence (and subsequent reconquest) of Burma. It was a daunting task, but one for which Slim was ideally suited. Concentrating on the welfare of his

men, he cut down disease, ensured an adequate supply chain and slowly built up his army to withstand an expected Japanese assault on Imphal.

When that materialised in early 1944, Slim displayed his genius for battle, refusing to be drawn by a feint attack in the Arakan and inspiring his troops to stand firm as both Imphal and Kohima were besieged. Resupplying the embattled garrisons by air, he ensured that the Japanese were contained and, when they finally began to retreat he gave them no opportunity to recover.

His greatest success came in February 1945 when, realising that the Japanese were drawing him into a potential trap, he outflanked their positions on the Irrawaddy River, taking the town of Meiktila and forcing them to withdraw. The subsequent British advance through central Burma, in which Slim used armour and mechanised formations in extremely difficult terrain, was a masterpiece of military skill, rewarded by the recapture of Rangoon in early May.

Slim's postwar career, as commander-in-chief Southeast Asia (1945-46), chief of the imperial general staff (1948-52) and governor-general of Australia (1952-60) merely confirmed his brilliance, showing that he was as much at home in the corridors of power as on the battlefield. Created a viscount in 1960, he died ten years later.

THE ELITE COMMANDERS
SPINOLA

Energetic commander and astute politician

Antonio Sebastião Ribeiro de Spinola was born at Estremoz, east of Lisbon, on 11 April 1910. The son of a leading civil servant of Genoese descent, Spinola was commissioned into the Portuguese cavalry in 1933. An excellent horseman, he was later to command the 2nd Lancers and made his reputation as a dashing cavalry commander while leading the 345th Cavalry Group in action against nationalist guerrillas in Angola from 1961 to 1964. However, this was not his first taste of active service since he had commanded Portuguese volunteers fighting for Franco in the latter stages of the Spanish Civil War in 1938 and had been an official observer of the German Army's operations on the Eastern Front in November 1941. On his return from Angola, promotion to Colonel having come to him in 1963, Spinola was successively Provost Marshal, Inspector of Cavalry and Deputy Commander of the prestigious National Republican Guard. He became a Brigadier in 1966.

In May 1968 he was sent, against his wishes, to command the forces in Portuguese Guinea as Gov-

Left: General Antonio Spinola, after a relatively successful 'hearts and minds' campaign in Guinea, became critical of Portugal's role in Africa. Below: Ex-Angolan guerrillas train under the watchful eye of a Portuguese instructor.

ernor-General and Commander-in-Chief. Believing the war to be unwinnable, he agreed to serve there for six months and to report on the situation inherited from his predecessor, Arnaldo Schultz. By the time he returned to Portugal in November 1968, Salazar had suffered a stroke and the new premier, Marcello Caetano, was prepared to give Spinola full powers to implement the radical new policies which Spinola believed necessary to win time for a political solution to the war against the nationalists in the African colonies. His arrival in the tiny colony of less than 14,000 square miles was to transform the Portuguese effort and turn what had appeared near defeat into virtual stalemate. The success Spinola achieved was

Left: General Spinola was dismissed by the Portuguese government in March 1974, but this acted as a catalyst for an army coup. Spinola was installed as head of the new government, but was forced to resign six months later by the more radical MFA elements.

all the more significant in that the principal guerrilla group in Portuguese Guinea, Partido Africano da Independência de Guiné e Cabo Verde (PAIGC), was by far the most effective opponent faced by the Portuguese in Africa, under the sophisticated leadership of Amilcar Cabral.

When Spinola arrived in Portuguese Guinea, the Portuguese forces were largely on the defensive and suffering problems of morale. Displaying an energy exhausting for men on his staff far younger than he was, Spinola was everywhere in conducting almost daily visits to his troops or the African settlements. Such visitations were unheralded in advance and Spinola ruthlessly weeded out incompetence. His impact upon the morale of troops was immense.

'SOCIAL COUNTER-REVOLUTION'

Above all, Spinola understood that insurgency was as much a political struggle as a military struggle and, in many respects, it could be said that he 'systematically stole' many of Cabral's ideals in what Spinola himself referred to as a 'social counter-revolution' to win the hearts and minds of the Africans. The resettlement programme begun by Schultz was extended to embrace 150,000 natives while, under the slogan of *Guiné Melhor,* Spinola's troops built houses, schools, hospitals and water points. Efforts were made to improve native crops and herds and to combat diseases such as cholera, yellow fever and leprosy. Spinola was to claim that he was winning back 3000 refugees a year from the neighbouring states of Guinea and Senegal while some 50 per cent of the 30,000 Portuguese troops in Portuguese Guinea were actually black, including units formed from guerrillas who had surrendered and the elite *Commandos Africanos.*

Spinola returned to Portugal in August 1973 as a national hero. He had been promoted general in 1969 and now received the highest Portuguese decoration of the Tower and Swords with Palms. However, he declined posts offered to him until appointed Deputy Chief of Staff with the rank of four star general in January 1974. But his belief in a social counter-revolution in the colonies had led him to advocate fundamental reforms in the structure of metropolitan Portugal itself. His views, which included a federal solution to the relationship with the African colonies, were expressed in the publication of *Portugal and the Future* on 22 February 1974. As a result he was dismissed on 14 March, an occurrence that played no small part in the overthrow of the Caetano regime by the Armed Forces Movement (MFA) on 25 April 1974.

Spinola was named as head of the new Junta of National Salvation and became President of Portugal on 15 May 1974. Yet, although both ambitious and no supporter of the old regime, Spinola's revolutionary credentials were regarded with suspicion by the more radical elements in the MFA. Faced with increasing rivalry among left and right wing factions, Spinola resigned the presidency on 30 September 1974 and was then retired by the new leadership in November. Implicated in an attempted coup against the radicals, he fled to Spain on 11 March 1975 and thence to Brazil. He has returned only briefly to Portugal since, despite being restored to the rank of general in 1978 and created a Marshal in 1981.

THE ELITE COMMANDERS

Raymond Ames Spruance (1886-1969) was commissioned into the US Navy in 1906. During World War II he was one of the most successful naval commanders in the Pacific, and is widely regarded as one of the greatest admirals of the 20th Century.

Following commission as a midshipman, Spruance spent a year in the North Atlantic aboard the USS *Iowa* before joining the USS *Minnesota* (1907-09). He was promoted ensign in 1908, and between 1909 and 1910 was instructed in electrical engineering. After service in World War I he became head of the Electrical Division at the Bureau of Engineering. From 1927 to 1937 he enjoyed three tours at the Naval War College (as well as one tour at the Office of Naval Intelligence) and was recognised as an able strategist. By 1939 he was a rear-admiral commanding the Tenth Naval District and in 1941 took over Cruiser Division Five, based at Pearl Harbor.

Spruance was still in this command when the Japanese offensive that led to the Battle of Midway opened in June 1942. Vice Admiral Fletcher, commanding the US naval forces (which, essentially, consisted of three aircraft carriers and their protective screen) was forced to relinquish command when his flagship, the USS *Yorktown*, was disabled; Spruance took over effective control of the US vessels for the major part of the battle. Although he had little experience of carrier warfare, Spruance led the Americans to a decisive victory in which the complex Japanese scheme to lure the US fleet into a trap was undermined by the success of the US carrier-borne aircraft strikes. All four of the aircraft carriers deployed by the Japanese Admiral Yamamoto were sunk.

Spruance was the first to admit that luck played a major part in the success of the US air strikes at Midway, but he had, nevertheless, shown an operational flair that was most impressive. He was awarded the Distinguished Service Medal, and Admiral Nimitz, commander of the Pacific Fleet, made him his chief of staff.

SPRUANCE

Above: Raymond Ames Spruance, considered by many to have been the best US naval commander of World War II. Below: Rocket bombardment of Japanese defences on Okinawa. The invasion of Okinawa was Spruance's last major engagement.

Spruance was noted for his calm ability to weigh up situations, allied to a natural aggressive instinct (a 'cold-blooded fighting fool' was the assessment of one of his contemporaries), and this combination stood him in good stead during his next post, head of the US naval forces in the Central Pacific. His Fifth Fleet attacked and took the Gilbert Islands in November 1943, despite heavy US casualties among the troops sent ashore.

After the Gilberts, Spruance's next target was the Marshall Islands. US naval forces were now operating thousands of miles from their major base at Pearl Habor, and the planning of these operations was very complicated because of the logistics difficulties. Spruance, however, mastered all the intricacies of this long-range offensive warfare. He used Marc Mitscher's fast carrier forces as a roving destructive weapon, destroying the Marshalls as a Japanese stronghold in January 1944.

THE PHILIPPINE SEA

In June 1944, the Marianas were the target for further US landings; Spruance hoped to lure the Japanese fleet into an action that would destroy it once and for all, but in the event could only engage it with carrier-borne planes. Although there was some criticism of Spruance for not having engaged in full-blooded pursuit of the Japanese with all his forces as soon as he knew their fleet was in the area, he was well aware of his enemy's willingness to sacrifice large forces to draw US elements into a trap; and his first priority was to safeguard the transports taking the troops to their targets of Saipan, Tinian and Guam. In any case, the result of this battle of the Philippine Sea was the virtual destruction of Japanese naval aviation.

In accordance with Nimitz's decision to split responsibility for US Central Pacific forces between two sets of staff (because of the enormous problems of planning these large-scale operations), Spruance was based in Pearl Harbor from August 1944 until February 1945. He then took over the naval forces that landed troops on Iwo Jima and Okinawa; the

THE ELITE COMMANDERS

Below right: The 'cold-blooded fighting fool', as Spruance was once described, on the deck of one of his carriers. Spruance had a naturally aggressive approach to naval warfare which was tempered only by a meticulous attention to detail and a refusal to take unnecessary risks. Below, main picture: Units of the US Pacific Fleet lie at anchor, with the carriers surrounded by a screen of escort vessels.

latter operation involved co-ordinating over 1200 vessels and 500,000 men. His flagship, the USS *Indianapolis*, was hit by a kamikaze plane, and he moved his flag to the USS *New Mexico*.

Spruance was preparing plans for the invasion of the Japanese mainland when the war ended. He relinquished command of the Fifth Fleet in November 1945, but almost immediately succeeded Nimitz as Commander-in-Chief US Pacific Fleet. He held this post until the following year. In February 1946, Spruance left active service and took up the post of president of the Naval War College. With him he took his Naval DSM (with two gold stars) and Army DSM and the Navy Cross, as well as a British Honour in the form of Honorary Companion of the order of the Bath.

THE ELITE COMMANDERS
STUDENT

The first great general of airborne forces

So far as the elite forces of the modern world are concerned, Kurt Student (1891-1978) has a special claim to fame. For he formed the first German paratroop battalions in the German Wehrmacht in 1938 and was the commander of the forces that carried out the successful airborne attacks of 1940, alerting the military establishments of the rest of the world to the fact that a new elite warrior – the paratrooper – had arrived.

As the 7th Airborne Division, Student's men were ready to go into action in Poland in 1939, but there was no need to use these new forces in the lightning victory won by the Germans. In western Europe, during the campaign of 1940, however, things were different, and paratroopers and airborne troops from Student's command carried out effective raids, taking strongpoints by surprise and securing essential communications centres. The most notorious were in Belgium, where the supposedly impregnable fortress of Eban Emael was captured by glider-borne forces that landed on the fort itself, but just as important was the taking of the bridges over the Maas estuary in Holland, and the establishment of units on the airfields at Rotterdam and Waalhaven.

Student himself had been wounded (unluckily, by a German bullet) during the fighting in Rotterdam, and was unable to, play a further part in the European campaign. His next important operation was at Crete in 1941, when in command of XI Air Corps, he planned the assault on the British and Commonwealth troops holding the island. Crete, however, was an expensive victory for the Germans, who lost 6500 casualties, and the future of such airborne operations was now in doubt. Hitler decided to cancel a proposed airborne invasion of Malta in 1942.

German airborne forces were never in a position to be used in large-scale offensive operations again, but Student's grandiosely named 1st Parachute Army desperately plugged the gaps in the German lines in the Low Countries in 1944, and was an important element in the German forces that successfully held the Allied offensive during Operation Market Garden. From November 1944 to February 1945 he led Army Group 'H' that held the German front from Roermond to the coast and his forces were to follow up any breakthrough achieved by the German Ardennes offensive of December 1944.

Student was an enthusiastic and dynamic leader, either in defence or attack, and the quality of the paratroop units of the German Army of World War II (who also proved their value as more orthodox ground troops in many actions, notably during the defence of Cassino in 1944) owed much to his example and energy. He was a visionary, who had an eye for the novel manoeuvre, and he combined this

Right: Student inspects German paratroops in May 1944, shortly before the Allied invasion of northwest Europe. Student had the confidence of his men; they realised his gifts as a commander of airborne forces, and his record in the early years of the war spoke for itself. Below: On manoeuvres, Student inspects the situation through binoculars. Whether in training or involved in actual operations, Student's calm, thoughtful manner was always impressive, although he spoke so slowly that Hitler, when he first met Student, believed that he must be a very stupid man. This early impression was soon reversed, however, and Hitler, always eager to take up new ideas, became one of Student's great admirers.

freshness of attitude with a personal manner that was calm and seemingly unflustered. Particularly impressive was his reworking of the original plans after the early losses during the invasion of Crete in 1941. In addition, Student had an attribute that was very useful in the German Wehrmacht of World War II: he was on good terms with Göring and Hitler.

Critics of Student, who include some of those who served under him, have complained that although he had a genius for grand concepts, he was less effective on the details of planning operations, and was, for example, vague on the provision of supplies during the build up to the Ardennes offensive. Nevertheless, he was the commander who first showed that airborne forces, now taken for granted but in 1940 a terrifying new weapon, could be decisive on the modern battlefield, and demonstrated that the speed and dash of such small, well trained units could have devastating effects.

THE ELITE COMMANDERS
TAL

Exponent of Israeli armoured warfare

Israel Tal was one of the most influential commanders in the Israeli Army during the 1960s and 1970s. As head of the Armoured Corps, he significantly improved its fighting abilities and during the Six-Day War of 1967 he played a leading role in the defeat of the Egyptian forces in the Sinai peninsula. He also guided the development of the Merkava main battle tank during the 1970s and its design embodies his ideas about armoured warfare.

Tal was born at Machanaim (now Zefat) on 13 September 1924, in what was then the British Mandate of Palestine. At the age of 18, in 1942, he joined the British Army and served with the Jewish Brigade. He saw active service in Italy in 1945. He left the brigade in 1946, returning to Palestine, where agitation for an independent Jewish state was at its height.

Tal then joined the Zionist military organisation Haganah (Defence). His experience was put to use in training the units that were to spearhead the Israeli forces during the 1948 War of Independence; and during this conflict, Tal served with the 'Oded' Brigade in the northwest of Israel, fighting against the Syrians.

After the end of this war, Tal remained in the new Israeli Defence Forces (IDF). In 1951 he took up the post of commanding officer of the Infantry Training School and moved on in 1952 to become Head of the Training Branch Headquarters. He continued to be associated with the infantry in the 1956 Sinai campaign, when he commanded an infantry brigade during the battle of Abu Aweigila. During this battle the main concentration of Egyptian forces was eliminated, but at the cost of high casualties. A prime reason for the number of casualties was poor preparation in both planning and equipment – something that influenced Tal's approach to warfare and made him determined to impose meticulous staff planning.

After 1956, Tal began his association with the Israeli Armoured Corps. First he took command of an armoured brigade and then served as Deputy Commander, Armoured Corps, under General David Elazar. During his time in this position, he was responsible for the formation of a committee, under Colonel Avraham Adan, to examine Israeli tank tactical doctrine, especially in the light of the adoption of Soviet-style tactics by the Arab armies, in the wake of the 1956 campaign. This committee came to the conclusion that massive frontal tank assaults should now replace the previous Israeli reliance on the indirect approach that had emphasised mobility on the part of the tanks and supporting infantry.

As a result of this, Tal began to support the acquisition of Centurion tanks by the IDF, in preference to the lighter armoured vehicles such as the AMX-13. The thick armour of the Centurion compensated for its lack of mobility by improving its ability to withstand enemy fire. This tank proved temperamental at first, but Tal believed that its problems could be overcome. When he took charge of the Armoured Corps in 1964, he implemented a programme to counteract what he regarded as the inefficiencies that were responsible for poor tank performance.

Tal's Armoured Corps received its first test in battle in the Six-Day War of 1967. The IDF attacked its Arab neighbours in anticipation of a suspected Arab assault. Tal himself was given command of a division on the Sinai front, with the task of clearing Egyptian forces from the Mediterranean coast as far as the Suez Canal. His first job was to drive the Egyptians from heavily fortified positions around

Rafah and El Arish. Careful planning enabled Tal's forces to avoid defensive minefields and to launch massed tank assaults. After hard fighting in the Rafah-El Arish area, Tal's men drove to the Suez Canal, overcoming all Egyptian resistance en route as part of a crushing Israeli victory.

Tal moved from command of the Armoured Corps to a position in the Ministry of Defence in 1969. Here he began to work on a scheme to build an Israeli-

THE ELITE
COMMANDERS

Above: General Israel Tal whose ideas on armoured warfare revolutionised the IDF's tactical approach, shifting the emphasis from conventional infantry-armour combat teams to all-tank formations. Previous page. Tal commanding the Armoured Corps at Rafah during the Six-Day war of 1967. Below: A Merkava main battle tank is put through its paces during manoeuvres on the Golan Heights. Tal nursed through the development of the Merkava which, with its low profile (making it a difficult target) and forward situated engine, provided its crews with extra protection.

designed tank. He remained at the Defence Ministry until his old commander in the Armoured Corps, General Elazar, became Chief of Staff of the IDF. In 1973, Tal moved to the position of Deputy Chief of Staff. At this time, Egypt and Syria were preparing for a new attack to recover the losses of the Six-Day War.

Tal's role in the Yom Kippur War of October 1973 has become wreathed in controversy. As Deputy Chief of Staff he opposed an attack across the Suez Canal, and preferred to see operations restricted to driving the Egyptians back out of Sinai. His opinions were overruled, however, and the Israeli forces fought their way across the Canal in the later stages of the war. Tal took command of the southern part of the Suez Canal front on 7 November, 15 days after the imposition of a United Nations' ceasefire. Despite this ceasefire, artillery skirmishes between Israeli and Egyptian forces continued. Tal ordered these exchanges to cease, claiming that the ordinary soldier was fearful that his 'trigger-happy' commanders would provoke a renewal of the fighting. Tal also had other disagreements with the Defence Minister, Moshe Dayan, and General Elazar over the disposition of his forces. His generally cautious conduct resulted in his replacement in December 1973, although he continued in the post of Deputy Chief of Staff. His behaviour at this time was far from the aggressive image he had gained during the Six-Day War. It is possible that his experience of rushed offensives during the Battle of Abu Aweigila, in 1956, made him wary of any operation that had not received the sort of careful planning which marked the Israeli offensive of the Six-Day War.

Tal returned to the Ministry of Defence in 1975 and brought his 'Merkava' project to fruition. The tank incorporates a number of unusual features in its design: unlike most tanks the engine is placed in the front of the vehicle, providing the crew with a considerable improvement in protection; the low height of the Merkava makes it a difficult target to spot, and spaced armour is used to counteract the effects of high-explosive squash-head anti-tank rounds. The tank is armed with a 105mm L7 gun and a comparatively large number of rounds can be carried. The emphasis on protection has left the Merkava somewhat underpowered, with a top speed of only 46km/h. It entered service with the IDF in 1979.

Tal retired from the IDF with the rank of major-general and took up a position with Tel Aviv University's Strategic Research Centre. Although a somewhat controversial figure, his military career was a success; and, no doubt, his soldiers greatly appreciated his concern for their lives.

TEDDER

Strategic Warfare Expert

Arthur William Tedder was born at Glenguin, Scotland, on July 11 1890. After graduating from Magdelene College, Cambridge, Tedder joined the Colonial Service and took up his first appointment – a cadetship to the administration in Fiji. Within a few months of his arrival, World War I erupted and Tedder applied for permission to return home and join up. His application was refused. Tedder resigned from the Colonial service and signed up for a commission in the Royal Flying Corps (RFC).

Following training, Tedder was posted to No. 25 Squadron in France in June 1916, and carried out bombing and photo-reconnaissance missions. In early 1917 he was given command of No. 70 Fighter Squadron. This was followed by a period with a training unit in England before a posting to Egypt in 1918. He was mentioned in despatches three times during the war.

In 1919, Tedder was commissoned into the newly formed Royal Air Force (RAF) as a squadron leader. He was particularly interested in the theory of air war and spent the early post-war years at the Air Ministry and the Imperial Defence College. In 1929 he took up a post at the RAF Staff College as an instructor and assistant commandant, and in 1931 left the Staff College as a group captain to take up command of the Air Armament School at Eastchurch. In 1934 he was posted to the Air Ministry as Director of training. Tedder spent two years in this post before accepting a nomination as Air Officer Commanding, Far East, which took him to Singapore. When he left that post in 1938 he had been promoted Air Vice-Marshal.

That year Tedder returned to the Air Ministry as Director-General of Research and Development, preparing for the imminent war – in particular he pushed for the rapid development of monoplane fighter aircraft.

When war finally broke out, Tedder joined the

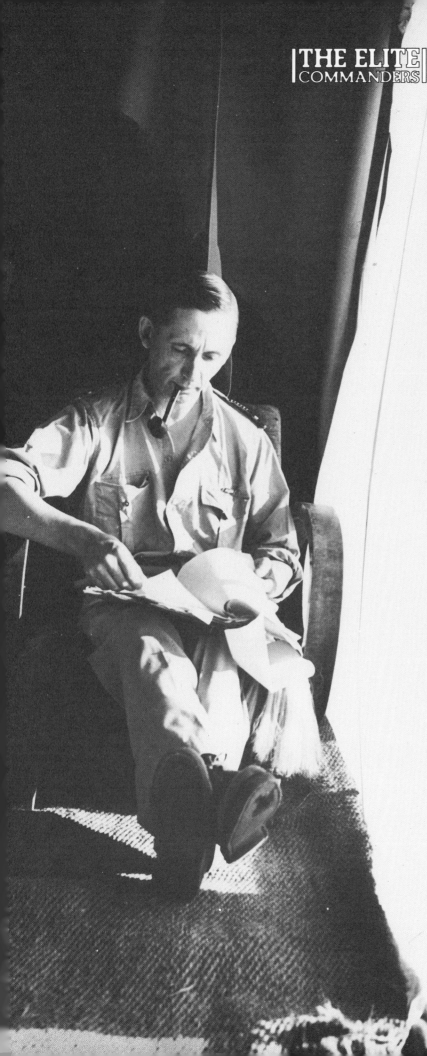

Ministry of Aircraft Production as a deputy member of the Air Staff for Development and Production. In late 1940, Tedder was appointed deputy commander of air forces in the Middle East and, in June 1941, succeeded Air Marshal Sir Arthur Longmore as Air Officer Commander-in-Chief. Churchill was unhappy with this appointment, so much so that Viscount Portal, the Chief of Air Staff, was forced to threaten resignation to prevent the recall of Tedder.

THE 'TEDDER CARPET'

As A.O.C-in-C in the Middle East, Tedder took on the task of revitalising a diminished air force, in the absence of reinforcements by sea and in the face of a strong Luftwaffe contingent based in Libya. By concentrating attacks on supply lines and airfields in North Africa, Tedder sought primarily to gain air superiority and, thence, more effectively support Montgomery's Eighth Army offensive at El Alamein. Tedder's system of pattern bombing and close co-operation with land forces proved a great success in clearing a path for the advance to Tunisia, and the sweeping bombing raids on enemy tank defences became renowned as the 'Tedder Carpet'.

In February 1943, Tedder was made Commander-in-Chief of Mediterranean Air Command, a position directly under Eisenhower. As C-in-C, Tedder was responsible for all Allied air operations in the Mediterranean theatre. As an Allied commander, Tedder excelled; by closely integrating air, land and sea forces, he was better able to maintain strong central control of air power. When the Axis forces surrendered in May 1943, Tedder finally gained Churchill's admiration, not only for his obvious military skills, but for the tact and diplomacy with which he had handled Anglo-American co-operation.

The success of his partnership with Eisenhower led to his appointment as Deputy Supreme Commander of the Allied Expeditionary Force. In this role he was responsible for the planning of the bombing of communications in preparation for the invasion of northwest Europe, and also for Allied air operations in western Europe. Tedder's strategy, advocating the bombing of French and Belgian rail links (called 'The Tedder Plan'), was to prove an invaluable contribution to the Allied invasion.

On 9 May 1945 Tedder signed the instrument of surrender on Eisenhower's behalf, and the war was over. In September 1945 he was appointed Marshal of the Royal Air Force and on 1 January 1946, as well as being promoted Chief of Air Staff, Tedder was created First Baron Tedder. He was later to take his seat as chairman of the Combined Chiefs of Staff Committee. Tedder's four year tour as Chief of Air Staff ended in 1949, but, in 1950, he was persuaded to represent Britain in Washington as chairman of the British Joint Services Mission and as UK member of the North Atlantic Treaty Alliance. After his retirement from active service, Tedder held many important civilian positions until his death on 3 June 1967.

Tedder's style of command was notable for its low profile, combining intelligent perception with gentle persuasion, and his skill in strategic warfare led Eisenhower to call him 'one of the few great military leaders of our time'.

Left: A.O. C-in-C Middle East Tedder mulls over plans at his HQ. His appointment was not popular with Churchill and it was not untill Tedder excelled in his next post A.O. C-in-C Mediterranean (page 156, below), that he won Churchill's approval. Page 156, above: The Tedder Plan in action, destroying French and German lines of communication in preparation for the Allied invasion of Europe.

THE ELITE COMMANDERS
TEMPLER

The man who smashed the terrorists in Malaya

The question of how to contain and defeat a determined guerrilla army has been one of the biggest problems facing the armed forces of the major powers since 1945. There have been few commanders of conventional forces who can justifiably claim victory in their attempts to suppress an insurgency, but among the ranks of this select few, pride of place goes to Field-Marshal Sir Gerald Templer (1898-1979) who, during his two-and-a-half year tour as Director of Operations in Malaya, mounted a campaign of unparalleled success.

Templer was commissioned into the Royal Irish Fusiliers in 1916. In World War II he held divisional command, and in 1945-46 was the Director of Military Government in the area of Germany controlled by the Anglo-Canadian 21st Army Group. From 1946 to 1948 he was Director of Military Intelligence at the War Office and then held the post of Vice-Chief of the Imperial General Staff until 1950.

In 1950, Templer was appointed as Commander-in-Chief, Eastern Command, a job which took him into one of the world's worst trouble spots. In Malaya communist insurgents had been achieving considerable success against the British-run administration and little headway had been made in stemming guerrilla influence. Templer was sent to Malaya in February 1952 as the new Director of Operations and High Commissioner.

Taking complete control of the campaign against the guerrillas, he immediately realised that the policy adopted by his predecessor, Sir Harold Briggs, which involved keeping a tight rein on the Chinese population among whom the guerrillas found most of their support, and effectively integrating the operations of the civil government, the police and the army, was the best approach to defeating the rebels. Although he had not devised this strategy, he applied the utmost energy to its execution.

Malaya had been divided into a number of administrative districts for the purposes of co-ordinating the elements of an effective counter-insurgency campaign. Under Templer, each district was controlled by a committee consisting of the District Officer, the Officer Commanding the Police District, and the Commanding Officer of the army battalion assigned to that area. As Director of Operations, Templer ensured that military action always remained subordinate to political considerations.

Templer channelled his considerable talents into turning the whole security apparatus into a responsive, flexible and adaptable instrument that could take on the guerrillas at every level. From large-scale military operations to carefully orchestrated propaganda campaigns within the Chinese sectors of the community, his counter-insurgency techniques pushed the terrorists back into the jungle where they could be tracked down and destroyed. By the time he retired from Malaya in June 1954, Templer had, in effect, broken the back of the rebellion, and although mopping up continued for another six years, any threat of a communist takeover had evaporated under his inspired leadership.

Templer went on to become Chief of the Imperial General Staff, from 1955 to 1958; but the pinnacle of his military career will always be seen as the years of success he enjoyed in Malaya.

Left: Templer on a tour of inspection in Malaya.

THE ELITE COMMANDERS

Partisan leader and Yugoslav ruler

Josip Broz, alias 'Tito', was born in 1892 near Zagreb in Croatia, which at that time was part of the Austro-Hungarian Empire. Tito was the seventh child in a

Left: General Josip Broz, alias 'Tito', (pictured here in 1943) was head of the Yugoslav Communist Party from 1937 until his death in 1980. Below: Tito's Partisans in action against the Axis forces of occupation.

family of 15. In 1907 he left home to become a metal worker in a nearby town. Tito's political ideas began to form at this stage – he became an active trade unionist, and was influenced by Marxist ideology.

Tito's first taste of military life came during the 1914-18 War. As a Feldwebel (sergeant) in the Austrian Army, he served on the Carpathian Front and was badly wounded and captured by the Russians in March 1915. Until 1917, Tito was a prisoner of war, but after the Russian Revolution he was released and became a Red Guard. After fighting in the Russian Civil War, he returned in 1920 to the newly created independent kingdom of Yugoslavia. He threw himself into the work of the Yugoslav Communist Party (CPY), and, from then until 1941, his influence grew steadily. During the Spanish Civil War he organised Yugoslav volunteers for the International Brigade, fighting for the Republicans, and in 1937 became head of the Secretary-General of the CPY.

Yugoslavia attempted to stay neutral when World War II broke out, but in 1941 Axis forces invaded and conquered the country in 10 days. Tito rose to the occasion, convinced that the struggle against the occupying German, Italian and Bulgarian troops also presented the opportunity to lead a communist revolution. Adopting the pseudonym of 'Tito' for the first time, he began to organise a network of resistance fighters, which he called 'Partisans' in a deliberate attempt to recall the spirit of the Spanish and Russian guerrillas that fought against Napoleon. By July 1941, Tito's men were carrying out acts of sabotage, and by the autumn he was able to launch a full-scale offensive which drove the Germans out

TITO

most of Serbia. Tito's Partisans seized control of two-thirds of the countryside and several towns including Uzice.

Tito's enemies included the Chetniks, a rival group of guerrillas led by Draza Milhajlovic, a fanatically anti-communist Serbian nationalist. Attempts at co-operation between the two groups collapsed in late 1941 and both sides struggled for the control of Uzice. Tito was victorious, but the Nazis were able to take advantage of the civil war to recapture most of Serbia.

OUTNUMBERED PARTISANS DEFEAT THE GERMANS

The Axis forces launched seven major offensives against Tito, who brilliantly utilised the rugged terrain of Yugoslavia to wage a savage guerrilla campaign. In the summer of 1942, Tito withdrew the bulk of his forces to Croatia, where the enemy was less concentrated. This gave the Partisans a vital breathing space, and by November Tito was able to boast of having three full divisions of three brigades each in Bosnia, Croatia and Dalmatia.

The Germans came closest to crushing Tito in their offensives of May-June 1943. Outnumbered six-to-one, Tito was almost surrounded on the mountain of Durmitor in Montenegro. However, in a classic guerrilla move, he fought his way out of the enemy encirclement. In spite of losing a quarter of his men, and half his equipment, Tito had again survived.

Two factors aided Tito's recovery. Firstly, discovering that the Chetniks were actively collaborating with the Nazis, the Allies began supplying Tito instead of Milhajlovic, and Tito was recognised as

Below right: President Tito of Yugoslavia, pictured in June 1978, shortly after his 86th birthday. Below: Tito recognised that the Partisans' strength lay in dispersing their forces to fight the Germans on a countrywide basis. Although he later formed more regular bodies of troops (below), to recapture territory, he never lost sight of his original guerrilla strategy.

the true leader of the Yugoslav people. He went to visit Stalin in Moscow, and Churchill in Italy. Secondly, the Italian withdrawal from the war in September 1943 enabled Tito to re-occupy Italian-held territory and to acquire a vast quantity of Italian arms. By early 1944 Tito had an army of half-a-million men. Aided by Allied air support from Italy, and the advancing Red Army, he re-entered the Yugoslav capital Belgrade in October 1944. By May 1945, Tito's men had reached Trieste on the Adriatic, where they met up with units of the British Eighth Army.

Tito was an outstanding leader. He played down the revolutionary aspect of the Partisans, appealing instead to patriotism and nationalism. This attitude underlay Tito's postwar policies as ruler of commun-

ist Yugoslavia. His strongly independent stance towards the Soviet Union reflected his unwillingness to become a docile Soviet 'client'. He broke with Stalin in 1949, and Yugoslavia has remained communist, but non-aligned, ever since.

Tito ruled Yugoslavia until his death in 1980. The supreme accolade to his qualities as a general lies in the fact that, of all the countries to be defeated and occupied by the Nazis, only Yugoslavia freed herself.

Formidable general and tough frontline commander

Walton Harris Walker was born on 3 December 1889 in Belton, Texas, USA. He began his military life attending the Wedemyer Military Academy. From here he went on to the Virginia Military Institute and in 1908 he moved on to the United States Military Academy at West Point.

He was commissioned from West Point as a second lieutenant in 1912 and took up his first posting with the 19th Infantry. His regiment had various US postings until, in 1916, they took up border patrols at Del Rio; Walker was promoted first lieutenant on 1 July 1916.

Promotion to captain followed in May 1917 and Walker took command of the 2nd Battalion, 57th Infantry. After this, he became a company commander with the 13th Machine Gun Battalion and went with them to France in April 1918. In June 1918, Walker received a further promotion to the rank of major (acting). He saw action at St Mihiel and Meuse-Argonne, received two citations for gallantry and won the Silver Star.

In April 1941, as acting colonel, Walker took command of the 36th Infantry at Polk, Louisiana. In June of the same year, he was promoted acting brigadier and given command of the 3rd Armoured Brigade at the same location. On 16 February, shortly after the US entry into World War II, he was promoted major-general (acting) and became commanding general of IV Armoured Corps. In October of the same year, Walker took over the administration of the Desert Training Centre. He had one final home posting before going overseas, in command of XX Corps, to joint Patton's Third Army in Europe.

XX Corps played an important part in the drive out of Normandy in 1944, and had reached the Moselle by November 1944. In February 1945, the push continued, with Walker's men crossing the Rhine

WALKER

and taking Kassel. His units also liberated Buchenwald before passing Chemnitz and driving south across the Danube to Austria. It was here that Walker was promoted to lieutenant-general by Patton himself, although again this was an acting rank. Along the way, Walker had also collected a Distinguished Service Cross and a second Oak Leaf Cluster to go with his World War 1 Silver Star.

Walker returned home in June 1945 to command the Eighth Service Command, until he moved on in June 1946 to command the Fifth Army Area. On 1 August 1947 he was promoted full major-general and in this rank he took over as Commanding General, Far East Command's Eighth Army. As such, Walker instituted a heavy training programme for his troops and when they were posted to Korea in June 1950, they had achieved a high degree of combat readiness. On 12 July Walker took command of ground forces in Korea under the overall command of General Douglas MacArthur.

The early part of the Korean War had gone badly

Right: Lieutenant-General Walton H. Walker, a successful World War II commander, achieved renown for his resolute defensive campaign in Korea.

for the US forces deployed into the peninsula and by the end of July they had withdrawn into a defensive beach-head, known as the Pusan Perimeter.

It was at this stage that Walker's abilities as a frontline commander were clearly demonstrated. He visited many of the frontline units and issued a famous 'stand or die' ultimatum, pointing out that there could be no effective withdrawal through Pusan.

With the arrival of reinforcements, Walker drew up plans for a massed counter-offensive aimed at driving the North Korean People's Army (NKPA) northwards. Despite NKPA offensives to the west, Walker quickly retaliated by moving the Marines into the threatened sector of the Naktong Bulge, and by 18 August he had driven the NKPA back across the Naktong River.

By continually moving various regiments into the battle areas Walker prevented enemy break-throughs, but only after large-scale tank battles, and the pressure in this area remained unaltered. Throughout August, the communist forces constantly attempted to breach the line with thrusts against defensive weak points. However, Walker exploited his interior lines to redeploy his forces, constantly shifted them around to block enemy offensives and reinforced battered units. This skilful and rapid manoeuvring eventually forced the NKPA onto the defensive in any areas where they achieved a local breakthrough and thus prevented them exploiting their advantages.

By the end of August, the 120-mile perimeter of the 4000-square-mile beach-head was effectively secured. Although in Walker's estimation, the communists still held the advantage, the perimeter had been held. This stalwart defence had set up the strategic situation that Douglas MacArthur exploited in the Inchon amphibious landings.

Walker's Eighth Army followed the retreating communist forces north in the aftermath of the Inchon landings; but in spite of this success, the intervention of Chinese troops late in the autumn turned the tide again, and the US forces were soon forced to pull back in their turn. Walker was killed in a car crash in December 1950 while making preparations to check the enemy offensive, and the US Army had lost a resolute commander.

Walker was a tough soldier and his abrasive, uncompromising character sometimes made him unpopular with the troops; he was, nonetheless, a formidable general and his skilful defence of the Naktong line is an undeniable military classic.

THE ELITE COMMANDERS

Bottom: Walker (centre right) discusses operations in the Pusan Perimeter, July 1950. Below: U.S. troops take the offensive in Korea, in September 1950.

THE ELITE COMMANDERS

The Soldiers' Soldier

Lieutenant-General Peter Walls was born in Salisbury, Southern Rhodesia on 28 July 1926, the son of a former acting Chief of Staff to the British colony's forces. Educated at Plumtree School, he enlisted as a private in the Southern Rhodesian forces in October 1944, but was selected for officer training at the Royal Military Academy, Sandhurst. From Sandhurst, he was commissioned into the Black Watch in the British army in March 1946 and served with the regiment until deciding to return to Southern Rhodesia in 1948. In Southern Rhodesia he re-enlisted – this time as a corporal – in the Permanent Staff Corps, but was quickly recommissioned and posted to a training unit. Bored with the duties, he considered leaving the army but was then seconded to the Kings African Rifles in British Somaliland in 1949. With promotion to Captain after returning from Somaliland, he was charged with raising C (Rhodesian Squadron) of 22 SAS, Malayan Scouts.

His service with the squadron in Malaya was undoubtedly one of the most formative periods of his career, Walls emerging as a Major and being awarded the MBE by the British for his services in 1953. He greatly admired the methods of the British High Commissioner in Malaya, Sir Gerald Templar, in defeating communist insurgency and conceived the need to recognise that such insurgency required both a political as well as a military response. Malaya also taught Walls the value of long range penetration operations and the use of the helicopter to insert

WALLS

Page 164, above: Lieutenant-General Peter Walls pictured after his appointment as Commander of Combined Operations (Comops) in March 1977, a post which, in theory, gave him authority to co-ordinate long-term counter-insurgency strategy. In practice, however, Comops became embroiled in the day-to-day planning of operations and rivalry with the army, with the result that a long-term strategy failed to materialise.
Page 164, below: Rhodesian soldiers patrol a frontier area to prevent guerrilla infiltration into the interior. Lack of manpower stretched 'the thin green line' of army patrols to the limit and led to the formation of Fire Forces – heliborne concentrations of troops and armaments which could be lifted into trouble spots.
Below: Walls (right) receiving the Defence Cross for Distinguished Service.

troops into key locations.

Malaya also led Walls to appreciate the needs of the ordinary soldier. Walls remarked on one occasion, 'I always thought of how they would read and understand the instructions'. He was, therefore, a man who, in the words of his deputy chief of staff, 'likes to get down to talking to troopies'. Walls was immensely popular with the army and became regarded by many white Rhodesians in the late 1970's as their chief salvation as the popularity of Rhodesia's prime minister, Ian Smith, waned. 'Tommy', as Walls was known to his friends, was a reassuring, solidly built figure admirably suited for such a role. Fond of informality, he was softly spoken but direct in manner and quietly humorous.

Following service in Malaya, he commanded the Tactical Wing at the School of Infantry (1954-56) and the Northern Rhodesia Regiment (1956-59); he served as Brigade Major of the Copperbelt and Northern Rhodesia districts (1961-62) and Adjutant General of the Rhodesian Army (1962-64). In 1964 he took command of the 1st Battalion of the Rhodesian Light Infantry and the opening of insurgency in Rhodesia in 1966 saw Walls in command of the 2nd Brigade. He succeeded to the appointment of Army Chief of Staff in August 1972.

Walls' appointment coincided with a major escalation of the war from early and amateurish guerrilla incursions to the opening of a new front by the military wing of the Zimbabwe African National Union (ZANU) in the Centenary district of northeastern Rhodesia in December 1972. In the war against the insurgents, Walls put into practice the military

lessons learnt in Malaya. In November 1973, he encouraged the formation of the Selous Scouts, for long-range penetration operations, and the Fire Force, to offset lack of manpower by concentrating firepower and mobility in heliborne forces. The war, however, steadily escalated in intensity, particularly after the Portuguese left their colony of Mozambique in 1975, and the *ad hoc* system of command, which had persisted since the early incursions of the mid 1960's, became inadequate for the task in hand. In March 1977, therefore, Walls was appointed Commander of Combined Operations, a post he was to retain until March 1980. He had been due to retire under army regulations and the appointment enabled him to remain in service.

COMOPS

In theory, Walls' new Combined Operations Headquarters (Comops) should have provided the kind of long-term planning that the Rhodesians needed to co-ordinate strategy. In fact, Walls and his staff became immersed in the day-to-day conduct of the war, with control over all offensive and special forces and responsibility for all external operations against guerrilla sanctuaries in Zambia, Mozambique and Botswana. Indeed, Walls increasingly directed such operations from a distinctive command aircraft rather than leaving operational control to field commanders – on one occasion his command Dakota came extremely close to being shot down by Zambian fighters.

In effect, Walls had forgotten the political lessons of Malaya and, although he continually stressed the need for political considerations to be understood in relation to the conduct of operations, in practice, the Rhodesian reaction was largely confined to seeking a military solution to insurgency. The situation was aggravated by Walls' failure to get on well with either Ian Smith, or his former deputy chief of staff, Lieutenant-General John Hickman, who became army commander in 1977. Walls was not actually superior in rank to Hickman or others in the security forces' command hierarchy, but Smith declined to give Walls the clarification of authority he sought.

POWER AND PRAGMATISM

However, it has been argued that by 1979 Walls was the most powerful man in Rhodesia, even if he maintained a largely apolitical stance, and he was undoubtedly the key figure in the Lancaster House negotiations, which brought about a ceasefire in December 1979, pending elections. Walls gained full credit from the British negotiators for his pragmatism and, although he asked the British government to declare the electoral victory of Robert Mugabe's ZANU void, because of the level of intimidation involved, he refused to countenance a coup by the Rhodesian security forces. He also accepted Mugabe's invitation to become head of the new Zimbabwe Joint High Command despite ZANU having once threatened to hang him during the war. It did not prove an easy assignment and, when Mugabe refused to give him the rank of full general in order to impose his authority on the warring guerrilla factions, he announced his intention to resign by the end of 1980. Going on pre-retirement leave in July 1980, Walls criticised the Mugabe government in interviews abroad. On 17 September he was dismissed from his command in his absence and special legislation was enacted on 25 September to prevent his re-entering the country. Walls subsequently retired to South Africa.

THE ELITE COMMANDERS

Steadfast at times of crisis

Archibald Percival Wavell, destined to become one of the most able British commanders of World

Below: General Wavell, C-in-C India, is pictured standing to the left of General Sir Harold Alexander (centre), GOC Burma, following a secret conference with other senior Allied officers.

War II, was born in 1883, the son of an army officer. Educated at Winchester, where he displayed strong intellectual ability, he went on to Sandhurst, from where, in 1901, he was commissioned into the Black Watch. After eight years with his regiment, during which he saw action in both South Africa and India, he attended Staff College at Camberley, although when war broke out in 1914 he preferred front-line duty rather than a staff post. He was badly wounded at the Second Battle of Ypres in 1915, losing his left eye, and thereafter he had no choice but to accept staff duties, initially in France and then under General Sir Edmund Allenby in the Middle East. By 1918 Wavell was carrying out the duties of a brigadier.

The restoration of peace saw Wavell return to his regiment (as a major), but his obvious command abilities had not gone unnoticed. During the peace his promotion was remarkably rapid: by 1930 he was a substantive brigadier, organising an experimental

Below left: During the campaign in the Western Desert, Wavell's forces launched numerous small-scale offensives along the Libyan-Egyptian border, despite being outnumbered by the Italian Army. Below: General Sir Archibald Wavell, in his capacity as GOC Middle East.

WAVELL

infantry brigade at Blackdown; eight years later he was General Officer Commanding (GOC) Southern Command in England as a lieutenant general. He was clearly destined for the top, having shown that he possessed all the right command qualities – bravery, leadership, administrative skill, an ability to inspire loyalty and, above all, an abundance of common sense. He needed them all when, in July 1939, he was promoted to full general and appointed GOC Middle East.

GOC MIDDLE EAST

His new command was vast and the responsibilities enormous. Covering an area some 1800 by 2000 miles, they included British garrisons in Cyprus, Egypt, Palestine, Transjordan, Sudan, British Somaliland and Aden. Wavell's duties, laid down in a precise government directive, were not merely to oversee these outposts but also to prepare them for potential war. The main threat came from Italy which, with huge forces in Libya and East Africa, (Ethiopia, Eritrea and Italian Somaliland), was in a strong position to attack the vital oil and communications routes through the Suez Canal and Persian Gulf. Wavell's forces, by comparison, were small and scattered. However, he approached his task with enthusiasm, ordering a survey of all Egyptian ports, prior to the creation of a wartime base in that country, and even demanding detailed plans for attacks into Libya should the Italians declare war. It was essential work.

Italy declared war in June 1940, presenting Wavell with a strategic nightmare. Within a month, the Duke of Aosta, Viceroy of Ethiopia, had pushed forces into the border areas of Sudan and Kenya, and a month later he invaded and occupied British Somaliland. In

THE ELITE COMMANDERS

The great irony of Wavell's career was that it spanned a succession of commands in crisis, from each of which he was removed once the threat had reached its peak. Nevertheless, his grasp of tactics and strategy was extraordinary. By setting up the Long Range Desert Group in 1941, Wavell created an intelligence and sabotage unit that was superbly suited to the battle zone of North Africa. Below: In the field, binoculars in one hand, Wavell outlines his plan of attack to a group of senior officers.

September, Marshal Graziani crossed the border into Egypt, while other Italian forces attacked Greece, an area Wavell could not afford to ignore, even though it was outside his command. His job was now to juggle his meagre forces in an attempt to reverse this process of enemy advance, and this he did brilliantly. In December 1940, he authorised General Sir Richard O'Connor to attack Graziani's overstretched units in western Egypt and, when this succeeded, he allowed the attack to develop. By February 1941, O'Connor had advanced to Beda Fomm, occupying the whole of Cyrenaica (the eastern province of Libya) and taking over 200,000 Italian prisoners.

By then, the reconquest of East Africa was already well advanced, with General Sir William Platt, commanding a small force from Sudan, having occupied much of Eritrea and opened the Red Sea to Allied shipping. At the same time, General Sir Alan Cunningham advanced from Kenya to occupy Italian Somaliland, liberate British Somaliland and probe deep into Ethiopia, the capital of which fell to South African troops on 6 April 1941. Thereafter, both British forces converged on the fortress of Amba Alagi where, on 17 May, Aosta surrendered, together with a further 200,000 men. It was a brilliant campaign.

This should have allowed Wavell to concentrate on North Africa, but in March he had been directed, against his own judgement, to transfer part of O'Connor's victorious army to Greece, where German forces were preparing to aid the Italians. It was a hopeless venture which left Cyrenaica poorly defended just as Rommel's Afrika Korps arrived on the scene. When Rommel attacked in late March, the British could not prevent his reoccupation of Cyrenaica, and when this coincided with disaster in Greece, it seemed as if Wavell's command was about to collapse. He held it together, finding sufficient forces to occupy Iraq and Vichy-French Syria to protect his rear, but it was clear that he had lost the confidence of the Prime Minister, Winston Churchill. In July, Churchill decided to relieve Wavell, replacing him with General Sir Claude Auchinleck in what has since been described as 'an amazing injustice'.

Wavell assumed Auchinleck's previous responsibilities as C-in-C India, only to arrive at a time when new disasters were looming. In December 1941 the Japanese attacks in the Far East caught the Allies unprepared and, despite Wavell's appointment as commander of all American, British, Dutch and Australian (ABDA) forces in the region, little could be done to prevent defeat. In February 1942, Wavell returned to India, where he then had to cope with the Japanese threat to the eastern border through Burma. Under pressure from the Americans and Chinese, he mounted an abortive attack into Arakan (on the west coast of Burma) in December, which convinced him that more time was needed to prepare his troops for jungle warfare. As a preliminary move, he authorised the creation of Orde Wingate's Chindits, repeating a policy already followed in North Africa, where it was Wavell who had given the go-ahead for the Long Range Desert Group.

In January 1943, Wavell was promoted to field marshal and given the essentially political post of Viceroy of India, a job he held under increasingly difficult circumstances until February 1947, the eve of Indian independence. Given his proven command abilities and unique grasp of strategic priorities, this was undoubtedly a waste of military talent but, as always, Wavell approached his task with quiet professional skill and good humour.

THE ELITE COMMANDERS

Left: William Westmoreland, soon after he assumed command of US forces in Vietnam, wearing airborne insignia. Before his new appointment, Westmoreland had been commander of the US XVIII Airborne Corps. Below: US troops deploy from a helicopter in the Central Highlands. The use of advanced technology failed, however, to give the Americans the advantage they needed to win the war.

Commander of US ground forces – Vietnam

William Childs Westmoreland was born in Spartanburg County, South Carolina, USA, on 26 March 1914 and was to become one of America's best-known generals. His early education included a year (1931-32) at the Citadel in South Carolina before entry into the West Point Military Academy in 1932. In 1936 Westmoreland graduated, was commissioned as a second lieutenant and posted to the 18th Field Artillery at Fort Sill, Oklahoma. In the same year, 1936, he was transferred to Hawaii where he joined the 8th Field Artillery. Westmoreland remained with this unit until 1942, when he was promoted to operations officer and joined the 34th Field Artillery, 9th Infantry Division, at Fort Bragg, North Carolina.

Remaining with the 34th Field Artillery, he first saw action in World War II in North Africa. This was followed by action in Sicily and then on Utah Beach in the Normandy landings. In 1944 he was promoted to Colonel and took up a position as Chief of Staff of the 9th Infantry Division. He held this appointment until

WESTMORELAND

1945 when he took command of the 60th Infantry Regiment.

Following the successful conclusion of hostilities in Europe, Westmoreland underwent a course of parachute and glider training before taking command of the 504th Parachute Infantry Regiment in 1946. In 1947 he was promoted Chief of Staff to the 82nd Airborne Division based at Fort Bragg. In 1950 Westmoreland moved on to become an instructor at the Command and General Staff College at Fort Leavenworth, Kansas. During this period he also taught at the Army War College. He was promoted Brigadier-General in 1952 and took command of the 187th Airborne Regimental Combat Team during their tour in Korea.

In the period 1953-4, Westmoreland took up a staff appointment as deputy assistant chief of staff (G-1) for manpower control at the Pentagon and in 1955 became secretary to the General Staff in Washington. In the following year he was again promoted and made major general. In 1958 he left his Washington appointment with the General Staff and took command of the 101st Airborne Division at Fort Campbell, Kentucky. He remained here until 1960, when he moved on to become the superintendent of the Military Academy. In 1963 Westmoreland became the commanding general of XVIII Airborne Corps at Fort Bragg.

In 1964 he was promoted lieutenant-general and given command of all US ground forces in Vietnam. In this role, Westmoreland was tasked with restoring a rapidly deteriorating situation. The Army of the Republic of South Vietnam (ARVN) was collapsing in the face of escalating communist pressure, while the government of South Vietnam itself was in the throes of dissolution, with military regime succeeding military regime in Saigon. Westmoreland at once set to work to apply theories of mobility and firepower to retrieve the position of the US ally. With the technical advantages that the US Army enjoyed, he was able to stun the communists with the initial deployment of his forces. In autumn 1965, for example, he deployed the fully airmobile 1st Cavalry Division into the Central Highlands to blunt an offensive by North Vietnamese Army (NVA) forces: this operation in the Ia Drang Valley stopped the NVA in its tracks.

Over the next two years Westmoreland mounted many more large operations, and between December 1964 and December 1967, it has been estimated that his formations inflicted over 300,000 casualties on the communist forces. Operation Cedar Falls, in January 1967, and Operation Junction City later that

THE ELITE COMMANDERS

Above left: Westmoreland with President Lyndon Johnson at a medal ceremony in 1966. During the first two years of his command in Vietnam, Westmoreland seemed to be enjoying great success, and was a nationally popular figure, touted in some quarters as a possible candidate for the 1968 presidential elections. Things were to change radically by 1968, however. The failure to inflict a decisive defeat on the communists and the mounting US casualty toll made Westmoreland unpopular and isolated. As a retired and older man (above right) he engaged in law suits against a television company that he claimed gave a false impression of his command during the Vietnam War.

spring were typical of the application of men and firepower to root out communist forces within set areas. Westmoreland believed that by inflicting heavy casualties on the communists in such operations he could destroy their will to fight.

The problem for Westmoreland, and for the Americans in Vietnam as a whole, was that such methods were not necessarily the way to win what was essentially a guerrilla war against the implacable, patient armies directed from Hanoi. The doctrine that Westmoreland employed so efficiently – that of using overwhelming force to secure an objective – was of little use where the basic objective could only have been to destroy the capacity of North Vietnam to support a war in the south. Westmoreland was unable to prevent the infiltration of communist troops and supplies from Laos and Cambodia via the Ho Chi Minh Trail and so he was always fighting on the strategic defensive.

By the end of 1967, (Westmoreland had, at one stage, claimed that victory would be achieved by the end of 1967) the administration of Lyndon Johnson was seriously concerned about the strategy being employed in Vietnam, and the Secretary of Defense, Robert McNamara, had lost all hope of any decisive victory. There were growing problems within the US armed forces in Vietnam: the strategy of attrition placed great emphasis on the 'body count', which led to inflated claims by officers eager for promotion, and encouraged the killing of civilians.

The communist offensive early in 1968 (the 'Tet offensive') and the siege of Khe Sanh in the same period convinced many in the USA that the armed forces were making little impression on communist strength. Westmoreland, on the contrary, realised that the communists had suffered severe losses during the offensive and believed that a new US effort was needed to take advantage of the situation. He called for another 200,000 troops to be sent into southeast Asia. Johnson called for an inquiry into the options open for the US forces; and shortly after, Westmoreland was recalled to the USA. He was promoted to chief of staff of the Army.

In 1972, Westmoreland retired, and was awarded the Distinguished Service Medal. He has since felt very strongly that criticism of his conduct of operations during the Vietnam War was often ill-founded. There is no doubt that Westmoreland was an expert in the application of firepower and the rapid transport of large numbers of men; but these gifts were somewhat out of place in Vietnam, where a far more subtle and (for the US Army) radical approach to the war was required.

THE ELITE COMMANDERS

WOODWARD

Task Force Commander

John Forster 'Sandy' Woodward, commander of the British Task Force sent to recapture the Falkland Islands from Argentina in 1982, was born in Cornwall in 1932. Unlike many officers in the modern Royal Navy, he had no naval background and was the son of a bank clerk. Educated at the Royal Naval College, Dartmouth, Woodward chose initially to specialise in submarines. At the age of 29 he was appointed to his first independent command as captain of HMS *Tireless*.

Until the Falklands campaign, Woodward's rise was steady but unspectacular. He was very much one of the new generation of naval officers, trained to regard computer systems and nuclear engineering to be as much a part of naval life as the more traditional skills of seamanship. Earlier in his career, as captain of the ill-fated Type 42 destroyer HMS *Sheffield*, he revealed this side of his character when he played an important part in the installation and testing of the Sea Dart missile system. Woodward also showed talent as an administrator, and in 1978 he was appointed Director of Naval Plans. In this key position, his chief function was to present the navy's case for government funds.

THE TOTAL EXCLUSION ZONE

In April 1982 Woodward was back at sea as a Rear Admiral and Flag Officer First Flotilla, commanding 16 ships in the annual 'Springtrain' fleet exercises. On 2 April the Argentinians attacked and captured the Falklands. Three days later, the carriers HMS *Hermes* and *Invincible* left Portsmouth to join Woodward's flotilla, now known as Task Unit 318:1 or, more simply, the 'Task Force'. Under the overall command of Admiral Sir John Fieldhouse (at Fleet HQ, Northwood), Woodward, flying his flag on *Hermes*, set sail for the disputed islands.

As Woodward's Task Force steamed south, the politicians and diplomats struggled for a peaceful solution to the crisis but, by 30 April, these attempts were clearly flagging. On arriving off the Falklands, Woodward's first priority was to secure a measure of air and naval superiority. Accordingly, he initiated a policy of isolation and steady military pressure on the Argentinian garrison on the islands. The previously declared Maritime Exclusion Zone was extended to

Above left: Admiral Woodward, commander of the British Task Force despatched to the South Atlantic in April 1982. Below: Ships of the Task Force en route to the Falkland Islands.

become a 200-mile Total Exclusion Zone through which the passage of aircraft or sea vessels would not be tolerated.

During the conflict the Royal Navy had three basic roles to fulfil: to enforce the Total Exclusion Zone, to protect itself against Argentinian attack, and to project power ashore. None of these tasks proved easy. The Argentinian navy was a formidable local force, based around the elderly, but still dangerous, carrier *25 de Mayo* equipped with A-4Q Skyhawk fighter-bombers. The carrier was supported by a variety of modern warships, including four diesel-powered submarines and two British-built Type 42 destroyers equipped with Exocet and Sea Dart missile systems. In the event, it was the Argentinian air forces that posed the major threat to the Task Force, for after the sinking of the cruiser *General Belgrano* on 2 May by the submarine HMS *Conqueror*, the Argentinian navy stayed in port.

Against some 142 Argentinian planes, Woodward could muster a mere 20 Sea Harriers based on the two vulnerable platforms *Hermes* and *Invincible*. The destruction of *Sheffield* by an air-launched Exocet on 4 May emphasised the vulnerability of surface vessels in a most dramatic fashion and Woodward was well aware that, should he lose a carrier, he would be hard put to continue operations. He, therefore, changed his tactics in early May and withdrew the two carriers to the east, out of air-attack range, leaving other ships to patrol the Total Exclusion Zone.

There is no denying that Woodward carried out his task in a thoroughly professional manner. Despite the reduced air cover, the unwelcome surprise that

Above: Woodward's flagship, the carrier HMS *Hermes*, returns to a tumultuous welcome in the UK. Woodward himself received a knighthood and promotion to the rank of Vice Admiral. Below: With a Task Force vessel close at hand, landing craft carrying men of 42 Commando, Royal Marines, plough through a choppy sea towards the landing point at San Carlos on East Falkland.

some of the Task Force's air-defence systems were less effective than expected, and the loss of six ships and damage to many others, Woodward maintained control of the sea until the very end. This enabled the land forces to be put ashore at San Carlos and to be supplied for the duration of the campaign. Woodward's aircraft were never able to gain complete air superiority – there were too few of them – but by the careful husbanding of his precious carriers, Woodward was able to ensure that air cover could be provided for most of the Task Force's operations. The disaster at Bluff Cove was an unfortunate exception.

Woodward was, rightly, cautious during the Falklands campaign, yet he displayed considerable moral courage in taking certain risks, such as sending the troop ship *Canberra* into the danger area of San Carlos Water. To have succeeded in assuring the safety of the assault landings and to have supported the subsequent military operations at the end of an 8000-mile logistic chain was a considerable achievement. Woodward was tasked with an extremely difficult and complex assignment which he carried out with skill and professionalism.

Sandy Woodward returned to the UK a national hero, to a knighthood, promotion to Vice Admiral and a post at the Ministry of Defence as Deputy Chief of Defence Staff (Commitments). He appears a self-confident, almost abrasive man as a mask for his essential shyness. He once described himself as 'an ordinary person who lives in suburbia... (not) a hard military man, leading a battlefleet into the annals of history'. It is ironic that Woodward's place in history is assured as the latter.

THE ELITE COMMANDERS

YAMAMOTO

Isoroku Yamamoto (1884-1943) was the man who masterminded the Japanese attack on Pearl Harbor, and whose ideas on strategy dominated the thinking of the Japanese Navy during World War II. He was one of the most clear-sighted and innovative admirals ever, with a firm grasp of the essentials of the war in the Pacific and a sound knowledge of the new opportunities afforded by naval aviation – opportunities that he put to good use.

Yamamoto graduated from the Japanese naval academy in 1904, and saw action in the Russo-Japanese War (1904-1905) during which he lost two fingers of his left hand. After service in World War I he spent several important years in the United States, both studying at Harvard and as a naval attaché. In the mid-1920s he was in charge of an air training school in Japan, and early realised the importance that aircraft might play in any future naval wars. He pushed hard for the development of naval aviation throughout the 1930s and by the time he became commander of the Japanese Combined Fleet in 1939 the Japanese Navy had a higher proportion of aircraft carriers than that of any other power.

Yamamoto was fundamentally pessimistic about war with the United States, believing that it could end only in defeat, but he hoped that the six months or so of victories that he reckoned he could achieve might enable Japan to negotiate a favourable settlement guaranteeing her a dominant position in East and Southeast Asia. His plan for Pearl Harbor took the Americans completely by surprise. US strategists had expected any Japanese strike to be directed at the British and Dutch possessions in Southeast Asia.

After Pearl Harbor, the Japanese destroyed Allied naval forces in Southeast Asia, sinking the British battleship HMS *Prince of Wales* and the battlecruiser HMS *Repulse* off Malaya, and then smashing Dutch, British and Australian units at the battle of the Java Sea. After this onslaught, the Allied

Above right: Admiral Isoroku Yamamoto consults his maps. He was a master strategist whose great strengths were his ability to co-ordinate far-flung forces and his awareness of the importance of naval aviation. Ironically, however, the success of US cryptographers in cracking Japanese codes enabled Chester W. Nimitz, the commander of the US Pacific Fleet, to place the few US aircraft carriers at precisely the right spot to disrupt Yamamoto's plans for the concentration of Japanese forces at the Battle of Midway in June 1942. The result was a catastrophic defeat for the Japanese Navy.

possessions in Southeast Asia were defenceless and the Philippines, the Dutch East Indies and Malaya fell to Japanese armies.

Yamamoto's string of victories, however, did not quite stretch for the six months he had hoped. In an attempt to cut the direct communications route between the USA and Australia the Japanese fleet suffered a setback at the Battle of the Coral Sea in May 1942; and then, at the battle of Midway in June, his forces suffered a major defeat.

Midway had been Yamamoto's most ambitious plan, splitting up enormous naval resources across the northern Pacific in order to lure the still outnumbered US Pacific Fleet into a trap near Midway Island. This was to be Yamamoto's master-stroke. Unfortunately, it relied on close co-ordination of all the units involved, and could be upset by problems of detail. US cryptographers had succeeded in cracking Japanese codes, and the Americans knew, therefore, some of the essentials of the Japanese plan. They were able to move all available aircraft carriers to Midway before the Japanese forces were in position. In a confused set of actions, during which luck played a major part, the four aircraft carriers that formed the core of the Japanese forces were sunk, and Yamamoto, the prophet and great exponent of naval aviation, found himself defeated by the same weapon. He had to order a withdrawal, and was never again able to take the initiative.

Henceforth, Yamamoto hoped to cause the US Navy heavy losses in breaking through a defensive perimeter, and then to use his Combined Fleet as a counter-attacking force to strike at the US forces that had got through the initial defences. Before he had time to implement this strategy, however, the great admiral himself was killed – once again, a victim of good US intelligence. On 18 April 1943, on a tour of inspection in the Solomons, his plane was shot down by US fighters that had been waiting in ambush following the interception of a radio signal giving the details of his flight.

THE ELITE COMMANDERS
YAMASHITA

'Tiger of the Philippines'

Tomoyuki Yamashita (1885-1946) will always be remembered for his great triumph in 1942, when he took the surrender of the British Empire and Commonwealth forces in Singapore, in Churchill's words, 'the greatest disaster to British arms which our history records'. But Yamashita was more than merely a commander who proved himself in one great battle. His exploits later in the war, in the Philippines, demonstrate just as clearly his excellence as a general.

Yamashita graduated from the Japanese War College in 1916, and his abilities were soon noted; he took up several important staff and command posts, and was given command of an infantry brigade in 1937, just as the Sino-Japanese War was beginning. In late 1940, Yamashita became inspector general of the Japanese Air Force, and led a military mission to Germany. He concluded that Japan should build up its air force and mechanise its army before risking war against Great Britain and the USA.

In spite of this report, war was declared in December 1941, and Yamashita was appointed to command the 25th Army that landed in Thailand and northern Malaya. The Allied forces facing him were superior in numbers and support weapons, but Yamashita fought a classic campaign using speed and surprise. His well-trained infantry units swarmed south, crossing areas, such as mangrove swamps, that the British considered impassable. The result was that, on 15 February 1942, the British were forced to surrender Singapore to a numerically inferior force.

After the successes of 1942, Yamashita was relegated to a relatively out-of-the-way command, in Manchuria in China, probably because the Japanese Prime Minister, Tojo, feared and disliked him. In July 1944, however, when the Japanese cause had become hopeless, Yamashita was recalled to the front line, and given command in the Philippines. Even though his sensible initial plans for defending the islands were rejected by the high command, he conducted a tenacious and skilful holding action on Luzon, refusing to engage in any fruitless, last-ditch defences before surrendering after the Japanese capitulation in September 1945.

In February 1946, Yamashita was executed for war crimes. He claimed that he would have prevented the atrocities committed by men under his command had he had the opportunity; and, in particular, that crimes committed by Japanese Navy troops in Manila in 1945 were against his wishes – he had ordered a withdrawal from the Philippine capital, and declared Manila an open city. Nevertheless, this defence was not deemed sufficient, and the 'Tiger of the Philippines' was hanged.

Far left: Tomoyuki Yamashita, an intelligent and far-sighted commander who was a master of the use of speed and surprise. Left: Japanese troops in the Philippines, where Yamashita conducted a stubborn but flexible defence against US forces.

Red Army Supremo

Georgi Konstantinovich Zhukov (1896-1974) played a major role in all the major battles on the Eastern Front after the initial German successes of the summer of 1941, and, in particular, he commanded Soviet troops in the three crucial engagements in 1941 and 1942 that broke the capacity of the German Army to defeat the Soviet Union; and he actively directed on the battlefield a greater weight of men and machinery than any other World War II commander. Like Montgomery, he showed himself a master of the material aspect of modern warfare; and, like MacArthur, he developed ways of fighting that suited the precise conditions of his theatre and the abilities of his troops.

Zhukov was conscripted into the Tsarist Russian Army at the beginning of World War I. In common with many other Russian soldiers, he found communism, and especially that brand preached by Lenin's Bolshevik Party, a far more realistic description of the nature of Russian society than any other political creed, and he supported the Bolshevik Revolution of 1917. He joined the Red Army upon its foundation in 1918, and served as a cavalry commander during the rest of the Civil War and the invasion of Poland.

After the war, Zhukov specialised in armoured warfare, and he taught the subject at the Frunze military academy. He also studied military science in Germany, during the period of military co-operation with the Soviet Union that marked the early years of Hitler's regime in Germany. Zhukov managed to avoid being implicated in the purges, those great examples of Stalin's megalomania that cut a swathe through the upper echelons of the Red Army during the late 1930s, and in 1939 he was given the posting that was the stepping stone to greatness.

In 1938, there had been clashes between the Japanese and Soviet forces in the Far East, where the Japanese presence in Manchuria gave the two states a mutual frontier, and in 1939 Zhukov was given

THE ELITE COMMANDERS

ZHUKOV

Previous page, above: Georgi Konstantinovich Zhukov, in the full panoply of a marshal of the Soviet Union. Previous page, below: Zhukov at the front in Manchuria in 1939. Leading Soviet forces against the Japanese in this short campaign, Zhukov made his reputation as a resourceful, vigorous field commander. Below: Victorious Allies in Frankfurt, May 1945. From left are Field Marshal Bernard Montgomery, General Dwight D. Eisenhower, Zhukov himself and Air Marshal Arthur Tedder.

command of Soviet forces in the area. In May, the Japanese instigated an attack on Mongolia, and the Soviets invoked a mutual defence treaty to go to the aid of the Mongolians. Zhukov directed a counter-offensive that began in August 1939; the Japanese Sixth Army was encircled and heavily defeated. On 16 September, the Japanese signed an armistice.

Having proved himself a more than capable field commander, Zhukov was created Chief of the General Staff, but after the early successes of the German invasion of the Soviet Union (Operation Barbarossa) he was soon given more direct control of forces in the field. In September he went north to Leningrad, menaced by German forces, and directed the defence that held up the Axis forces and was to result in the long siege. Then, in October, he was appointed C-in-C of the whole western front. The central sector was particularly threatened by the renewed German drive on Moscow, but Zhukov fed reinforcements and war material into the line to slow and then halt the German offensive. Once the impetus had gone from his enemy, he launched a counter-attack, beginning on 4 December. Caught off-balance, the German Army was all but annihilated around Moscow, although by February the front had stabilised.

Zhukov was appointed Deputy Supreme Commander of the Red Army in August 1942, and remained in that post until the end of the war. But this central co-ordinating role did not prevent him now taking a part in the turning point of the war in the East: he did much of the planning and personally organised one of the wings of the offensive that surrounded the German Sixth Army at Stalingrad in November.

In his post as second only to Stalin in Soviet direction of the war, Zhukov was closely involved in all the subsequent Soviet offensives, either at the planning or command stage, and took a close personal interest in the winter 1944 offensive and the final move on Berlin in 1945. He was always ready to visit a front to issue orders directly, and to prevent any slackening of the impetus of an attack. He was not prepared to countenance any incompetence among his subordinate army commanders, and his example was critical in the way that the Red Army, which in 1941 had been woefully unprepared for a large-scale mobile war, was able to deploy massive amounts of war material to shatter the German armies during the great offensives of 1944 and 1945.

POSTWAR PROBLEMS

With the shortage of information about Soviet decision-making during the war, it will always be difficult to make a final assessment of the Soviet commanders. However, Zhukov's key part in the resolute defence of Leningrad, his major role in launching the 1941 offensive outside Moscow, and his contribution to the victory at Stalingrad, give him a place in the pantheon of great World War II military leaders.

Zhukov's postwar career was somewhat chequered. In 1946, he was relegated by Stalin to a regional command, and did not return to prominence until 1955, after Stalin's death. Then, in july 1957, he became a full member of the communist party praesidium, the highest state rank ever achieved in the Soviet Union by an active soldier. He was soon to disappear from public view again, however, and his achievements were not openly acknowledged again until the mid-1960s.